KU-372-829

THE
LEADER
AS
COMMUNICATOR

36189812

LIS - LIBRARY

Date	Fund
21/3/14	bs

Order No.

DONATION

University of Chester

THE LEADER AS COMMUNICATOR

STRATEGIES AND TACTICS TO
BUILD LOYALTY, FOCUS
EFFORT, AND SPARK
CREATIVITY

R OBERT M AI AND
A LAN A KERSON

AMACOM

American Management Association

New York • Atlanta • Brussels • Buenos Aires • Chicago • London • Mexico City
San Francisco • Shanghai • Tokyo • Toronto • Washington, D.C.

Special discounts on bulk quantities of AMACOM books are available to corporations, professional associations, and other organizations. For details, contact Special Sales Department, AMACOM, a division of American Management Association, 1601 Broadway, New York, NY 10019.
Tel.: 212-903-8316. Fax: 212-903-8083.
Web site: www.amacombooks.org

This publication is designed to provide accurate and authoritative information in regard to the subject matter covered. It is sold with the understanding that the publisher is not engaged in rendering legal, accounting, or other professional service. If legal advice or other expert assistance is required, the services of a competent professional person should be sought.

Library of Congress Cataloging-in-Publication Data

Mai, Robert, 1943-
    The leader as communicator : strategies and tactics to build loyalty,
focus effort, and spark creativity / Robert Mai and Alan Akerson.
        p.   cm.
    Includes bibliographical references and index.
    ISBN 0-8144-0740-4 (hardcover)
    1. Communication in management.   2. Communication in organizations.
    3. Leadership.   I. Akerson, Alan, 1945-   II. Amacom.   III. Title.

HD30.3.M34   2003
658.4'5—dc21

                                                        2002155174

© 2003 Robert Mai and Alan Akerson
All rights reserved.
Printed in the United States of America.

This publication may not be reproduced,
stored in a retrieval system,
or transmitted in whole or in part,
in any form or by any means, electronic,
mechanical, photocopying, recording, or otherwise,
without the prior written permission of AMACOM,
a division of American Management Association,
1601 Broadway, New York, NY 10019.

Printing number

10   9   8   7   6   5   4   3   2   1

Contents

LIST OF FIGURES

Acknowledgments

Many people helped us in many different ways to put this book together, and we'd like to thank them. Dave Arseneault, Larry Bruozis, and Dave Hilliard, exemplary leader-communicators, graciously cooperated with us to get their "stories" told with facts and accuracy. George Cesaretti and Paul McKnight gave us invaluable insights that we hope to have captured well and accurately. Fred Fernandez, Peggy Gardner, Keith Hartje, Marsha Littell, Dan Mc-Mackin, Jeff Pritchard, Jerry Rucker, Dave Senay, Katy Sherrerd, and Ken Sternad also helped us bring real-life examples into our narrative, and our book is the richer for their efforts.

Our range in finding source material for the rather broad subject we've attempted to write about was extended significantly through the help of colleagues and friends like Len Baenen, Lisa Richter, and Peter Wilson. Special thanks go to Christine Luebbert for tracking down elusive sources. Monique Becker also helped here, and we thank her too.

We want to thank Adrienne Hickey and Erika Spelman for their encouragement in getting us started and for moving our project along. Putting together the "finishing touches" on a book like this one involves other kinds of support as well, and we appreciate Dawn DeLaria and Mark Polzin's help in closing some loops.

Lastly, we would like to express our gratitude to all the leaders we've known over the years who taught us, through their approaches to dealing fairly and sensitively with people they work with, what communication might really look like when it succeeds and serves the best ends of their organizations.

Introduction

*"The major problem with communication is
the illusion that it has occurred."*
—GEORGE BERNARD SHAW

The stakes have perhaps never been higher for leadership
communication. Organizations of all kinds are engaged
with a more mobile and demanding workforce, and they
feel a growing need to gain full value from employee knowledge
and expertise. Leadership reputations for honesty and integrity have
taken some heavy blows, and the erosion of trust in corporate senior
leadership in particular has done significant damage to relationships
with the people they want to lead.

How well leaders connect with the people in their organizations
has enormous consequences for the contributions these people
make and the likelihood they will choose to stay with the organization. Yet leadership communication is typically relegated to a minor
role in organizational strategy. More often, it is treated simply as a
technical skill to be developed (i.e., public speaking, business writing, listening skills, etc.).

As two communication professionals working with executives
from some of America's leading corporations, as well as with government agencies, schools, and not-for-profits, we see leadership
communication as something much more important. We regard it
as *the* critical leadership competency for guiding organizations
through conditions of heightened transition and turmoil.

Above all, leadership communication entails nurturing and
maintaining a workplace environment in which communication
flows freely and quickly *in all directions* with minimal distortion or

lag time. The leader of an organization is automatically the designated chief communication officer and is accountable for all communication in the organization—not only his or her own, but that of the entire workplace community. As such, communication demands a deeper understanding, and some new perspective.

A NEW CONTEXT FOR LEADERSHIP COMMUNICATION

Organizations today are looking for ways to accomplish three related goals:

1. Create a workplace community that attracts, engages, and retains talented people.
2. Maintain an even keel and a steady course through times of transition and difficulty.
3. Stay at the leading edge of change in their business through a process of continuous innovation and renewal.

Each of these goals demands a well-designed, well-executed leadership communication strategy. As organizations are challenged to be more nimble and creative, more able to move together to mobilize around opportunities with "short windows," and more able to attract and keep talented people whose career inclination is to hop around, communication with and among employees takes on increased strategic importance. This, we believe, is the new context for leadership communication.

REBUILDING TRUST

Creating and sustaining a climate of trust and a sense of community within the organization must be a priority for any organization's leadership. How leaders extend trust, share information, provide direction and orientation, and in general develop a feeling of a common stake in the organization's future represents, in sum, what is preeminently a communications challenge. Adding to the challenge is the very real fact that organizational life as we know it today is often the kind of environment that can breed mistrust, cynicism and low concern for the organization. The toxic effects of layoffs, mergers, and bankruptcies make the challenges of leadership communication only more daunting, even as they are more critical for an organization's success.

COMMUNICATION ROLES FOR LEADERS

We believe that the most practical way to approach these challenges is to describe and examine a set of specific communication *roles* that leaders can play. Each role can be learned. Each must be thoughtfully and skillfully exercised. Taken together, these communication roles can help shape focused, motivated, and inquiring employees; a workplace characterized by social trust; and an organization that is flexible and quick to take advantage of opportunity. Together, these roles can enhance the organization's strength as a community, its readiness to align with real priorities, and its ability to adapt and renew itself, three key organizational goals.

The goal-driven communication model we work from defines each communication role by the service it renders to the organization. It's based on more than fifty years of combined experience with organizational leaders of all kinds, but especially with leadership coping with the unique challenges of contemporary organizations. It is applicable to leaders at all levels, whether a CEO or an ad hoc team leader. Its aim is to frame communications around truly compelling leadership agendas and so to make communication a more *strategic* leadership concern.

SETTING THE STAGE

We begin our argument in chapter 1 with a short vignette, built from a composite of several senior leaders with whom we've worked, that illustrates the consequences of being a good planner but not an effective communicator. This sketch of an incomplete leadership profile is used to raise questions about the role of leadership communication in the twenty-first-century organization, where employee retention and knowledge assets are increasingly important, and increasingly at risk.

Given the changes we've seen in staffing strategies for the new workplace, and in the expectations held by talented employees for their organizations, we examine key implications for leadership communication in chapter 2. Using some of the research on the "new deal at work," we identify some of the most pressing challenges facing organizational communications as leaders cope with new organizational relationships with their employees. We also examine how leadership communication plays a role in developing intellectual and social capital, two new currencies used to gauge organizational strength and performance.

THE LEADER AS COMMUNITY BUILDER

How do leaders help employees align their personal goals and sense of mission with those of the organization? Research on the leader as *meaning-maker* suggests that this is a role of emerging power to inspire and retain talented people. Chapter 3 examines the ways in which leadership communications can effectively create platforms for building alignment between employee and organization based on a sense of common stake and shared values. One strategy we explore is the technique of creating a continuous narrative about the organization's future that invites individuals to share and embrace. Another is to continually build a big-picture context for the organization's decisions and actions.

The concept of storytelling and narrative communication takes on special significance for leadership communications. It represents both a means for leaders to convey meaning and direction and the way employees may best remember and make sense of their own role in an organization and where the organization is headed. In chapter 4 we tell some stories about leaders telling stories, ones that serve to build awareness, solidarity, and motivation.

We have come to learn that *social trust* is immensely important as a criterion for cooperation and mission fulfillment. How can leadership communications strengthen social trust within an organization—particularly at a time when the "new deal" in employee relations is increasingly contractual and impermanent? Chapter 5 links recent research on the role of social trust and social capital in organizations to some logical implications for how we might best communicate with each other. We look at ways in which leaders talk, then "walk the talk" to create a climate of integrity and mutuality in the life of the organization. And we also demonstrate the value of the leader as an *early intelligence source,* helping employees to stay abreast of organizational decisions, to become smarter about the environment and ways to succeed in it.

THE LEADER AS NAVIGATOR

What makes "nimble" companies nimble? How do some organizations manage to change focus, but remain focused? At a time when organizations are challenged to change signals quickly in response to evolving market and environmental conditions, the ability of leaders to keep people always aware of the score, tuned into what's important and why, is crucial. And as companies revitalize, if not reshape, their corporate *brand* to keep pace with change, each new brand promise must be matched by the ability of the organization and its workforce to deliver on that promise and to "live the brand." Chapter 6 examines communication strategies for sustaining an emphasis on doing the right things right. It discusses several strategies that leaders can use to communicate with clarity and urgency—and to engage other managers to follow suit.

When companies come to anticipate restructuring and merger as a *normal* course of doing business, there is a heightened risk of employee disorientation, and consequent loss of productivity and morale. Yet many companies have adapted well to this organizational turbulence and have even become stronger and more focused. Chapter 7 looks at the role of leadership communication in keeping the ship steady and on course during times of transition. We pay special attention to how leaders maintain their credibility when directions seem to be shifting and how they create a sense of opportunity, rather than confusion, in the face of change.

Most organizations contain a variety of different functional units, and often these units work according to their own rules and professional cultures. Many larger organizations are further segmented by different operating units and sales offices located around the globe. Organizations that can orchestrate such complexity are organizations that communicate well. The key leadership competency addressed in chapter 8 is the ability to communicate across professional and operational boundaries so as to effectively link functions and resources for the common good. The communication skills of such a leader range from those of a diplomat and emissary to those of a translator and cross-cultural interpreter.

THE LEADER AS RENEWAL CHAMPION

One of the real challenges to leaders of successful enterprises is how to resist standing pat, thereby becoming too locked into yesterday's solutions. How do leaders best communicate that it's okay to report an inefficient operating practice, pass customer complaints upward so they can be effectively dealt with, and in general challenge the status quo? How do leaders let their people know that they can add more value to the enterprise by sponsoring constant evaluation of present practices, with an eye to improving them? And how do they provoke the surfacing of *mental models*—the fundamental business assumptions that underpin the way we do business now?

Chapter 9 addresses leadership communication strategies for combating smugness and complacency and for championing watchfulness and inquiry. It emphasizes in particular the leader's role as questioner, and the ways in which leaders can routinely raise questions and invite others to do so as well.

Dynamic organizations that actively challenge the status quo as a means of staying fresh and competitive require leaders who can use conflict and tension for positive ends. Chapter 10 discusses the critical role that leadership communications can play in fostering healthy contention and sponsoring debates that bring alternative ideas into play. We look at several techniques for making such debate (especially in staff meetings) more productive and less painful.

In the past decade, we were tutored on the importance of being a learning organization, able to constantly adapt and renew our companies and so stay ahead of change. While few argued against such a model, we are still notably ill informed about how to make organizational learning *happen* in our companies. Chapter 11 looks at the roles leaders can play in supporting continuous improvement activity. We focus especially on ways that leaders can get their people to share what they know, making tacit understandings more explicit so that others can benefit from them.

Organizations that lead change, rather than merely react to it, are organizations that know how to sponsor knowledge creation and then implement the best new ideas. Chapter 12 examines how leaders effectively stimulate experimentation and innovation, and create a communication climate that supports free knowledge exchange and feedback. We highlight an unusual basketball coach whose team reinvented its style of play and dramatically changed its performance.

In the concluding chapter, we try to kill two birds with one stone. We introduce two families of assessment questions, one about self-assessment and the other about seeking audience feedback, and we use both to suggest how to organize a leadership communication assessment and to review the ten communication roles we've just discussed at length.

THE LEADERSHIP COMMUNICATION DEVELOPMENT PROJECT

Our final chapter begins by offering some guidelines for determining how your present leadership communication profile matches the attributes of the model discussed above. We provide two audit templates, tools to use to take a snapshot of your own situation, and some general strategies for assessing strengths and weaknesses. We conclude with a discussion of the importance of thinking about communication as strategy, and about using assessment and observation to develop leadership communication competency.

RISKY BUSINESS

A book about leadership communication runs several risks. Its contents can seem too obvious, belaboring ideas that are so common-sensical that they bring more yawns than insight to readers. It can focus too narrowly on "things famous people said"—the *great speeches* approach to leadership communication that makes for entertaining reading but leaves you not with usable strategies but with quotable quips. Or it can get too mechanical—"follow these twelve steps to successful presentations"—leaving the reader with a bunch of formulas that rarely translate into anything natural enough to feel right or have the effect you want.

Our interest in how leaders communicate *with* their people and how they enable people in their organizations to communicate with one another has led us to write a different kind of book. We're fascinated more with how leadership communication works as a strategy to serve the three critical organizational agendas discussed above. This book is therefore about what leadership communication looks and sounds like when these three agendas are being well addressed and well supported. It's a book about things leaders do to make communication a force for accomplishing important organizational purpose.

In writing this book, we have set two goals for ourselves: first to make our case to leaders and potential leaders that communication carries a make-or-break importance; second, to provide comfortable, easy-to-remember, easy-to-use communication *tactics* and *tools* that support key leadership objectives. We hope as you read on that you'll see yourself in many of the situations we describe, that you'll feel reinforced in some of the things you're doing, and that you'll want to try some of the things you haven't done yet.

I

The Agenda for Leadership Communication

"We are raising the bar on understanding one another. We demand much more mutual understanding than we ever did in the past."

—Daniel Yankelovich, *The Magic of Dialogue*

Two significant developments in the lives of present-day organizations have important implications for those who lead teams, business units, or the entire organization. First, new generations of employees, particularly knowledge industry and other professional employees, expect to be not only well informed about their organization, but a part of the dialogue about where it is going. They want to know what management is thinking, and they want to have their opinions heard.

Second, organizations are more and more prone to merge, re-structure, and rebrand. Because of this, employees increasingly experience discontinuity and disruption in their work and in their relationships with their company and one another. Indeed, because the terms of the "new deal" in the workplace typically limit the company's long-term commitments to employees, discontinuity is almost a given.

We contend, especially in the work environment of the twenty-first century, that communication takes on even more importance because organization effectiveness is now measured more by human factors like intellectual capital (intelligence creating value) and social capital (relationships creating value) than by older factors like efficiency, waste, and absenteeism. Each one of these new human factors in turn is influenced by how employees *feel about* and *contribute to* their organization and its work. At stake here are relationship issues of trust and morale and, ultimately, of productivity and retention.

Employees today have higher expectations for work communication than ever before. What these expectations look like and why leaders need to adjust their own approach to communication in response are the subjects of the next two chapters.

1

Leaders as Communicators

> *"[M]anagers are leery about communicating. Although some are willing to communicate before they have all the answers, they are concerned about the consequences of making a mistake."*
>
> —Patricia Milligan,
> "Regaining Commitment"

*A*nd therein lies the dilemma. Leaders today often feel caught between "telling it like it is"—for many, the instinctive thing to do—and holding back (or just not telling it quite the way it is). Speeches about organizational goals and values, while easy enough to deliver, these days provoke questions and, in some cases, doubts that give leaders second thoughts about offering substantive information in the first place. After all, responsible leaders don't want to be caught setting expectations they can't stand behind, or making promises they can't keep.

And there's another concern—about the amount of open discussion and give-and-take that can be tolerated within the organization as it strives to move smartly together in the same direction. Employees seem to have more things to say and more questions to raise these days, but it's still the leader's responsibility to make the decisions and live by the consequences.

CAN WE TALK?

The problem is complicated by the traditional nature of leader-employee relationships in many organizations, and the ease with which employees and leaders fall into dysfunctional communication. Ronald Heifetz has suggested that "authority constrains leadership because in times of distress people expect too much. They form inappropriate dependencies that isolate their authorities behind a mask of knowing. And then everyone rationalizes the dependency."[1]

Under such circumstances, leadership communication can be little more than ceremonial: repeating platitudes and avoiding real dialogue. The senior leadership rituals of making cameo appearances at company events, conducting parade reviews at remote plants, and talking to the workforce via canned video broadcasts are perhaps the most obvious manifestations of this tendency. But to some extent, talking over (or around) employees is a risk that all leaders run. Unfortunately, many organizational leaders aren't even aware of such examples of their failure to communicate, of not connecting with their teams.

A FABLE

Once upon a time, there was a brilliant Fortune 500 corporate CEO. In fact, he was not only brilliant but also gracious, down-to-earth, affable. People inside the company who knew him generally liked him. Now the corporation was at a crossroads. Like many venerable Fortune 500 companies, this one needed to enter new and unfamiliar markets, continue to make big profits at its old businesses, and somehow engage its tens of thousands of employees around the world in this uncharted and difficult process.

But our CEO had a plan for the strategic change. It was big, daring, yet ingenious. Somehow it even answered the age-old consultant's dilemma about organizational transformation, namely, "How do you change a tire on a car going 90 mph?"

Picture the plan for success sketched out on a marker board, with a proud and satisfied CEO speaking to his troops on closed circuit video. He had worked hard, built the right equations, and now conveyed that deep sense that this was the right and best direction to go.

Without doubt, he had communicated and worked with his direct reports in choosing and planning the changes that would have to happen. In addition, once the concept was largely in place and ready to go, he informed his thousands of employees about the changes. He did this through all the typical, conventional, but high-quality employee communication tools at his disposal. Moreover, he did not just tell them once, but numerous times in many different ways.

Despite this, the employees . . . well, some didn't get it, some got it but didn't like it, and some liked it but believed it would never ever work. Employees grew cynical and frustrated as they saw jobs being changed, moved, or eliminated altogether. Many of those employees close to the marketplace saw the on-the-ground customer concerns and challenges much more clearly and much earlier than "corporate" did. But their insights and intelligence gathering from the marketplace never really worked their way into the CEO's thinking.

The CEO's plan unfolded, and initially it was successful to a significant degree. But success was built as much on the serendipities of marketplace preferences as on strategy. Later, when the numbers went south, the CEO confronted growing problems of morale, cynicism, and mistrust among the workforce. As repeated downsizing took place, the company lost important parts of its institutional knowledge and culture, including a significant number of more senior and longer-tenured employees.

Our CEO became frustrated, skeptical about the workforce and its inability to get behind the new plan. He understood the change strategy so well, recognized the need for it so clearly. Why couldn't the employees grasp it, buy into it, and go with it? After all, there were repeated announcements and explanations.

This fable represents a composite of real people we've seen coping with real challenges. For us it illustrates how many leaders come up short as communicators, not because they lack oratorical skills but because they see communication as little more than oratory. They grossly underestimate the importance of communication strategy and of communication *as* strategy.

WHAT WE MEAN BY LEADERSHIP COMMUNICATION

Since we're about to launch a baker's dozen chapters' worth of discussion on how leaders can effectively manage communications in their organizations (with particular focus on three key agendas), we think it wise to stake out the territory a bit. So here's what we mean by the concept.

First of all, as we tried to imply in the fable, leadership communication is a much bigger affair than simply delivering information or making "effective presentations." Our basic definition of leadership communication is that it involves the communication that leaders have *with* people, not simply words spoken, or information passed, *to* them. In this sense, thinking about leadership communication must address three topics:

1. What you say and how you say it
2. Whom you talk with
3. How you get people talking with you and with each other

Leadership cannot exist in the absence of dialogue with those who agree to be led. Command and authority are conferred, but leadership is created jointly, a product of the words shared and the conversations held that together establish and develop relationship. Lew Platt, former Hewlett Packard CEO, actually defined his job as "managing conversations."[2]

Thus, leadership communication is about relationship building, in all of its many dimensions. When leaders manage communication effectively, work relationships are strong, well informed, and purposeful. Both leaders and their teams are more engaged and in sync. Trust levels are higher, and information is freely shared. And there's a commitment to mutual education and feedback, such that things learned are spread and used within the organization.

Second, leadership communication is both an instrument of strategy *and a strategy in itself.* It is the means by which leaders build community and trust; create workforce alignment around mission and tasks; and engage employees in an ongoing, continuous improvement dynamic that shapes and reshapes the nature of the work, our three key organizational agendas. As a strategy, leadership communication can either accomplish successful realization of these three agendas or fail to do so.

LEADERSHIP COMMUNICATES: SO WHAT?

The problem with this subject is that it's easy to ignore. Everyone communicates—it's like breathing—and we all learn to do it as we grow up. So what's the issue? To be sure, the last thing we want to do in this book is to complicate a simple subject, or clothe it in so much jargon and consultant talk.

Instead, we invite you to step back a bit and to look at leadership communication from an organizational perspective—three organizational perspectives, to be exact. Stepping back is critical here, because our life in organizations is like being in the middle of a stream. We're caught in its constant flow. We typically take the water and the flow for granted because we don't have time to do much more than keep our boat headed in the right direction, and stay afloat. We don't think much about the very medium that carries us along, even while it changes speeds, turns corners, throws some things in our path and obscures others. What we want to invite you as readers and leaders to do is to step out of the water and reflect on communication as a medium we can skillfully direct and thereby gain advantage.

Immersion in the stream of organizational life can indeed hinder our ability to see and hear clearly what's going on around us. But leaders are potential victims of another source of disorientation, for as they move higher up the organizational ladder, they may be distancing themselves from two critical sources of organizational news: frontline employees and customers. The joke about the person at the top being the last to know is really an insight into the difficulty of leaders staying in touch. And a current strategy to counter this problem, reducing the distance from top to bottom by "delayering," can lead to other communication problems. As Henry Mintzberg reminds us, "delayering can be defined as the process by which people who barely know what's going on get rid of those who do."[3]

The three perspectives we employ to explore leadership communication have always been important in organizations, but in recent times they've gained new dimension and significance. In chapter 2, we examine each one in turn to establish just why they're important to the health of an organization and how they dictate communication strategy by leaders.

NOTES

1. Ronald A. Heifetz, *Leadership Without Easy Answers* (Boston: Belknap Press/Harvard University Press, 1994), 180.
2. Anne B. Fisher, "Making Change Stick," *Fortune* (April 17, 1995), 122.
3. Henry Mintzberg, "Musings on Management," *Harvard Business Review* (July–August 1996), 62.

2

Critical Issues for Leadership Communication

"Organizations have to market membership as much as they market products and services— and perhaps more. They have to attract people, hold people, recognize and reward people, motivate people, and serve and satisfy people."

—PETER DRUCKER, "THE NEW SOCIETY OF ORGANIZATIONS"

W e decided to write this book because leaders we've worked with continually express concern about three "people" issues that we, biased as we are, consider to be preeminently communication issues:

1. Commitment to the organization and its goals (calling for leaders to act as *community builders*)

2. Awareness and understanding of organizational goals and priorities (calling for leaders to act as *navigators* and *direction setters*), especially during change and transition
3. Willingness and ability to help the organization become better (calling for leaders to act as *renewal champions*)

A major section of the book is devoted to each of the three issues. Our approach in these sections is to explore the various communication *roles* leaders can play to manage the issues effectively. This chapter expands a bit on the issues, both as a source of concern to leaders everywhere and as an example of the critical nature of leadership communication in sustaining healthy, productive organizations.

ISSUE 1: COMMITMENT TO THE ORGANIZATION AND ITS GOALS

"Many executives now use the phrase, 'you want loyalty, get a dog.' "

—PETER CAPPELLI, *THE NEW DEAL AT WORK*

When commitment to the organization and its goals is weak, symptoms range from halfhearted work efforts to an ongoing exodus of your good people. Retaining talented people you want to keep has become a key issue for organizations in which knowledge assets are critical and where breaks in continuity can damage organizational effectiveness. Yet surprisingly, a recent study showed that "over 50% of firms surveyed had a strategy to recruit new talent, typically away from competitors, but only about 30% had a strategy for retaining the talent they already had."[1]

Commitment to an organization rests largely on relationships with one's boss. In one study, the quality of such relationships was found to be "three times more powerful in predicting organizational commitment" than variables like years in the job, job level, and organization size.[2] And the reverse is true too: human resources professionals tell us that people quit their boss more than they quit their organization.

Trust in the leadership of many organizations has been seriously rocked by a number of high profile scandals in recent years. This is over and above the mistrust generated by a decade or more of the layoff and merger craze. And trust, once lost, is hard to regain. Employee commitment to their leaders and to their organizations will come at a higher price, and it will come more slowly. It will require stronger demonstrations of leadership integrity and openness than ever before. The topic of trust is addressed later on in this chapter.

Organizations as Communities

> *"Most Americans harbor an unsatisfied hunger for community."*
>
> —DANIEL YANKELOVICH, *THE MAGIC OF DIALOGUE*

Work organizations have always provided a kind of community for employees. Our workplace is a source of colleagues and friends, supporters and allies, and the sense of self we develop around our job skills and position in the organization. Even in an era when lifetime employment seems a thing of the past, and constant change has meant constant restructuring of the work "community," the workplace remains an important (if not primary) social environment for most people.

Work organizations allow us to connect in meaningful ways to others. The conversations we have in the workplace are as much about simply socializing as about sharing job-related information. As one social scientist points out, people talk to establish bonds of social relationship with one another. "Small talk in this sense— about the weather, about mutual friends, about personal problems— universally constitutes the bulk of conversations from societies of hunter-gatherers to present-day postindustrial ones, and exists primarily for the purpose of enmeshing people in a web of social relationships and obligation."[3]

The workplace can, of course, be a strong, supportive community for its employees, or it can be something else. Some of the most important criteria for building a strong sense of workplace community can be inferred from research conducted over several decades by the Gallup organization. Gallup has sought to discover how employees determine the "strength of a workplace"—"the core elements needed to attract, focus, and keep the most talented employees."[4] The research focuses on a dozen factors that describe a strong, desirable workplace. Most of the areas deal with aspects of the workplace as a community, in which employees find friends, support, direction, and opportunities to speak out and be heard (the other four areas concentrate on job definition and material support).

The factors that refer to the workplace as a community are:

- ☐ Knowing what is expected of you at work
- ☐ Receiving regular recognition or praise for good work
- ☐ Feeling that your boss or some other manager cares about you as a person
- ☐ Having someone encourage your growth and development
- ☐ Feeling your opinions seem to count at work
- ☐ Feeling your job is important because of the mission and purpose of the organization
- ☐ Having a best friend at work
- ☐ Receiving periodic feedback on your work performance[5]

We believe the workplace issues raised in the Gallup research contain critical implications for leadership communications, and we refer back to them in ensuing chapters. For now, we'd like to treat them as a rather straightforward list of qualities that define effective organizations: the kind of organization that engenders strong employee commitment and loyalty.

The "New Deal" in the Workplace

Since the 1980s, employee commitment has been severely tested and, in fact, redefined, by the growing tendency of employers to regularly reconfigure, and often reduce, their workforce. We have come to speak of a new "social contract" and a "new deal at work" to describe the terms of organizational work, chief of which is the absence of long-term commitment by either organizations or employees. The new deal, in the words of Peter Cappelli, is "an openended agreement that is continually being negotiated between employer and employee, based on the state of the labor market."[6]

Under such fluid circumstances, many organizations have revised their thinking about employee commitment and how commitment actually adds value to the enterprise. "Commitment to what?" is a useful question for leaders to ask, because commitment to the organization as a whole is, in many instances, both an unrealistic expectation and perhaps no longer so important as it was in the days of lifetime employment.

Furthermore, given what employee research discloses about the factors employees value most in an employer (see the Gallup research above), commitment to the organization is not always that vital to high performance. "What is required," suggests Cappelli, "is probably as simple as commitment to colleagues, to a work team, or to a project. Commitment is much easier to establish with other individuals than with an abstract entity such as a corporation."[7]

Notwithstanding the above, many or most company leaders still believe that commitment and loyalty to the larger organization remains possible to some degree and, in many cases, worth working at. Strategies here range from building pride in the organization's mission, its standing in its industry, or its role as a good corporate citizen, to strengthening employee ties to the corporate community through family-friendly benefits and company-sponsored social events.

Cappelli's research identifies a variety of organizational strategies that correlate with greater employee commitment in the era of the new deal. Most of them have clear implications for leadership communication practices, including:

❐ More formalized work activities, including well-defined rules and policies
❐ Employee participation, and working with greater autonomy
❐ Indications to employees that the organization respects and appreciates their efforts
❐ Making employees feel that their contributions are important[8]

In addition to these practices, many companies are resorting to other approaches that refocus the sense of community around smaller work groups, where team and department leaders are challenged to create more open, free-flowing communications. We take up each of these findings in later chapters, when we discuss specific leadership communication tactics to build community.

Trust and Commitment

Trust is a condition of commitment and the glue that binds members of a community. In organizations, it is based on expectations, as well as demonstrations, of leaders being open, honest, and fair. Employees who have frequent communications with their leaders are generally more satisfied in their work, and they perform better as well. Employee commitment is also directly related to how open their organization is with information.

In the past ten years, employee trust in its leadership has been eroding. As one contributor to a Conference Board report put it,

"Management	But . . .
❏ Never seems to get its fair share of pain.	They're getting rewarded.
❏ Always seems to get a chair when the music stops.	The pay gap widens while layoffs pile up.
❏ Isn't leading with a clear vision.	They're maximizing shareholder value . . . by cutting payroll."[9]

This erosion of trust—especially in senior leadership—has centered on employee perceptions that the interests of the leadership team do not align with the rest of the organization. In corporate America, we have seen increasing instances of executive compensation tied to the price of stock. That in turn has led to complicated stock manipulations, sometimes at the expense of the longer-term health of the organization and its employees. In the wake of the Enron/Andersen affair, where both employees and stockholders were deceived, people have new reasons to question the trustworthiness of their leadership. Senior corporate executives are rightly concerned over the damage to company reputations in particular and to business repute in general.

Employee trust in leadership rests on two factors. The first is the way leaders execute their duties and obligations in support of the work contract, however formalized that contract is. The second involves a less formal set of relationships, which unfold on a day-to-day basis and turn on such leadership behaviors as fairness and supportiveness. As the new deal makes the first factor more limited in scope, the second gains in importance. How leaders communicate with their people is clearly key to how trustworthy they appear and how well they in turn extend trust to employees. Trust is reciprocal in organizations: I'll be more likely to trust you if you express trust in me.

A Valued, but Vulnerable, Commodity

What's especially interesting about the evolving workplace is how leader-employee relationships are becoming more informal and collegial. There is a feeling of greater egalitarianism in many organizations, which in turn implies higher levels of mutual trust. But this trust is severely tested when organizations restructure and people are moved around or laid off. In the worst case, employees come to feel that the casual, friendly work climate is just a sham, a superficial kind of relationship that doesn't represent the real terms of the new deal.

Other tests that trust in leadership must weather are tied to how the organization represents itself and is seen by the outside world. In almost any instance in which an organization is publicly accused of wrongdoing, the harm done to its external reputation is felt inside too. Employees become suspicious about the motives and ethics of their leadership and can deny them the kind of trust they may have freely extended before. On an operational level, work productivity can suffer because failed trust leads to employee confusion, reluctance to act, and time wasted in defending reputations (as well as performing damage control).

Over the past few decades we've come to see trust in organizational leadership as adding real value to team and organizational performance. Social scientists have coined the concept of "social capital" to describe how strong relationships built on trust constitute a measurable asset, leading employees to more willingly subordinate their individual interests to those of the organization. When social capital declines, so does cooperation, selflessness, open sharing of information of ideas, and willingness to go the extra mile for the organization. When social capital declines, so does the strength of community.

Issue 2: Awareness and Understanding of Organizational Goals and Priorities

Getting everyone in the organization on the same page, focused on the priorities of the moment, is a challenge at any time. In an era characterized by constant change to organizational structures, systems, and objectives, the obvious danger is that the workforce will lose its focus and spin its wheels. When "the right thing to do" is a moving target, at best you'll hit it infrequently; at worst, you'll give up in frustration. The importance of clear, regular, and up-to-date communication as an antidote to this danger is also obvious.

Effective leadership communication is the most powerful tool for managing change and transition in your organization. It is critical in minimizing employee fear, paralysis, and disaffection that in turn can hurt organizational performance. Yet many organizations, especially companies engaged in merger and acquisition activity, communicate too little too late about new directions and what they mean. The poor track record these initiatives have shown is certainly a consequence of a failure to communicate well.

Part of the problem is that leaders are reluctant to involve too many people in plotting the course of change—in being part of the change conversation. Richard Pascale suggests that the problem "is that the whole burden of change typically rests on so few people. In other words, the number of people *at every level* who make committed, imaginative contributions to organizational success is simply too small."[10] This kind of problem in communicating has two dimensions to it. One is the issue of who needs to know and be involved. The other is how best to create and sustain a meaningful dialogue with people who *can* help shape change to the advantage of the organization (and themselves). We address both in Part IV.

Straight Talk, and More of It, Please

Even in less turbulent, more "normal" circumstances, practically every employee attitude survey cites communication as a problem. Employees don't feel they're well informed about what's going on and what's important. And it's not always because they don't get enough information; sometimes they say they get too much and have difficulties sorting the relevant from the irrelevant. They say that leadership relies too much on broadcast rather than face-to-face communication, a form they consider less clear and reliable. They complain they're often confused when leaders speak too "globally" when they need a more "local" focus and context. And they feel disappointed, as well as uncertain about what to do, when important news is fired out at them but leaders don't follow up to explain what it means.

Ironically, at a time when many leaders say they want to be more accessible and open with employees, and with e-mail and intranets providing the means for more regular and easy communication, too many employees feel out of tune and out of touch with the organization. Yet with nimbleness and flexibility becoming more important, the workforce needs to be well informed and aligned with what's important now more than ever before. Leaders must share information more regularly, and, more important, they need to explain what "it really means" to employees. If you can't explain why an objective or a task is important, then you can't expect others to rally around it.

Simple, Direct, and Often: Information Sharing at Emerson

Sharing information and keeping people informed are so important at Emerson, a leading global manufacturing company, that division presidents are required to develop an annual communications plan, and are evaluated on its implementation. "Effective communication is key: it breeds involvement," says CEO David Farr.[11] A standard element of the plan is a state-of-the-business address that covers market conditions, the business plan, costs, priority concerns, and what people can do to help. This annual address is supplemented by quarterly updates, typically delivered by the division president or the plant manager.

Prior to these quarterly communication meetings, Farr delivers a Webcast to all company executives worldwide on the corporate picture, reviewing subjects like profitability, inventories, and any major issues the company is dealing with. "I communicate very openly throughout the organization, so everyone in the organization can hear clearly 'this is what's important,'" admits Farr, who adds "I use e-mail a lot." The Webcasts create context for the dialogue at the division level. When Emerson wants to alert employees to some fast-breaking news, it also resorts to its Webcast method.

One of the established tenets of leadership behavior at Emerson is to "keep it simple." From a communication standpoint, this has some obvious, as well as some less obvious, implications. Leaders at Emerson are expected to be direct, open, and forthright in their communications with employees. Somewhat ironically, Farr mentions developing "simple plans" as another aspect of this management tenet. And when you think of it, a plan that has been carefully examined and forged through much discussion is ultimately a simpler plan to communicate and implement. It's got most of the ambiguities knocked out of it and most of the "i's" dotted.

As a third dimension of keeping it simple, Emerson prides itself on having minimal bureaucracy to slow down and complicate organizational message delivery. The distance from Farr's office to any plant operator is among the shortest in the industry. Simple plans, simple messaging, simple organization: they all contribute to a clear mandate for leadership communication at Emerson.

Issue 3: Willingness and Ability to Help the Organization Become Better

"The only thing that increasingly will matter . . . is management's performance in making knowledge productive."

—Peter Drucker, *Post-Capitalist Society*

In the twenty-first century people want to work for dynamic *learning organizations* that give them continuous opportunity to put their knowledge to work. We want our bosses to listen to us when we have ideas about how to make things better. And we want to be acknowledged and respected, if not rewarded, for the thought contributions we make to the organization.

That's good news, because smart leaders will look for any knowledge advantages they can find to incorporate into the way business is done. The challenge for leadership is to recognize these potential "knowledge assets" and to leverage them effectively. As Drucker notes, "making knowledge productive" is increasingly the way leadership contributes value to the organization.

Intellectual Capital with No Return

What makes this challenge a communication issue is that knowledge is only an asset if it is shared and applied. Unfortunately, organizations and their leadership don't always know how to do this, and there are significant organizational barriers to turning valuable knowledge into valuable practice. Expertise is often locked in the heads of individual employees, and it doesn't get out. Sometimes this is simply because ideas are not fully articulated. Or they aren't shared because employees can't put them adequately into words. They're embedded in their work practice: they know how to apply the knowledge but can't quite tell you everything they do.

But just as often, employee knowledge is withheld for want of a motive to share it or for fear that bringing an idea forward will result in negative, rather than positive, consequences to the individual. When fear of criticism and backlash from leadership causes people to keep their thinking to themselves, then intellectual capital is squandered, and the return is minimal to nonexistent.

For almost ten years one of us witnessed a vivid illustration of this phenomenon while working with corporate clients to set up and administer team suggestion systems. Our approach involved employee teams meeting for about twelve weeks to generate cost reduction ideas, with each team member sharing in a significant award for any submitted ideas that were approved. The idea was that by training team leaders in problem solving and cost accounting, teams would be able to work together during the twelve weeks to come up with some usable ideas.

Without fail, however, there was a disproportionate number of great ideas submitted *during the first few days of the program,* which could not possibly have resulted from much team deliberation since in most cases they would only have met once by that time. Rather, individual employees who had been carrying around ideas, sometimes for years, on how the organization could cut costs were finally given a good enough reason to bring them forward.

Intellectual Capital Is Invested Socially

Clearly, leaders must open doors for good ideas to come out, and create opportunities for employee conversations to spread knowledge and expertise. These challenges are much more complicated than building an intranet and flooding the field with employee input. They involve understanding what makes employees reluctant to offer their best thinking, and how these barriers might be countered. They involve as well being proactive about reducing fear—including clearing the "trolls" out from under any bridges you want to invite your people to cross. Knowing that you're their champion when it comes to offering a critique of the status quo or, at least implicitly, a criticism of present practices ordained by present leadership, is critical to your people's willingness to speak out.

Connecting more closely with your employees, and helping them connect more regularly with one another, primes the pump. As the Conference Board concluded, "If employees are vital assets, management can no longer afford to be isolated from the people in their organizations. Leadership in the context of the new deal means involving employees and mutually defining goals. It also means having visible leadership, where actions speak louder than mission statements."[12]

Intellectual capital is most likely to deliver returns when its owners feel free to share it, question it, and build on it. Dialogue focused on acquiring, examining, creating, and applying new knowledge is what puts intellectual capital to work in an organization and what delivers both short- and long-term returns. It's all about leaders bringing the right people together and getting them talking in the most open, informed, and productive ways. We talk more about this in chapters 9 through 12.

Getting Practical

We're now ready to take you on a tour of our three-dimensional model—how leaders can most effectively use communication strategies and tactics to deal with issues of community and trust, focus and alignment, and learning and renewal. We address these issues using insights from organizations we've worked with and heard about, tactics we've seen demonstrated by a variety of leaders at all organizational levels, and ideas we've picked up along the way in our experience as students and teachers of communication. Our aim is to be as practical as possible, providing you with things to do and say that make good sense.

NOTES

1. Peter Cappelli, "Managing Without Commitment," *Organizational Dynamics* (spring 2000), 14.
2. T. J. Larkin and Sandar Larkin, *Communicating Change: Winning Employee Support for New Business Goals* (New York: McGraw-Hill, 1994), 15.
3. Francis Fukuyama, *The Great Disruption* (New York: The Free Press, 1999), 179.
4. Marcus Buckingham and Curt Coffman, *First, Break All the Rules* (New York: Simon & Schuster, 1999), 28.
5. Ibid.
6. Cappelli, "Managing Without Commitment," 11.
7. Peter Cappelli, *The New Deal at Work: Managing the Market-Driven Workforce* (Boston: Harvard Business School Press, 1999), 218.
8. Cappelli, "Managing Without Commitment," 19.
9. Patricia Milligan, "Regaining Commitment," *The New Deal in Employment,* Report No. 1162-96-CR (New York: The Conference Board, 1996), 8.
10. Richard Pascale, "Changing the Way We Change," *Harvard Business Review* (November–December 1997), 127.
11. David N. Farr, speech delivered at the Dean's Breakfast, John Cook School of Business, St. Louis University, September 25, 2001. All subsequently quoted material by Farr comes from this source.
12. Brian Hackett, "What's New About the New Deal?" *The New Deal in Employment,* Report No. 1162-96-CR (New York: The Conference Board, 1996), 30.

II

The Leader as Community Developer

> *"Effective leaders put words to the formless longings and deeply felt needs of others. They create communities out of words."*
>
> —WARREN BENNIS, "THE LEADER AS STORYTELLER"

N o matter how small a work organization may be, it still represents a kind of community for its employees, a place where members share a common purpose and come to know one another. Organizational leaders have long played on this sense of community, with its concomitant attributes of loyalty and commitment to the organization. In today's workplace, strong ties to the organization are perhaps even more vital as leaders seek to involve employees more fully in all aspects of the enterprise.

In particular, leaders want employees who are motivated to think creatively on behalf of the organization. As Chris Argyris suggests, "To bring this about corporate communications must demand more of everyone involved. Leaders and subordinates alike, those who ask and those who answer, must all begin struggling with a new level of self-awareness, candor, and responsibility."[1]

This section on the leader as *community developer* unfolds around several related discussions. Chapter 3 looks at how leaders help integrate employees into the work community by inviting their allegiance to organizational goals and what goal attainment might mean both to the organization and to them. In chapter 4, we examine how leaders can deepen feelings of community membership and affiliation through storytelling, a powerful communication medium that links people to a common culture and common values. Chapter 5 examines how leaders present themselves as trustworthy communicators, the tactics they use to build trusting work relationships, tips on listening and managing dialog, and communication practices that create a climate of trust throughout the organization.

Throughout the book, we blend organization vignettes, research insights, and practical tips to guide leadership communication practice. And we wrestle with the paradox that people struggle with in most organizations: wanting to believe in each other and, in particular, in their leadership, yet all the while knowing that one of the reasons the Dilbert comic strip is so funny is that it is all too often true.

Note

1. Chris Argyris, "Good Communication That Blocks Learning," *Harvard Business Review* (July–August 1994), 85.

3

Meaning-Maker

*"Work both reflects our interests and forms
them."*

—KENNETH BURKE, *PERMANENCE AND CHANGE*

O ne of the challenges for leaders in any organization, at any
level, is to help their employees find intrinsic reward in
their work. The good news here is that sources of intrinsic
reward are various and plentiful.

Many of us, in fact, feel rewarded simply by doing a job well.
We don't need anyone to tell us about it; we know it when we've
done it. For those involved directly in the competitive side of the
organization's affairs—selling, developing proposals, maintaining
client relationships—the intrinsic rewards can come from winning
and sustaining wins. Here, organization leaders can enhance this
kind of reward by actively recognizing wins, calling attention to
their significance, and celebrating their accomplishment.

But we can go further with the idea of intrinsic rewards. Beyond knowing that a job's well done or well won lies a vast territory
of intrinsic work rewards that can be influenced by an organization's leadership—in particular, by leaders talking with their people
about the meaning of the work. In managing such conversation,

leaders can become nothing less than *meaning-makers* for their organizations, helping people make sense of their work and jobs in two ways:

1. They create focus and context for the work of the organization.
2. They "offer legitimate channels for members to act in ways that will increase their feelings of significance and their actual importance to the community."[1]

MAKING JOBS BIG ENOUGH FOR PEOPLE

"Most of us are looking for a calling, not a job. Most of us, like the assembly line worker, have jobs that are too small for our spirit. Jobs are not big enough for people."

—STUDS TERKEL, *WORKING*

There is another, more fundamental, level at which we derive satisfaction from work. It involves how we think about the meaning of our work, and about the work of the organizations that employ us. It is the level at which work helps to create our sense of identity—our basic definition of ourselves, the values we hold, and the roles we adopt. In its extreme form, we come to speak of work in terms of a "calling"—where our job attaches to a strong sense of mission and fulfills some deep-seated personal needs and desires. We see this occasionally with occupations in organized religion, the military, and perhaps professions like medicine or social work.

Most of us probably don't view our jobs as a calling, but we can still take significant satisfaction from our work because of its very nature. In many cases, the personal meaning we derive from work comes with the territory. People in the health-care industry contribute to the physical well-being of others and can readily confer a special meaningfulness to their jobs. People in the entertainment industry amuse us and contribute to our emotional well-being; they can take satisfaction from this sense of their work, irrespective of their actual role in it.

The equation that links an industry's work to some societal benefit, and hence some readily derived societal meaning for one's work, is doubtless stronger in some cases than others. But the potential is almost always there to make work meaningful above and beyond the actual details of a job and how it's performed. This is especially true when our work involves us in some kind of purposeful activity from which we can derive a sense of both personal meaning and belonging to a group. The research cited in chapter 2 is quite clear about this and supports the propositions about work, identity, and satisfaction illustrated in Figure 3-1.

A few years ago there was an unusual and amusing series of television ads for an online job search company. They featured several young kids, staring into the camera, saying things like "When I grow up, I want to earn a living wage," or "When I grow up, I want to be downsized." The tone of the messages was heavily ironic: the speakers' sense of a personal vision was the antithesis of the American dream. Most people we know who saw the ads felt they really hit home and made a strong statement about the importance of work identity. The tag lines for the ad series highlight an increasingly important dimension of work life and its potential to satisfy us: we want our work to have meaning and to connect us in meaningful ways to other people.

Researchers Linda Smircich and Gareth Morgan go so far as to define leadership as the "management of meaning": "the way leadership actions attempt to shape and interpret situations to guide organizational members into a common interpretation of reality...."[2] Meaning-making is all about constructing a sense of what is real

Figure 3-1. Propositions about work identity.

❑ The workplace is an important *community* for most people, one in which we spend significant proportions of our time.

❑ People want to feel a sense of status in their workplace, an identity that can command a certain respect.

❑ People want work to be meaningful, to have a purpose.

❑ People want to feel good about the contribution they make through their work.

and important, both for the individual and for the organization. Meaning-making becomes a critical dimension of the leader's role because when people have a clear sense of what they are doing together and why it's important, they understand better the nature of the enterprise and are more strongly committed to it. In our view, those "leadership actions" referred to above are mainly about communication. Leaders make a distinct contribution here simply by exercising a routine of strategic communication.

MAKING WORK MEANINGFUL: TWO LEADERSHIP COMMUNICATION TASKS

> "One might just as well say that leadership is the process of making sense of what people are doing together so that people will understand and be committed."
> —WILFRED H. DRATH AND CHARLES J. PALUS, *MAKING COMMON SENSE*

As a meaning-maker, the leader has two broad communication tasks: helping people strengthen their feeling of membership in, or affiliation with, the group or organization; and creating "frames" that people can use to understand better and define their work and its meaning.

1. *Defining Membership.* Leaders who help people feel they are part of a larger community that supports them and serves their interests can command a more abiding sense of loyalty and higher levels of work satisfaction from those people.

2. *Framing Work.* Leaders who help colleagues and employees articulate for themselves a greater sense of meaningfulness in their work roles can strengthen the intrinsic reward potential of work and so energize the workforce. Leaders who help people recognize the value and meaning of their work are able to tighten the alignment between personal and organizational goals and enjoy

higher levels of commitment, perseverance, and dedication as well.

Leaders can be *meaning-makers* for their people in the sense that they can communicate how work may acquire meaning that is positive and fulfilling. In the following pages, we discuss several fundamental strategies for how leaders can play this meaning-maker role by effectively managing these two critical communication tasks.

MEANING-MAKER TASK ONE: DEFINING MEMBERSHIP

> *"[L]anguage evolved to facilitate the bonding of social groups, and . . . it mainly achieves this aim by permitting the exchange of socially relevant information."*
>
> —ROBIN DUNBAR, *GROOMING, GOSSIP, AND THE EVOLUTION OF LANGUAGE*

Cultural anthropologists tell us that people (as well as primates) are preeminently social animals. We live as members of families, teams, communities, and larger societies and cultures because that's how we've evolved. We seek out membership in groups because we tend to profit from them as individuals: they help us cope and provide us with comfort and security.

It's Only Natural

Interestingly, researchers in a variety of evolutionary fields (anthropology, linguistics, physiology, etc.) suggest that both prehistoric communities ("bands") as well as more contemporary human groups seem to favor "an upper limit for group size compatible with everyone's knowing everybody"—in other words, being able to address people based upon some kind of personal recognition. We seem to affiliate naturally with groups that are not so big that we can't get to know each member in some relational way—which according to the researchers tops out around "a few hundred," a figure that, for instance, represents approximately the number of students a school principal can claim to know by name.[3]

Most of us work for an organization that provides us, at minimum, with some form of compensation, along with an infrastructure and tools with which to perform our job roles. But beyond that, organizations can represent for their employees both a community of friends and supportive colleagues and a source of identity through association with a larger entity. *To be part of something that's bigger than ourselves is a natural instinct that can be either well or poorly served by the organization we work for.*

Some organizations manage to communicate to their members a ready sense of belongingness, a status of membership with privileges. Others do not. How to deliver this communication successfully is a major issue we'll want to address in this chapter. From a structural standpoint, the need to affiliate, to feel membership in a community, would seem to be better served by a smaller organization (a few hundred members or less) than by a larger one.

Larger organizations represent, in this sense, more of an *abstraction* of community that we must come to terms with in different, sometimes more artificial, ways. For one thing, the tendency of larger organizations to organize themselves bureaucratically presents the threat of dehumanizing relationships and compromising affiliations. Therefore, the ways in which leaders manage through their communications *the natural human instinct toward group affiliation* is critical in creating, or failing to create, opportunities for employees to secure satisfying and rewarding experiences from group membership.

A Sense of Inclusion

Many organizations in fact solve this problem of heavily formal, bureaucratized communication by flattening the organization's structure: creating work units and departments that maintain reasonable size limits. But more to our purpose, the challenge to create and sustain opportunities for satisfying affiliation needs is often best served by a variety of leadership communication strategies.

At the top level, for example, leadership communication wants to emphasize a sense of *inclusion in a close and supportive community.*

Leaders want to constantly affirm the rights of employees to "full membership status," even while maintaining different levels of such status. Jack Welch came up with a folksy kind of metaphor to describe the GE environment: "We came to work everyday open to ideas from anywhere, trying to create the atmosphere of the informal corner grocery store in a large business—a family business that didn't count where you came from or how many stripes you had on your sleeve."[4]

Welch is addressing here a special dimension of the affiliation strategy: the challenge to make organization members feel closer to the *center* of things, where their voice counts and can be heard. If we construe meaning-making as a shared activity between leaders and their people, then, as Drath and Palus point out, "People closer to the center naturally participate more fully in creating, nurturing, and evolving the meanings of the community."[5] Strengthening the opportunity to affiliate brings with it the opportunity to play a more active role in "co-constructing" meaning. Meaning-making becomes a collective endeavor that binds organization members more tightly together in a cooperatively shaped future.

Phil Jackson and Leadership Communication   At a ceremony honoring the achievements of NBA basketball coach Phil Jackson with the Chicago Bulls basketball club, a former player spoke about what made the experience with Jackson so rewarding for his teammates and himself, apart from winning six championships. Addressing his coach, the player shared these sentiments: "Phil, you gave all of us the love of this game back. . . . You let us embrace the game and see the beauty it can be on the floor. . . . But most important of all, you allowed us to believe in what team is all about."[6]

So what might this ability to bind people together look like from the standpoint of specific communication strategies: things you might say, and ways to make your words well understood? Figure 3-2 lists four basic themes that can be played on in different ways, continuously.

For each theme, you'll need anecdotes, examples, illustrations of how they play out in your organization. Moreover, talking about these themes heightens employee sensitivity to their presence, or the extent of their presence, in your organization. The best approach is to acknowledge that the organization is less than perfect

Figure 3-2. Communication themes to strengthen affiliation.

1. We share a common stake in serving a worthy purpose.
2. We share allegiance to commonly held values.
3. Everyone is important; everyone is part of a community.
4. We think and work as a team; we succeed when we're united.

in each of these areas, but cite examples of where these themes are in evidence and where they need to be strengthened.

Perhaps the best illustration of pulling together a large group of people by emphasizing all of these affiliation themes is the way in which the American government, together with public and private institutions and the media, rallied Americans in the months following the September 11 tragedies. As Americans, we often take our identity as citizens of a nation for granted. Our affiliations are focused on smaller associations and group identities. But we claimed our citizenship loudly and passionately as we responded to an unprecedented national crisis, and our leaders wove all of the themes cited above into their speeches, as they sought to rally us around a new and uncertain future.

Community Dialogue

In an obvious way, we affiliate with an organization when we can freely converse with its members. The more dialogue we have, and the more people we talk with, the more affiliative ties we tend to make within the organization. As a leader you want to have conversations, in myriad forms, with everyone. You also want to make it easy for everyone to hold their own conversations, share information, ask and answer questions, and speak their mind. For an organization to take on the feel of a community for its members, the communication role of leadership needs to promote inclusion and shared responsibility: "We're all in this together."

Bureaucracy, rank, and privilege work against a dynamic sense of community in an organization. They convey distance between bureaucratic levels and patronize, rather than engage, fellow workers. Not to "stand on ceremony" is one important tactic to use here. Examples range from Japanese auto executives eschewing perks and large corner offices and making themselves physically accessible to others, to GE's emphasis on informality as a code of behavior, to Emerson's constant flattening of its organization to minimize the distance between leaders and frontline workers. Wherever possible, leadership communication must emphasize strong community affiliation and membership by trading on concepts of solidarity, stewardship, and collaboration.

We have found three strategies in particular to be effective in leveraging communications that strengthen the sense of membership and affiliation:

1. Encouraging people to make public their commitments to the organization, its goals, and its objectives
2. Holding group gatherings to build relationships
3. Publicizing the organization's role as a corporate citizen

A discussion of each of these strategies follows.

Encouraging People to Make *Public* Their Commitments to the Organization, Its Goals, and Its Objectives

Psychologist Robert Cialdini reports that "there's strong evidence to show that a choice made actively—one that's spoken out loud or written down or otherwise made explicit—is considerably more likely to direct someone's future conduct than the same choice left unspoken."[7] We've observed this behavior on many occasions, as in the following example.

Testifying for Quality A group of team leaders was being challenged to raise quality indicators at a "Big Three" American automotive components plant. The group was generally cynical about such initiatives and collectively did not express much enthusiasm for the effort.

Company management took an unusual step and invited team leaders to do two things: write a paragraph or two about what they thought quality meant to them and what kinds of quality they could commit to; then forward the paragraph to headquarters and receive a jacket with the company logo and a statement of quality commitment prominently displayed on it. To most people's surprise, the

invitation was widely taken up, and the written statements conveyed genuine, if not eloquent, expressions of the importance of
quality work. On a personal level, the subject of quality struck a
responsive chord. The initiative was in turn much better supported
than management had expected. Team leaders stuck by their words
and wore their jackets proudly. Figure 3-3 suggests how leaders
might initiate a public commitment of this nature.

Advocates and Ambassadors A variation of this strategy involves
asking employees to play the role of organization ambassador or
(increasingly) of "brand ambassador." When employees assume the
responsibility of speaking for the organization to outside audiences,
they often internalize their speeches and their message points and
wind up feeling more strongly affiliated with the organization. We
all tend to feel more strongly about something when we actually
speak out for it: in effect, we become what we say. Leaders are often
mystified by the lack of commitment shown by their reports, when
in fact these people might readily ratchet up their commitment levels considerably simply by having opportunities to "testify," as leaders more routinely have to do.

There are many opportunities for employees to affiliate by becoming advocates and spokespersons both inside and outside the
organization. Invitations to describe work team successes at staff
meetings allow people to feel good about themselves as team mem-

Figure 3-3. Making commitment public.

Leaders should consider when and how it might be appropriate to invite
their people to register a commitment in some public way. We suggest a
three-step communication routine to maximize effectiveness:

1. On a voluntary basis, *ask* people to "sign on" or to "make a pledge"
   or to verbally commit in some way to an objective or a cause.
2. *Share* the commitments with a larger audience (people want to
   appear consistent with what they've said). This can be done simply
   by announcing the number of people who have signed on or, more
   ambitiously (if appropriate), by actually listing names of pledgers,
   publishing pledge statements, etc.
3. *Respond* both privately and publicly to public commitments: "I
   think Tom and his team's plan is right on target and begs our support. Let me know how I can help."

bers, without the awkwardness of seeming to brag about themselves as individuals. And being asked to speak before community groups and associations as a representative of the company or even to generate sales referrals for products they feel proud of has the potential to strengthen their feelings and loyalties toward the organization.

Holding Group Gatherings to Build Relationships

Finding positive occasions to bring people together is another easy way to reinforce the sense of community most employees desire. Many organizations have a knack for holding large gatherings that are both fun and effective at building solidarity. Southwest Airlines has long been known for the frequency and liveliness of its group celebrations ("The party never ends"[8]). These routinely festive occasions strengthen affiliation in several ways, from simply allowing employees to have fun together, to celebrating group and organizational accomplishments, to envisioning the future together.

In fact, any group celebration creates a forum for leaders to reinforce the ties that link employees to one another and to the organization. Leaders might focus on any or all of the following topics to highlight the benefits of organizational membership:

❒ Group or team contributions to the organization's success
❒ Organizational accomplishments brought about by great effort
❒ The organization's history and the continuance of strong traditions
❒ A positive, healthy future for the organization and its people

There are of course other occasions besides "celebrations" for assembling large groups of organization members. Educational meetings, planning retreats, and conferences can do double duty: Accomplish the primary objectives of the gathering *and* strengthen the positive feelings that people have for the organization and for their membership in it, as well.

When Kindred Spirits Come Together Fleishman-Hillard, one of the world's biggest public relations/communications agencies, traditionally convenes a "worldwide conference" every two or three years, as much to expand and enhance relationships across far-flung offices as to share corporate goals, plans, and best practices. For a recent worldwide conference, Dave Senay, then general manager of Fleishman-Hillard's headquarters office, sent the memo shown in Figure 3-4 to his troops to help them make the most of their conference attendance.

It's also worth saying that efforts to build on the sense of community within the organization don't have to be major productions. While the annual conference, company picnic, or holiday party might be a great way to support affiliation, there are many other informal occasions for bringing people together for conversation: luncheons for honorees, brown baggers, golf and bowling events, and so on. Never underestimate the value of these gatherings in helping to define continually for employees just what it means to be a member of the organization.

Publicizing the Organization's Role as a Corporate Citizen

An important dimension of one's identity as an organizational employee is how that organization connects with the larger society, especially with the communities where employees live. Membership in an organization is strengthened when that organization is known to be a responsible, if not generous, corporate citizen. Unfortunately, many leaders ignore this dimension of organizational life, even when their company might be actively engaged in philanthropic or other civic activity.

Taking Pride in Corporate Citizenship UPS is an example of a company that both maintains a strong philanthropic program and actively encourages its people to get involved as community volunteers. Managers and other employees are actually allowed to perform some volunteering on work time, and an unusually high proportion of UPS people serve on boards, committees, neighborhood improvement projects, etc. Imagine how you'd feel as a UPS employee when your company runs national full-page ads like the one picturing Dave Smith, UPS package car driver (in his brown uniform), and Elder P. J. Thomas—cofounders of Manna Ministries, Alabaster, Alabama—over this quote from Mr. Smith:

Figure 3-4. Fleishman-Hillard memo: getting the most from employee conferences.

Friends:

If you haven't been to a worldwide conference before, you're in for a real treat. The only problem is how fast the two-plus days fly by. Suddenly it's Saturday, you're on a bus to the airport, and you're wondering where the time went. I wanted to share some thoughts gained from WWC's of the past, and hope you can add them to your own list of ideas.

1. Don't let the conference just "happen to you." It's designed as a free-wheeling dialogue throughout, both in the structured times, and unstructured times. Mix it up, intellectually, socially.
2. Have a plan. Many of you have worked across office lines on accounts and probably have at least a person or two for whom you would like to match a voice and face. Don't leave without finding each person you'd like to meet. And that person you're standing next to in the lunch buffet line? By all means introduce yourself. . . .
3. We have new partners. . . . they really want to know about FH. Be generous with your time, show them the way.
4. Avoid one another. OK, not really. But if you are exclusively "hangin' with your home boys or girls" during this gathering, well, it will be a pity.
5. Believe it or not, there's a certain mystique to being from the "corporate headquarters." Some of the mystique is good; some ain't. As ambassadors of all that is good and right with the world, not to mention FH, your neighborliness, humility and hospitality will go a long way to solidifying our role as intersection of all roads through FH.
6. You may never be surrounded again in your life by such a high concentration of intelligent, energetic, personable and kindred spirits as you will at this conference. It's the global nation of FH. And it's a feast. There is real joy in this event. Celebrate it. Add to it.

See you there!

Dave

Reprinted with permission.

LIBRARY, UNIVERSITY OF CHESTER

> My partner P. J. and I cofounded Manna Ministries
> 12 years ago with just a couple of cans of food.
> Nowadays, we feed 478 families a month. My em-
> ployer, UPS, has been supportive through it all.
> Helping me balance delivering packages with vol-
> unteering 60 hours a week, stocking our pantries
> and donating money when I won the UPS Jim
> Casey Community Service Award.[9]

When an organization like UPS contributes to civic improvement, its reputation climbs with two audiences: the public (including clients) and its own workforce. Some companies might choose
to avoid the spotlight for civic contributions, but they do not need
to hide their philanthropic role from employees. By making this
role "public" inside the organization, leadership is merely acknowledging that *everyone* in the organization should take credit for, and
feel proud about, these contributions.

One final note on communication strategy in support of affiliation and building an identity around the organization. Sometimes
the best way to build social cohesion and a strong group identity is
to define the organization through its competitive situation. "We
work together so as to triumph over our competitors. We're a team
whose identity is strengthened through contest and through the
drama of contests that pit teams against one another." Though the
call to compete, to do battle, if you will, can be overused and over-
done, it can still help develop employee affiliation. People often
cohere as an organization simply by understanding what makes their
own organization different from the competition.

MEANING-MAKER TASK TWO: FRAMING

*"Framing provides a means of constructing a world, of
characterizing its flow, of segmenting events within that
world, and so on. If we were not able to do such framing,
we would be lost in a murk of chaotic experience and
probably would not have survived as a species in any
case."*

—JEROME BRUNER, ACTS OF MEANING

On December 10, 2001, four Americans were memorialized for their roles in the conflict in Afghanistan. All of them had given their lives in actions against the Taliban. One, a former marine and CIA operative, was to be buried in Arlington National Cemetery. The three others, Green Berets who were felled by "friendly fire," were honored in a separate ceremony at Fort Campbell, Kentucky.

One of the eulogies included these words: "They changed lives for the better and freed them from oppression. What more of a legacy could anyone hope to have?" Another concluded that "these warriors gave themselves for the pursuit of something greater than themselves because they knew it was the right thing to do. They gave themselves not just for a cause, but so that people beaten down by an oppressed authority might be liberated . . . to know the experience, the blessings of liberty of freedom that we citizens of this precious land know and cherish so deeply."[10]

Eulogies are opportunities to talk about people in larger contexts, as distinguished and remembered by the causes they lived (and died) for, the people they helped, the callings they served. We use eulogies to commemorate the meaning of lives. They are occasions in which the things people do and did are linked to a significance that summons our respect and admiration. Eulogies, however, are not the only opportunities where we can cast deeds and actions in larger, more significant molds. We don't have to wait so long.

Framing Work Experience

Our lives and our day-to-day tasks always have the potential to take on larger meanings when we see them tied to larger, ongoing organizational purposes. When you cast the work of the organization in such a way, you are framing the work experience in a clearer, more significant context. The frame changes the meaning of work, especially for those who do the work.

Framing represents a critical communication role that leaders perform to make work and work life more meaningful. Framing, we argue, occurs all the time. Leaders inevitably create contexts for work throughout their communications, whether deliberately or not. How they describe specific situations or challenges gives meaning to the work that must follow. Leaders are clearly in the meaning construction business ("meaning-making" is just a more elegant and alliterative way to say it). Leaders construct meanings around work and work tasks with varying degrees of intentionality. They find themselves regularly playing all three roles in the parable of the three umpires: "The first one said, 'I calls them like they is.' The second one said, 'I calls them as I sees them.' The third and cleverest umpire said, 'They ain't nothin' till I calls them.' "[11]

A consciously planned framing strategy can help a workforce clarify and enlarge its sense of the meaning of work. We see four dimensions to this framing strategy:

1. The "big picture"
2. Vision
3. Values
4. Change and refocusing

Leaders have occasion to create enhanced meaning for organizational work through these four dimensions. Let us examine each, while not ignoring the fact that there is considerable overlap among them in almost any framing discussion.

Framing the "Big Picture": Naming the Game

In the past decade or so, organizations have come to realize the value of making employees more knowledgeable about the environment in which they operate. This has been particularly true in business. Companies in a variety of industries have educated their people on such subjects as changing customer needs, new technologies, evolving regulatory climates, and shifting competition. These subjects are taught both formally, through organizational media and educational programs, and informally, in staff meetings, briefing sessions, and the like.

Leaders invest in this communication effort largely to help the workforce understand company direction and objectives and to be able to perform better. By delivering candid and forthright information about the forces that affect the organization's well-being, such a meaning-making strategy can raise employee comfort levels about the future and reduce uncertainty and anxiety. Increasing business (or operating) literacy across the organization is essentially a framing strategy. It involves expanding the employee perspective on the organization. When leaders can readily frame work experience in the context of big-picture issues, they command higher levels of attention and action from their colleagues.

Big-picture framing can include any or all of the topics in Figure 3-5.

One approach to big-picture framing we like in particular involves creating a sort of illustrated information sheet or map that simulates the journey ahead for the organization's "players." This tabletop approach for sparking conversation and learning involves groups of employees reviewing organizational challenges and suggesting actions to deal with them. AT&T sales employees have used a board-game device to broaden their business literacy, and Sears has used a product called a "Learning Map."[12] A company discussed in chapter 6, MidAmerican Energy, has taken the tabletop concept even further to engage large numbers of work teams across the company. MidAmerican uses the concept as part of a guided discussion that cascades through the organization. Leaders carry these conversations down to their respective work groups, while crafting their own versions of the frames in the process.

Anchoring the Big Picture A leadership team retreat offers an excellent opportunity for crafting, or recrafting, the material for big-

Figure 3-5. Framing for business literacy.

- ❏ *Organization History:* Where have we been?
- ❏ *Industry and Market Trends:* What's happening in the arena we play in?
- ❏ *Customer Profiles:* Who are our customers, and what do they want?
- ❏ *New Customers Won, Current Customers Lost:* Why did they come? Why did they go?
- ❏ *Performance Indicators:* How's our financial performance? What do customers think and feel about us? What about the investment community? What about employees?
- ❏ *Cost of Doing Business:* What are our leading cost categories? How do we make a profit?
- ❏ *Competition:* What are we up against? Whom do we worry about?
- ❏ *Other Topics:* How is technology changing the game? What about the regulatory climate?

picture framing. Boards or senior management teams usually get
together at least once a year for the ritual of hatching next year's
plans. As a kind of "warm-up" for this rather choreographed exercise, senior management groups sometimes step back a bit and ask
basic questions of themselves, such as What does the market look
like? Where do we want to be in it? and What's our value proposition? Some management teams also take the next step, attempting
to reach some consensus around the answers to these questions, and
then work them up into several message points that they can all use
with various audiences in the ensuing months.

The message points taken together tell a story. They represent
the building blocks for framing future events, directives, and analy-
ses that leaders can draw on in their conversations. Some organizations (see the tale of two high-tech companies in chapter 4) are
quite deliberate in shaping these building blocks. We recommend
three simple criteria for crafting effective big-picture message
points:

1. *Clear*—intelligible to all audiences you want to reach, from
   employees to industry analysts
2. *Comprehensive*—applying to all that you do, an umbrella
   under which the whole organization fits
3. *Compelling*—capable of engaging interest; enthusiasm; support; and, most important, action

And just to repeat: The purpose of taking the time to compose
these messages as a leadership group is to jump-start the meaning-
maker role that all leaders play whether they realize it or not. Big-
picture message points serve as templates for developing fuller statements and explanations "on the ground," as needed. They serve to
convey clear and consistent meaning to the ongoing happenings of
an organization. They don't aim to be "visionary" or aspirational so
much as they mean to describe in the simplest of terms the organization's basic plan: "This is our situation, and here's what we're
going to do."

Framing Around Vision

Leadership framing, the tactic of enhancing the meaning of work
by providing focus and context, serves several purposes. Big-picture

framing, naming and explaining the game, adds knowledge and substance to the ways we understand our work and its significance. But framing can motivate and inspire as well, as in this example from an October 22, 1962, address to the nation by President Kennedy, describing his plans for dealing with the Cuban missile crisis:

> **The path we have chosen for the present is full of hazards, as all paths are—but it is the one most consistent with our character and courage as a nation and our commitments around the world. The cost of freedom is always high—and Americans have always paid it. And one path we shall never choose, and that is the path of surrender, of submission.**

Unfortunately, the concept of vision in the context of organizational life has been corrupted by the institutionalization of the "vision statement." We discuss a critical distinction for leaders in framing around vision in the section below.

The "Vision Thing"

> *"The last thing IBM needs now is a vision."*
> —Lou Gerstner (on taking over as CEO), *New York Times*, March 10, 2002

Since the 1980s, most self-respecting companies have invested in developing vision statements. But as Dilbert and others have pointed out, vision statements tend to rely on the same few words ("number one," "be the best") and the same tired clichés ("people are our most important asset"). And since they seem to draw from such a small pool of images and ideas, they don't distinguish one organization's work from another. Corporate vision statements are mostly nondescript: put a bunch of them in a hat, draw them out one at a time, and you'd be hard pressed to identify the owner of each. They live on our organization's walls but have no life in our planning, our decision making, or our reflection on the organization in general. They have, in many cases, taken on the communication impact of wallpaper. In sum, they don't make meaning for people's work.

Our treatment of framing around vision is therefore more of an *on-the-go task,* seizing opportune moments to put a situation in the right context, lay out a problem, or link a specific work task to larger goals of the organization. It's about making figure/ground distinctions or, rather, naming the ground in order to clarify the figure and its significance. This kind of framing is most often an act of spontaneous leadership conversation, rather than the product of behind-the-scenes message crafting by communication "elves."

Talking Vision

> **"The greatest inhibitor to enlisting others in a common vision is lack of personal vision."**
> —JAMES M. KOUZES AND BARRY Z. POSNER,
> *THE LEADERSHIP CHALLENGE*

Framing can connect people to the organization and its work through the logic of its message or because its themes and content touch people at deeper levels, in deeper ways. Some of the most powerful frames leaders create are in fact those that trade on the so-called soft concepts used by leaders throughout history to challenge our spirit and ennoble our cause. People in organizations want to be mission driven; they say so in employee survey after survey. *They want to be engaged in a meaningful journey toward a worthy destination.* Leaders who can integrate statements of aspirational vision into their talks and conversations are leaders who are able to leverage this natural motivational force in their people.

So where does that leave the task of framing work around vision? Precisely where it's always been: in the hands of leaders who don't require or rely on a prepackaged statement or slogan but who instead "talk vision" when it's appropriate to do so and who do it sincerely, often, and with some passion. In the aftermath of September 11, it was then-mayor Rudolph Giuliani whose vision of dedication and recovery, of rebuilding and moving ahead captured the hearts and minds of not only New Yorkers but the rest of the country as well. Giuliani's pulpit was highly mobile: He shared his vision for the work ahead in city hall, in churches, and just walking down the block with a bunch of reporters' microphones under his nose.

When leaders are both relentless and effective at communicating their visions, they succeed in establishing a powerful frame for talking about work and work priorities. We once participated in a sales presentation for a big piece of business, a project to help a major wood products company refocus itself on new business goals. Part of our pitch addressed the importance of framing the company's "rebranding" effort around a clearly articulated vision for the company and its people.

"If that's so important," the head of the company's proposal evaluation team challenged, "how well can you state your own company's vision?" In what must have looked somewhat comical to the client team, all five of us responded spontaneously and more or less in unison, with a one-sentence description, using basically the same words, of what our firm tried to be for its clients. Afterward, the head of the team told us that we had won the business right then and there.

Aligning Visions Leaders who drive home the vision of the enterprise help their colleagues connect personal aspirations to those of the larger organization. They work to *align* individual visions with organizational goals on a level at which people can make common cause. Because they speak both for themselves and for the organization, the "personal visions" of leaders must be intelligible as well as captivating.

When you frame organizational work around vision, your words must be *clear* enough to understand, *comprehensive* enough in scope to connect with a variety of people in the organization, and *compelling* enough—through their appeal to higher motives and ends—to energize those people for action. It's hard to think of a better example than the following, from another American president trying to reframe events for a somewhat shaken and disoriented audience of citizens with an uncertain view of their future:

> It is for us, the living, rather, to be dedicated here
> to the unfinished work which they who fought here
> have thus far so nobly advanced. It is rather for us

to be here dedicated to the great task remaining before us . . . that this nation, under God, shall have a
new birth of freedom; and that government of the
people, by the people, for the people, shall not per-
ish from the earth.

The "us" in Lincoln's 1863 Gettysburg Address is "the living,"
which can't be much more comprehensive in scope. The task is
clear: dedication to "unfinished work." And the cause is indeed
compelling: freedom underwritten by (in one of Lincoln's most
memorable lines) "government of the people, by the people, for
the people."

Such framing opportunities come most readily, of course, when
leaders speak before groups. It is always a missed opportunity when
business leaders choose to frame the work of their organization (and
its people) not in a sense of larger purpose, but rather in the cold,
mundane language of profit and loss. Think of all the meetings you
have attended where the appeal to action, to dedication, was made
exclusively in terms of hitting financial goals and targets, and where
elements of vision and purpose were left unspoken. Yet it is vision
that energizes us and sustains our focus.

Framing Around Values

> "It's fine to emphasize what we must shoot for, but
> we also need to know what we stand for."
> —SUMANTRA GHOSHAL AND CHRISTOPHER A. BARTLETT, THE
> INDIVIDUALIZED CORPORATION

When Mayor Giuliani presented the theme of New Yorkers caring
for each other (extending the selflessness of the police and fire-
fighters to all New Yorkers), he was framing the task that lay ahead
by laying claim to a *value* not readily ascribed to residents of "the
Big Apple." But it worked, and he carried it off. New Yorkers became noticeably friendlier. They adopted roles of caregivers and
supported one another—even as strangers—during the ensuing
weeks. They came to see themselves in a different light from before,
and their collective efforts at recovery from an unprecedented and

horrible disaster were marked by high energy and deep commitment.

Using human values like service, honesty, diligence, and cooperation to frame work practices and to establish workplace priorities is a practice likely to be found in many organizations today. Whether or not an organization chooses to officially identify and publicize its values (in which case it risks the kind of sterilization that afflicts many vision statements), the habit of citing "our values" has become quite commonplace.

At its inception, Saturn very consciously built its approach to selling and customer service around a specific set of values: "commitment to customer enthusiasm, commitment to excel, teamwork, trust and respect for the individual, and continuous improvement." So that Saturn employees would have ready access to these values, laminated pocket-sized cards were made for everyone. So far, this sounds pretty familiar, right?

But Saturn saw the values as a frame through which a variety of decisions would continuously be made by leaders and their teams. Saturn people always talked values. They hired their retail teams on the basis of affinity for the values and the likelihood that a new hire would feel comfortable implementing them. They looked for people whose own values aligned with theirs and who would feel satisfied and rewarded in a nontraditional automotive retail setting. In the process, Saturn rewrote the book on the car ownership experience and continues to be ranked at or near the top of the J. D. Powers car-buying experience survey.

While working for Saturn as a consultant, one of us once made a suggestion that was at first questioned, then rejected because "it would not be true to one of the Saturn values." The reaction showed how integral the Saturn values had become to the way in which people actually ran the business; everyone on the Saturn team we were engaged with could have come to the same decision using the same rationale.

Values Drive the Business Values that don't deliver success for the enterprise aren't valuable. And values that individuals can't personally embrace aren't much good either. The good news is that most universal human values are ones that bring benefit to most organizational work: the challenge is to really communicate them well and to live by them. Perhaps the most effective way by which leaders

communicate values is to recognize and reward behavior that con-
forms to or demonstrates them. The old saying "What's important
is what gets rewarded" is as good as any indicator to the real values
of an organization. Leaders who model organizational values define
them through their actions. Leaders who recognize and reward performance consistent with key organizational values help to frame
the meaning of work accordingly.

Under Jack Welch, GE touted "the four E's"—to have *energy*,
to be able to *energize* others, to have an *edge* (to be able to say yes or
no, not maybe), and to be able to *execute*—to get the plan done.
Company leaders are actually rated on their adherence to values,
and evaluations involve input beyond their bosses. Using key organizational values as a basis for performance evaluation is indeed a
strong way to communicate their importance.

Welch was quite candid about this when he talked about who
gets promoted at GE. Discussing a kind of manager who succeeds
"on the backs of people," Welch explained how important it was
to convey forcefully that this kind of practice was contrary to GE
values (specifically, the value of energizing and developing others).
The most definitive way to communicate on this values issue was
to get rid of those individuals who couldn't live by it. "An organization that doesn't root them out can't talk about values," was
Welch's conclusion.[13]

Indeed (Enron notwithstanding), we seem to be living in an age
where the role of values in the workplace is on the rise, judging at
least by the solid trend in management literature (from Peter Block's
Stewardship to the more recent *Servant Leader* by James Autry).[14]
We've seen more and more organizations mentioning values, in
both formal meetings and more informal conversations. Leaders are
apparently getting increasingly comfortable in talking about them
and in using them to frame "what's important around here."

The following story from our own consulting experience might
add some extra dimension to how critical values have become in
framing priorities. One of us was explaining to a hospital leadership
team how a new idea generation program could produce significant
cost savings by tapping into the ingenuity of hospital staff. The program would be powered by the opportunity for "idea teams" to
earn merchandise awards based on the worth of their submitted
ideas. This element of the program drew immediate and impas-
sioned fire from the nursing contingent. "Our jobs are about saving

lives, not earning trips and toasters!" "How dare you insinuate any other motive, any competing values!"

These challenges were potential showstoppers. Lengthy discussion and a lot of backpedaling took place before we could move ahead. As it worked out, once the program got under way, nursing teams were active participants and made significant contributions. But each successive time we introduced this program at another hospital, the same values issue had to be dealt with in the same way. We needed to let the health-care professionals testify about their strong adherence to a specific set of professional values and then frame the program initiative in a way that those values would indeed be honored and respected.

Framing Around Change

> *"The future of the past is never very sure. The only certainty is that the past will be what we make it, that what we choose to note about the present, to remember about the past, will change as our own concerns change."*
>
> —EUGEN WEBER, *FRANCE, FIN DE CIÈCLE*

As companies routinely reorganize, restructure, and rebrand themselves in response to technology, marketplace, or regulatory shifts, leaders have special communication challenges to face up to. While we address the issue of change management communications more fully in chapter 7, there is a framing dimension to change that should be looked at here.

The issue is primarily about how change affects the meaning of organizational work, both on a big-picture, organizational level, and on the level at which individuals assess the meaning and significance of their own jobs. Change naturally disrupts the ways we see ourselves in our work. Organization leadership needs first to be sensitive to the ways transition and change may affect their people. After that, leaders need to help those affected (usually everybody, in some way or another) to establish a new, satisfactory basis for *alignment* between individual and organizational meaning of work. In other words, the new frames of the individual and the organization must fit together.

Certainly, most leaders would like to define, both for themselves and their people, the events they are living through and the forces they're reacting to. While change communications can't always be controlled by the "It ain't nothin' till I calls it" tactic, transition and the reasons for it all require definition, explanation, and rationale. People want to know that their leadership has a solid grasp of where the organization is going and why, even as they need to know what's going to happen to them and their jobs.

On another level, middle and frontline management often want a say in how reorganization might best be designed. They want to contribute in some significant way to the creation of new frames and new stories for their organization. For change to be managed as a normal part of organizational life, a reasonable expectation for many organizations today, decisions about the change campaign cannot, to borrow a phrase, be left to the generals. So too do leaders at all levels of the organization need to be engaged in meaning-making activity.

Leaders create appropriate frames for people, themselves and others, to make sense of change. Part of the reframing challenge can in turn involve new metaphors and terms or apply old vocabularies in new ways. Intel transformed itself from a memory products company to a maker of microprocessors, the guts of computers. Nortel changed its image from a black-box manufacturer to a business communication solutions company. Both these companies, and hundreds of others too, have faced the task of reframing, and then helping employees come to terms with the changes and their consequences.

Themes for Change

In general, leaders need to build their framing around change using any or all of the following themes:

- ❐ Need and urgency
- ❐ Opportunity for improvement and betterment
- ❐ Shared responsibility: common stake, common fate
- ❐ The right thing to do

In defining the forces of change and the impact it will have, leaders will also want their frames for the future to include expressions of:

❏ Appreciation of the past and where the organization has been
❏ Sympathy for the disruptions, inconvenience, and confusion brought about by change
❏ Honesty and candor regarding critical timetables, delayed consequences, and accounts of how many people may have to leave the organization
❏ Support for and interest in individuals as they work to shape their own meaning for the future, both those who will stay and those who will leave

MEANING-MAKING AS SHARED ACTIVITY

While much of this chapter has concentrated on how leaders can give meaningful shape to the organization's work, it is just as important for leaders to provide opportunities for people to shape their own meaning and to align personal meaning with that of the larger group. In a simple sense, this means creating forums and platforms that allow people to say what's on their mind. *Leaders can help colleagues put words to their thoughts by setting this as an expectation for everyone.* As Karl Weick coyly notes, we talk in order to "discover thinking. How can I know what I think until I see what I say?"[15]

The most available subject for such conversation is work that's already been done. Weick reminds us that "meaning is retrospective and only elapsed experience is available for meaningful interpretation."[16] By prompting conversation about work practices and jobs completed, the leader can help people assign new dimensions of significance to their own work: They can discover for themselves "how to see what they say about the things they do," to paraphrase Weick. Something as simple as prompting "shoptalk" among employees can contribute to useful meaning-making. And if people are encouraged to talk about their work not just in terms of how they do what they do (shoptalk), but also what it contributes and why it's important, they will gain a clearer sense of the meaning of that work.

Continuous process improvement is an excellent topic for extending the conversation about work. One of the authors has consulted with scores of companies engaged in a team suggestion process, where team members generated cost-saving ideas (and earned significant awards for those that were accepted). As team members built a cost-benefit case for their idea, they often developed in the process a more sophisticated understanding of how their organization did business.

The other outcome, of course, was pride that their team was making a contribution above and beyond day-to-day job requirements. Both of these consequences, as postprogram surveys revealed, helped participants expand on the meaning of their work and feel more aligned with the work of others in the organization. And as people in organizations grow more articulate about their work and the enterprise in general, they are better able to target the right things to do and to do the right things right.

NOTES

1. Wilfred H. Drath and Charles J. Palus, *Making Common Sense: Leadership as Meaning-Making in a Community of Practice* (Greensboro, N.C.: Center for Creative Leadership, 1994), 18.
2. Linda Smircich and Gareth Morgan, "Leadership: The Management of Meaning," *Journal of Applied Behavioral Science* 18 (1982), 261.
3. Robin Dunbar, *Grooming, Gossip, and the Evolution of Language* (Cambridge, Mass.: Harvard University Press, 1997), 121 and Jared Diamond, *Guns, Germs and Steel: The Fates of Human Societies* (New York: W. W. Norton, 1999), 271.
4. Jack Welch, "Jack Welch: Icon of Leadership," interviewed by Stuart Varney at Fairfield University, *CEO Exchange,* WWTW Chicago, (December 30, 2001).
5. Drath and Palus, *Making Common Sense,* 11.
6. Terrence Armour, "Bulls Fans Get Their Phil," *Chicago Tribune,* May 6, 1999, Sports Section, C1.
7. Robert B. Cialdini, "Harnessing the Science of Persuasion," *Harvard Business Review* (October 2001), 76.
8. Kevin Freiberg and Jackie Freiberg, *Nuts!: Southwest Airlines' Crazy Recipe for Business and Personal Success* (New York: Broadway Books, 1998), 176.
9. These advertisements for UPS ran in several American magazines during 1999–2000.
10. Kimberly Hefling, "A Farewell to 4 Fallen Americans," *St. Louis Post-Dispatch* (December 11, 2001), A1, 5.
11. Karl Weick, *The Social Psychology of Organizing,* 2nd ed. (New York: McGraw-Hill, 1979), 1.
12. See Anthony J. Rucci, Steven P. Kirn, and Richard T. Quinn, "The Employee-Customer-Profit Chain at Sears," *Harvard Business Review* (January–February 1998), 92–95.
13. Jack Welch, "An Interview with Jack Welch," interviewed by Geoffrey Colvin at the University of Michigan Business School, (*C-Span 2,* April 9, 2001).
14. See, for example, Peter Block, *Stewardship: Choosing Service Over Self-Interest* (San Francisco: Berrett-Koehler, 1993); and James Autry, *The Servant Leader* (New York: Prima 2001).
15. Weick, *The Social Psychology of Organizing,* 165.
16. Ibid., 245.

4

Storyteller

"The right anecdote can be worth a thousand theories."

—WARREN BENNIS, "THE LEADER AS STORYTELLER"

Who doesn't like to hear a good story? Stories are the way we think, remember, communicate; the way we create meaning, coherence, and trust. Storytelling is pervasive in our lives: Even a set of directions for baking a cake or assembling a machine is really a story or a narrative. What's more, we make decisions based on how well stories hang together, their "narrative logic." We listen to a new story line, we compare it to other narratives we already use, and we decide if the new story, or some combination of new and old, makes more *sense* or is better able to describe the reality of our business. Then we adopt it and use it to create a new explanation of who we are, what we do, or how we do it.

TELL ME A STORY

Stories create a sense of the way things connect. They arrange a jumble of events and decisions into a logical sequence. They interpret the meaning of separate actions and suggest causal relationships between them. They put decisions and actions into a larger perspective so that we can better evaluate them. Stories carry emotion into the facts of organizational life and help us attach our own feelings to our jobs. Telling a story can relax the person doing the telling and secure the attention of listeners. Storytelling involves strategy and skill, but it's also something that we all come by naturally. While some of us are more gifted storytellers than others, we all possess the gift and use it every day.

In organizations, stories help us both create and communicate meaning, the meaning of events, decisions, and shared experiences in particular. In this sense, storytelling or narrative making is a critical attribute of leadership communication. Leaders add meaning to the experiences of work and work life by describing them in stories about individuals and groups and the organization itself. Leaders' storytelling thus performs several critical functions in the quest for meaning-making:

❐ Giving meaning to experiences that lack meaning in themselves
❐ Identifying or inventing an underlying theme or subject
❐ Providing rationale and legitimacy for actions taken or planned
❐ Bringing closure to a series of decisions or events[1]

Finally, stories create the basis for making judgments so that we might set actions and happenings in a moral context. Stories help leaders establish for their people what's right and what's wrong.

A Story About a Story

Wyman Center is a nonprofit organization that builds youth development programs around camping experiences. Its extensive operation serves young people from many different communities and goes far beyond the traditional "summer camp." At the heart of the Wyman Center's work is one of the oldest operating youth camps in the country, Camp Wyman. Since 1897, this camp, located just west of St. Louis, has provided rich character-building experiences for more than half a million children and teens.

In recent decades, the Wyman Center has expanded from an agency providing summer camp experiences for underserved youth to a nationally recognized youth services organization that strives to build a comprehensive support structure for each child by engaging family, school, and peers in a variety of developmental activities. Wyman was the first nonprofit organization ever featured by *Inc.* magazine and has attracted continuous national and international attention as a path breaker in extending the reach and impact of the outdoor camping experience.

CEO Dave Hilliard is a charismatic leader and a self-confessed storyteller (he actually attends an annual storytellers conference "to replenish his repertoire"). He has built a strong organization of resourceful, committed professionals who continually push the envelope in redefining the role of camping experiences to build character and resilience in young people.

Recently, the organization prepared to take another step forward in its evolution: working with a global corporation to design and operate a nationwide youth development resource. Centered around Wyman's proven success with delivering programs that develop life skills and leadership capabilities, the program involves young people in as many as five consecutive summertime camping experiences. Perhaps more significantly, the program also involves taking "camp" into the neighborhood and communities where kids live. The aim here is to create collaborations with families, neighborhood agencies, schools, and other community institutions, using the philosophy and traditional activities of the camp experience as a core from which to further cultivate character and leadership in participating youth.

Hilliard faced a critical challenge as he prepared the organization for the new corporate-sponsored effort. He needed to engage his leadership team in rethinking Wyman's mission. More specifically, he wanted to advance the concept that *leadership development* might become a central goal in the expansion of Wyman's youth work. Hilliard was, in effect, proposing a significant new focus for the organization and a revised sense of professional identity for the people who would take this concept forward. The leadership team needed to wrestle with this concept before each of its members could fully embrace it.

Wyman had already made significant strides toward piloting

more extensive and continuous programs, and in partnering with other agencies on youth development projects. But when Hilliard and his communications director presented the team with a draft of a proposed new mission statement that began with the line, "Wyman Center guides youth toward being *great leaders*," it was met with uncertainty and skepticism. "Can we really say this—can every kid be a 'great leader'?" was one response. "That seems a little 'over the top'" was another. *Leadership* was itself hard to define, and staff feared they would have to spend too much time explaining what it meant. Wyman's mission might not seem so clear as it did before.

Over the next three days, Hilliard and the team discussed how the proposed mission statement might actually impact Wyman programs and initiatives and suggest new priorities for Wyman staff. The leadership team is acutely mission driven. Many had left higher-paying jobs in the corporate sector, and the caliber of professionalism is unusually high across the team. This shift in mission was not something they would consider lightly. Team members had to process what the new "purposing" of Wyman would mean to their professional lives and values, as well as to the children and families they served and the organization's long-time supporters. Each would want to try it on for size and test it for fit.

On the second day, sensing lingering unease with the new mission statement, Hilliard tried a different approach with the "great leaders" concept. He began by saying, "Let me tell you a story." The "story" was actually several recollections about past campers, all from inner-city neighborhoods, who had kept in touch over the years and who had become, in various ways, leaders in business, government, and their communities. The story also contained a very personal statement of Hilliard's belief in the power of the Wyman experience to develop character and leadership in participants. He simply sat at the U-shaped table and told it—no stirring oratory, just some clearly remembered accounts of how past Wyman kids had grown into leaders. It was just a story and, at the same time, a moving testimonial to the power of an idea.

Later, the meeting facilitator, seeking to find out how the story had gone over, asked a participant whether the restated mission would appeal to potential donors and supporters. She had been reflecting on the story, and she had a ready, though unexpected, response. "You know," she said, "as a mother, I think I *want* my two daughters to become leaders. They might be leaders of a corporation, or leaders of a Sunday school class. But being leaders is, I guess, an important and worthwhile thing to become, and I think it's a very appropriate part of our mission." It was clear that Hillliard's story had resonated with her at a deeper level than a well-organized presentation of the merits of the idea ever could have. The story brought the idea home to her.

What had started as an unsettling proposal to change the focus of the organization was now becoming a compass point for staff leaders to orient themselves in the future. The idea for a new positioning of what had been a rather one-dimensional organization was evolving into a compelling, shared platform on which a highly committed group of professionals could renew their energies and direction. There was never any vote taken, and Hilliard did not force the issue during the meeting. But clearly his story helped the senior management team connect its deep professional commitment with a bold vision for what the organization could become.

In the wake of Hilliard's storytelling, his listeners began crafting their own narratives, trying them on for size, and coming to understand how they themselves could be "characters" in the new story. Their subsequent conversations and reflections have continued to shape how the Wyman Center could serve this mission and what competencies they would need to develop.

Leaders like Dave Hilliard use anecdotes and recollections as story material, but with the purpose of delivering deeper meaning and greater impact. They create big-picture stories by enlarging on more detailed, case-specific accounts. Philosopher Paul Ricoeur says that "To make a plot is . . . to make the intelligible spring from the accidental, the universal from the singular, the necessary or probable from the episodic."[2] Meaning-making depends on storytelling, both for its ability to suggest larger meaning and for its power to engage and hold our attention.

NARRATIVE-BUILDING STRATEGIES

What are the criteria for stories that people in the organization will listen to, believe, and accept? We're back to the *3 C's* of good organizational communication: Stories need to be clear, comprehensive, and compelling.

- ☐ *Clear* narratives are simple, direct, and told in plain language and include reasons and explanations when they are called for.
- ☐ *Comprehensive* stories have several requirements:
  - ○ That we don't leave things out
  - ○ That we show continuity between where we've been and where we're going
  - ○ That we help all listeners find their place in the story
- ☐ Stories can be made *compelling* by applying a variety of dramatic techniques, of which eight (see Figure 4-1) are probably the most commonly used by organizational leaders.

Because leaders must define the meaning of events in terms of their significance to the organization, they need to build individual events into bigger stories. They need to show how those stories fit into the larger drama. Ronald Reagan was particularly good at this. When the space shuttle *Challenger* burst into flames on January 29, 1986, killing all of the astronauts on board, Reagan described the tragedy, in an address to the nation, as part of the greater story of America's venture into space: " 'I know it's hard to understand that sometimes painful things like this happen. It's all part of the process of exploration and discovery, it's all part of taking a chance and expanding man's horizons. The future doesn't belong to the faint-hearted. It belongs to the brave.' "[3]

Figure 4-1. Storytelling techniques.

- ☐ Make them action oriented: people getting things done.
- ☐ Link them to shared values and common ground.
- ☐ Cast organization people as leading characters.
- ☐ Cast *everyone* in the organization, by implication or extension, as a character in the drama.
- ☐ Cast the competition as the opposition (the antagonist).
- ☐ Portray the past as a prologue to a new story.
- ☐ Portray the present as the beginning (or the middle) of a journey toward specific goals and aspirations.
- ☐ Portray the future as a destination where goals are to be realized (or renewed).

USING STORIES TO BUILD COMMUNITY

Stories are good for helping people feel connected: They're prime tools for building a sense of belonging and a reason to affiliate. "A community," explains David Carr, "exists by virtue of a story which is articulated and accepted, which typically concerns the group's origins and its destiny, and which interprets what is happening now in the light of these two temporal poles."[4] For Dave Hilliard's senior leadership, a story helped prime some thinking about how the team might reconnect around a new mission.

How does storytelling figure in your organization? Do organization members know about its history? Would they be likely to describe the same future scenario for their organization? Do they share the same tales about particular people, past and present?

When stories about an organization are told and retold, they take on added significance and stature. They become part of the organizational lore and culture. One of us once worked for an organization in which a popular activity was to swap stories about a certain corporate leader who had a gift for indiscretions with clients. One tale, a particular favorite, had him telling a group of Toyota sales executives, "We're going to make you the Cadillac of your industry!" These stories were told over and over again and never failed both to entertain and to reinforce a feeling of camaraderie.

COAUTHORING STORIES

When leaders tell compelling stories, they influence others to pick up the same story line and retell it. Leaders' stories that frame decisions and future plans will spread throughout the organization as other people retell them and rework them in their own words. Leaders want stories to be retold and spread. "Talking is remembering," says psychologist Roger Schank.[5]

Storytelling is contagious. We all create stories for ourselves, and we play roles in one another's stories. Organizations define themselves through stories authored by their members. In a very real sense, an organization exists in the texts of the stories people tell about it and accept as being real and true (even when they're not!).

Leaders don't have a monopoly on storytelling. Instead, their stories are edited, retold, distorted, and revamped, whether they like it or not. If anything, leaders need to invite their colleagues to contribute "material" to an ongoing narrative that describes the work of the group or team. This might mean working to bring more voices into play during staff meetings or issuing project "post-mortems" that seek both to learn from and celebrate work that's been completed. Throughout, leaders will want to thread smaller stories into larger ones, weaving them together so that they illustrate and reinforce key organizational messages.

Stories can also help to bring out craft knowledge and best practices that might otherwise remain unspoken and thus hidden to the organization (this subject is dealt with in more depth in chapter 12). Leaders can help people share knowledge and insights about getting the work done by encouraging them to tell stories at staff meetings about how they solved a particular problem or succeeded in pleasing a customer. Most people enjoy doing this, especially if they're not singled out and made uncomfortable.

Creating *forums* for telling and hearing stories is a critical task for the organization's leadership. Over time, people will come to link one story to another and to fit their own material into larger, available story lines. Novelist Robert Hellenga has a character explain, "I used to think that the bigger stories explained the smaller ones, that the bigger rings gave meaning to the rings that they enclosed, but now I think it's the other way around, and that each story illuminates and gives meaning to the larger story of which it is a part, till you get to the farthest ring. . . ."[6]

CHANGE AND TRANSITION STORIES

In recent years, organizations have become more conscious of the role narrative can play in facilitating major transitions, in particular, restructurings brought about by mergers, acquisitions, and spin-offs. Leaders responsible for knitting a new organization together have found it especially important to dwell on organizational histories. The intention here is both to honor past accomplishments and to identify those aspects of the past that need to be carried forward, as well as those that must be left behind. Commemorating past achievements and paying homage to past heroes are good methods for mitigating or softening the feelings of pain and loss brought on by these jarring transitions. Stories told about where you've been, and the people who helped you get where you are today, can build confidence in the future. Such stories preserve the organization's self-respect and leave its people more comfortable with the agenda for change.

Of equal importance in managing transitions is the way in which leadership can create credible, plausible narratives for the future. We'll speak more on change communication in chapter 7. The current chapter addresses the role that storytelling can play in refocusing and reenergizing people in a new and different organization. In several companies we've worked with—each one going through a major restructuring—there has been a systematic storytelling "roll-down" to get several layers of leadership involved in shaping a different kind of future for the organization. Senior leadership first sketches out the contours of the story from a "big-picture" perspective, with three or four plot elements describing where the organization is headed and why.

The stories typically start with some statement about a challenge or a dilemma that had to be faced. From there, the story line might describe a chosen direction and how the people in the organization might best pull together to take the organization forward. Often the story is then picked up by other levels of management who are asked to develop it further, adding details about actions that need to be taken, and getting more specific about who will do what.

Royal Dutch Shell Group offers a good example. "The group's managing directors first penned their own story lines about needed change and the future and then engaged the next layers of management in crafting their versions. Tales were told of years of profitable growth and technical leadership but also spoke candidly to present-day predicaments. . . ."[7] These tales were then retold throughout the company and in the process, passed through operating divisions in more than one hundred countries. The result: "All concerned understood the case for change and told each other what they would have to do to bring the 'new' into being."[8]

As stories like these are handed down through an organization, a larger, organizational story, with many tellers, is crafted. This kind of collectively told tale becomes the basis for how people in the organization will understand both its history and how the future might best be designed. Stories that help people make sense of change typically let people know:

- ❐ Where the organization is going
- ❐ Why the change is necessary and important
- ❐ What specific steps will need to be taken
- ❐ How people can help make the change a success
- ❐ What's in it for them

Because coauthorship strengthens group ownership of stories of change, you want to engage others in plotting important details.

A Transformation Story with "Corporate" Authorship

A major print communication company realized it needed to engineer significant transformation to continue to grow in an industry brimming with smarter, faster competition. Building outward from its core print business, the company planned to rebrand itself as a provider of all kinds of communications solutions. In the process, leadership would have to tell a new story to its customers and to its employees, one about where the organization was heading and how it would get there.

The first step was to touch base with a range of company leaders, from corporate staff to frontline leadership in the field. What did they think about the future, and how might the organization best tell its new story internally, so that employees could get behind it? Phone interviews and focus groups across its global divisions yielded good insights about likely reactions to new story lines. Key message points were tested for clarity and credibility, and reactions were folded into a report that would guide communications moving forward.

The company also chose to take a close look at its various story telling media, in particular some rather costly company magazines and a recently launched Web site. It found that the magazine was clearly not the best medium to use to reach its worldwide employees, and that people relied much more on their division leaders to tell them about new directions and the business case for change. In fact, continued reliance on traditional print communication vehicles would likely fail to improve a rather superficial employee awareness of its overall business strategies. Armed with fresh input from its research, however, the company could now create a new, coauthored story and deliver it in the most effective ways.

CREATING THE "BASIC PLOTLINE"

Most organizations like to capture the essence of who they are and what they do in a few brief statements, sometimes called an "elevator speech." This is the *basic plotline* of the organization, and it can anchor all sorts of spin-off stories for a variety of audiences. The basic requirement of the basic plotline is that it is *intelligible to any audience*. The plot can combine elements of an organization's vision and mission, refer to key values, or target important goals. But it must be told in a simple, straightforward, and consistent way, so that customers, employees, suppliers, investors, . . . whoever, all understand the story in essentially the same way. All in one elevator ride.

Basic plotlines are useful for several reasons. First of all, they enable senior leadership to be on the same page with one another when talking among themselves or with others. One of the key tests employees apply to leadership communication is whether it is consistent through the ranks. If not, leaders lose credibility. It's critical that leadership teams subject their plotline to regular reviews (say every year or so) to guarantee accuracy, relevance, and continuity. This exercise also engages leaders in an act of collective narrative building (AKA meaning-making), where they can update and refresh their stories together.

Second, revisiting the basic plotline often reveals the existence of different or conflicting stories that need to be reconciled or negotiated. In some cases, resolution may require a new plotline, leading to a new consensus around a new direction. Finally, the basic plot serves as just that: a foundational story on which stakeholders can build their own, more extensive plotlines and narratives. Here is an account of two relatively young, hard-charging companies who each decided to invest some time in "negotiating" such a basic plot among their senior leadership ranks.

A Tale of Two High-Tech Companies

Two Internet service companies, both with positive balance sheets and positioned for future growth, decided to catch their breath for a moment and see if all senior management team members had similar conceptions of those futures. One of these teams was in fact still assembling its leadership team, and two members had less than three months' tenure with the company. Both companies took the step of holding a (facilitated) senior leadership discussion on the subject of "Who do we think we are?" and "Who do we want to be?" Their common purpose was to generate answers not only for themselves, their boards, and their stockholders, but for their employees and their customers as well. It was the first time that either company had done this exercise.

With these meetings they wanted to develop a set of agreed-on message points they could all use to tell their story. They also agreed to the same criteria for these messages. The message points and the story they formed must be clear, comprehensive, and compelling (see the big-picture framing discussion in chapter 3). What happened in both cases was unexpected. For one thing, there was hardly unanimity among team members in defining either present or future. Discussion within each team revealed differing opinions on marketplace issues and action priorities. Neither of the groups was ready to draft and disseminate. It was, as one of the participants suggested, something like the parable of the blind men and the elephant, with each one touching a different part and coming to a different conclusion about what they had in hand.

Armed with the knowledge that they were far from aligned, participants went to work on the problem and ended up with richer, more encompassing statements. They surprised themselves at their own willingness, even motivation, to "wordsmith"—certainly not their intention coming into the meeting. It was as if they realized that *some* tentative agreement about the words would enable them to agree about other issues more easily in future discussions. Framing the big picture with clarity and some consensus would allow them all to paint more effectively inside the frame later on.

In one of the two discussions, a young CEO sat quietly and pensively as his colleagues complained about how their chief competition had made considerable gains and captured the fancy of "the Street." When he finally spoke up, he asked to try out a new scenario for what the company might become. His ideas were prompted not only by what he had been hearing about the competition's gains but also by his perception of where the market was headed and how the company might reposition itself to capitalize on it. In effect, he was composing a new story for the company ("I've been kicking this around for some time, actually . . .").

Good discussion—open, candid, and thoughtful—emerged and shaped a new story line, and that in turn led to the drafting of a clear, comprehensive, and compelling statement of new business purpose. That statement would be worked over more in the ensuing weeks and would ultimately frame for all a new picture of their future.

The End of the Story

Storytelling is about meaning-making. From basic plotlines that reveal the essence of a company and its mission, all the way to stories that heal wounds, create alliances, or rally troops around new challenges and opportunities, stories help us make sense of the organizations we serve, and our place in them. So it's not surprising that leadership communication relies heavily on storytelling: telling the right stories to the right audiences at the right time and involving others in the work of authorship as often as possible.

NOTES

1. Lewis P. Hinchman and Sandra K. Hinchman, eds., introduction to *Memory, Identity, Community: The Idea of Narrative in the Human Sciences* (Albany, N.Y.: State University of New York Press, 1997), xxvi.
2. Anthony Paul Kerby, "The Language of the Self," in Hinchman and Hinchman, *Memory, Identity, Community*, 135.
3. Adam Clymer, Defining a Leader by His Words," *New York Times*, September 16, 2001, 4.

4. David Carr, "Narrative and the Real World: An Argument for Continuity," in Hinchman and Hinchman, *Memory, Identity, Community,* 20.

5. Roger C. Schank, *Tell Me a Story: A New Look at Real and Artificial Memory* (New York: Charles Scribner's Sons, 1990), 115.

6. Robert Hellenga, *The Fall of a Sparrow* (New York: Scribner, 1998), 26–27.

7. Philip Mirvis, "Can You Teach Your People to Think Smarter?" *Across the Board* (March 1996), 26–27.

8. Ibid., 27.

5

Trust Builder

> *"Trust in authority relationships is a matter of* predictability *along two dimensions: values and skills."*
>
> —RONALD HEIFETZ, *LEADERSHIP WITHOUT EASY ANSWERS*

Trust is a valuable asset for organizations, the ultimate expression of social capital, as shown in chapter 2. But we live in the "Age of Dilbert," in which cynical employees dismiss leadership trust as an oxymoron and frequently used platitudes become "the great lies of management."

Great Lies of Management*

1. "Employees are our most valuable asset."
2. "I have an open-door policy."
3. "You could earn more money under the new plan."
4. "We're reorganizing to better serve our customers."

---

*"Great Lies of Management" from *The Dilbert Principle* by Scott Adams. Copyright © 1996 by United Features Syndicate, Inc. Reprinted by permission of HarperCollins Publishers Inc. For additional territory, contact United Media, 200 Madison Avenue, 4th Floor, New York, NY 10016.

5. "The future is bright."
6. "We reward risk takers."
7. "We don't shoot the messenger."
8. "Training is a high priority."
9. "I haven't heard any rumors."
10. "We'll review your performance in six months."
11. "Our people are the best."
12. "Your input is important to us."

Perhaps it's always been this way. But in these days, when organizational life seems so dominated by change and uncertainty, with corporate "spin doctors" and "corporatespeak" turning up everywhere, it seems harder to trust what our leaders say. Yet, given the challenges to organizations to keep their feet while they're knocked around in unsteady environments, trust in leadership is a must for survival. It's also one of the most important "intangibles" that talented workers look for in choosing an organization and a key factor in keeping them loyal, satisfied, and productive, once they're on board.

This chapter addresses the qualities and behaviors that help leaders of organizations create and sustain trust. We look at specific communication strategies and tactics that make leaders more trust-*worthy* and that establish a climate of trust that allows everyone to communicate more openly and candidly inside the organization. In short, we describe how leaders communicate and support others in communicating, in honest and credible ways.

INDIVIDUAL VOICE AND ORGANIZATIONAL TONE

At a recent management conference we attended, a speaker introduced himself as a "slow-talking Midwesterner." "In order to deal with people from the East Coast," the speaker went on, "I took a 'speed-talking' course. I got up to 48 words per minute, but I was making too many mistakes." Our take-away from this tale is not to beware of fast-talking Easterners (one of us was, after all, born in New York City). Rather, we find here a basic piece of communication advice that most good leaders follow naturally: *Be yourself and speak in your own voice.* Contrary to a common belief, effective presentations involve neither acting nor impersonation. Instead, the first job of the leader making any sort of presentation is to convince the audience that the person they are seeing and hearing is who that person really is.

This advice is not as easy to follow as it may seem, however. For one thing, leaders often feel a need to assume different identities as they address different audiences. In one instance, they can be speaking with fellow board members. In another, they're addressing a group of subordinates. And in another, they're speaking to reporters, or industry analysts, or any "outsiders" whose understanding and interpretation of a speech can in turn feed back to people inside the organization.

Informality as a "Big Thought"

One way to move beyond this identity confusion as a speaker is to be direct and informal as often as possible. Jack Welch has suggested that "the story about GE that hasn't been told is the value of an informal place. I think it's a big thought. I don't think people have ever figured out that being informal is a big deal."[1]

Informality is a leveling force. It provides an excellent way to let your talk flow out of the real you, not the manufactured one. It cuts away the stiffness and artificiality that bureaucracy can breed. It allows communication to be freer and less guarded, less "political." It makes it easier to be yourself. It also allows for communication that bypasses the normal chain-of-command pathways, enabling leaders to seek out and deliver information more directly with people across the organization. They can be specialists or generalists, bosses or subordinates, but they're also members of the same community and can relate to one another as colleagues.

Welch explained in another interview the importance of informal "schmoozing" as a communication mainstay. "When you start out a meeting Monday morning that's pretty critical, a budget review or something like that, we spend the first half-hour or so talking about what happened on the weekend: 'Did you see Tiger Woods sink that putt?' . . . Business is a game. It's not some serious, pompous ass thing!"[2] While informality may not work for every organization or every leader, its impact on an organization's ability to sponsor open, candid dialogue is hard to ignore.

Informality does not need to inhibit tough talk. GE and Emerson, two organizations that intentionally cultivate informality, are also known for their occasionally rather brutal (as in brutally honest) dialogues. That's why both companies go out of their way to create social occasions for different levels of leadership to hold conversations. Developing professional relationships on a personal level creates the conditions necessary for the candor and directness so important to effective business dialogue, which can then, ironically, be more depersonalized. You don't feel so much under attack when you know you'll be drinking together in another couple of hours.

Be Personal, but Don't "Make It Personal"

Informality can open communication channels, encourage participation, and build trust. It can strengthen the bonds that exist between leaders and their coworkers. But when a leader has to counter or criticize, she or he will want to "depersonalize" the criticism: Direct that criticism toward the *idea* or the *decision* and away from the *person* presenting it; keep the person's dignity intact, help him manage his "face," even as you administer the lethal injection to his proposal. This is a "critical leadership communication moment": Done the right way, it expands the opportunity for continued openness and trust; done poorly, it introduces fear and resentment into the relationship.

Telling It Like It Is

Technology insinuates itself into our organizational give-and-take more and more each day. The trend in M.B.A. hiring has brought a more self-conscious professional dialogue to business. Company leaders are finding it increasingly difficult to avoid using jargon, alphabet soup acronyms, and technical terminology as they try to explain themselves and their operations. But credibility suffers when leaders fall prey to management fads and the special vocabularies that come with them. "Customer delight," "servant leadership," and "the learning organization" are but a few of the ideas that at first capture our attention for the best of reasons but then have a habit of deteriorating into empty slogans as more and more people use them too casually and too glibly. Jargon and technical language can make you seem vague, condescending, even deceitful ("If he *really* wanted us to know what was going on, he wouldn't use all that gibberish; he'd just say it.")

Sometimes leaders hold back on what they know for fear of sounding too much the expert. As a sign posted on a university bulletin board once had it, "No gurus is good gurus." Yet expertise is in itself a value that leaders can bring to the enterprise, and you should neither hide it under a bushel nor assume that it's self-evident. When you want to mount a persuasive argument, don't be afraid to let people know what you know in order to lay claim to the natural respect people accord earned expertise. The trick is to communicate knowledge in a relevant (not gratuitous) way and to take care to meet the audience at least halfway with language that clarifies rather than mystifies.

The simple way to say this is to keep it simple. But as we've found, "it ain't that simple" to simplify and to be consistently concise and clear. Figure 5-1 contains some approaches that can help.

Abstractions aren't the only trap that leadership communications fall into. Euphemisms are right up there too. For instance, how many ways can we invent to say "We're going to fire some people?" Over the past decade, as organizations shrink and contract to stay competitive, we've heard phrases like *downsize, right-size, reduce head count, reengineer, restructure,* and *optimize the labor force.* True, we're all reluctant to deliver unpleasant news, but inventing euphemisms doesn't change the meaning. It just makes you sound as if you're afraid to simply say what needs to be said, so people can deal with it and get on with their business.

Euphemism has indeed escalated as lawyers, management consultants, public relations professionals, and others intrude more and more into the things leaders say. At its worst, it suggests that leadership is avoiding the truth, or is hiding something. At best, it still works against a leader's ability to engage the full trust and commitment of the people in an organization. We can't pin the blame completely on the handlers, though, because the responsibility to speak directly and candidly always remains with the leaders themselves.

Figure 5-1. Tactics for keeping it simple.

1. *Open a discussion by saying: "I'm going to try to be as simple and straightforward as I can."* This statement can be both a reminder to the speaker and a promise to the audience: You're putting yourself on notice, as it were, and your audience will measure you by how well you live up to that commitment.

2. *Avoid saying at the outset "I'll be brief" or words to that effect.* This line is much overworked. In addition, it seems from our experience to be a promise that most speakers cannot, or never really intend to, keep.

3. *In your mind, equate simplicity with honesty and let honesty be the motive that drives your discussion.*

4. *For more formal presentations or speeches, do a dry run with representative members of your intended audience; get their feedback on what's clear and what's not.* Look for better, shorter, clearer words and expressions with which to make your points.

5. *Develop three or four (but no more) key message points, the backbone of what you want to say, and hone them until they're as precise and concise as they can be.* Work them into your discussions. They will keep you focused on why you wanted to talk in the first place, and they will dramatically increase your chances for success in getting your ideas across.

6. *Read your audience, not just once or twice but continuously.* Look for heads nodding (a good sign) or blank, quizzical expressions (a bad sign). Use real-time feedback and make adjustments accordingly to regain attention, reiterate key points, or just move the whole thing along faster.

7. *Routinely interrupt your talk to check on how it's being grasped and to make sure you haven't lost your audience.* Don't just ask, "Am I being clear?" (often perceived as a challenge to their intelligence rather than your ability to speak clearly). Instead, repeat some version of your opening statement (to reaffirm your desire to be well understood). Then ask if there are any points they might like you to clarify or expand on: "I know we've covered a lot of ground in the last few minutes. Is there anything I could elaborate on, or maybe make a little clearer? Anything that I might have covered too lightly? Anything you want more detail on?"

8. *Listen to yourself.* Record yourself giving the presentation once or twice to audit your own speaking habits and mannerisms. You'll be surprised at what you can learn and what you can change and improve.

9. *Consider how you might incorporate any of the following "principles of plain English" (from the SEC booklet of that name[3]—prepared as a guide for writing financial disclosure documents) into your way of speaking:*

❏ Use the active voice with strong verbs—for example, instead of saying *Some changes will be implemented by the division in the future*, you may want to say *We will make some changes—next week.*
  ○ "Strong verbs are guaranteed to liven up and tighten" your speech.
  ○ Audiences "understand sentences in the active voice more quickly and easily because it follows how we think and process information."

❏ Use personal pronouns—for example, instead of saying *Division leadership wants to keep its people well informed*, you might say *We want to keep you well informed.*
  ○ "Personal pronouns aid your [audience's] comprehension because they make clear what applies to [them] and what applies to you."
  ○ "They allow you to 'speak' directly to your [audience], creating an appealing tone that will keep your [audience listening]."

❏ Bring abstractions "down to earth"—for example, instead of using an abstract concept like *the learning organization*, try to describe it in terms of behaviors, such as *a place where people continually acquire, create, and use knowledge to improve the way they work*
  ○ "Most people don't have an image in their minds when they hear abstract words . . . [a]nd yet it's far easier to comprehend a concept or a situation when your mind can form images."[4]

MAKING YOURSELF VISIBLE

Leadership communication is generally perceived to be more credible if delivered in person. You've got to be seen to be trusted. At Saturn, this direct, in person approach starts as a welcome to the company for new hires, where a plant or unit manager typically tells the newcomers about the company's aims and philosophy. "That's the first thing you get when you join Saturn. I can't tell you how many people from General Motors . . . came to Saturn and said, 'I've been with General Motors for 25 years and I have never met a plant manager, let alone the president of the company.'"[5]

Making a habit of holding face-to-face encounters, as we saw in the examples from the previous section, conveys honesty and candor in leadership communication. It's the opposite of the "seagull" style of leadership communication: Fly in, squawk a lot, and fly out. Jan Carlzon, the legendary leader of SAS, was definitely not a seagull-type communicator. "In his first two years at SAS, Carlzon spent up to 50% of his time communicating directly in large meetings and indirectly in a host of innovative ways: through workshops, brainstorming sessions, learning exercises, newsletters, brochures, and exposure in the public media."[6] Chuck Knight and his successor Dave Farr at Emerson spend more than half their time in what they call "planning" activities, really conversations with their unit managers around the world.

"Where's Waldo?"

People like to have a sense of what their leaders *do*. They don't necessarily want to know in detail—they've got their own jobs to contend with. But keeping in touch with leadership is useful and reassuring. "CEO sightings," for example, typically generate good, positive employee buzz, especially if they're managed with some frequency and consistency.

Leadership presence can be communicated even when leaders are not present. That's good news, because leaders who are perpetually out of sight can prompt all kinds of less-than-charitable speculation and rumors about what they're doing (and what they're up to). We've seen several measures leaders have taken to prevent the kind of speculation that ultimately erodes leadership credibility. As a leader, taking the initiative to let people know when you're out of town is a nice "heads up." It also helps to build cohesiveness in the workplace.

We used to receive regular e-mails from a colleague whenever he went on a trip, and the entry in the "subject" box was always "Where's John?" While most of the time we really didn't care where John was, we appreciated the gesture as a courtesy. It underscored a sense of commitment to our department.

One company conducting a major corporatewide idea generation program offered this unusual example of "staying visible." Part of the program involved evaluation committees, consisting mainly of managers with budget responsibility, sitting in closed-door meetings to evaluate idea submissions. Because it was important to communicate to all employees participating in the program that their ideas were receiving serious, thoughtful consideration, evaluation committees across the company would post signs outside their meeting rooms whenever they were "in session." The signs said simply, "The following members of the Great Ideas Program Evaluation Committee are meeting to evaluate submitted ideas." Not only did this let people know the whereabouts of specific leaders; it also advertised the fact that the committees really did meet.

More Visible Than You Think

Visibility is as much about how and with whom you communicate as it is about the number of times you're out and about as a leader. Strengthening the sense of community in an organization involves the way leaders interact with and touch the people in their organizations.

One of us used to work for Maritz, a family-owned firm and the largest planned incentive company in the world (with travel, marketing research, communications, and training components). The CEO was Bill Maritz, who, like his father before him, seemed to know by name a large percentage of the more than five thousand employees. Once, the author was going over job responsibilities with a newly hired secretary when Bill walked by. He stopped, introduced himself, and welcomed the woman to the company. A week later, the secretary received a short note (Bill had remembered her name) wishing her good luck in her new job. The note of course made the rounds and made more than one person's day.

Recently, another CEO note went way past its designated audience and landed on the first page of the *New York Times* Business Section, in an article titled "A Stinging Office Memo Boomerangs: Chief Executive Is Criticized After Upbraiding Workers by E-Mail."[7] The memo was originally sent to the managers of a global healthcare software development company, and it charged them to do something about what the CEO saw to be lackadaisical employee work habits. Its tone was direct and threatening, expressing in no uncertain terms both the CEO's extreme displeasure over the work hours he perceived headquarters employees putting (or not putting) in, and the punitive actions he was prepared to take.

There were two reasons this memo reached a wider audience than its author had intended: Its classic "Theory X" style and tone made great copy, and it was sent via e-mail (allowing it first to be leaked around the company, then later posted on Yahoo). The CEO became instantly visible to a huge audience, including all his employees, and not in a way he wanted to be.

The most obvious lesson this story holds for leaders would probably be, "Don't use e-mail if you desire confidentiality." But in this age of interactive telecommunications, the better counsel for leadership communication would be to write everything as if it *might* end up in the *New York Times*. Because it just might.

Making Your Thinking Visible Too

Trusted leaders are those whose abilities people rely upon, and whose values people know and respect. A leader's knowledge and skills are most reliably demonstrated, and measured by employees, over time, in the way they perform. But that can take a while. Sometimes it's helpful to let employees know about what you can do and what you've done. We're not talking about regaling employees with war stories. People will acknowledge and defer to expertise if it's not paraded and flaunted, but rather provided as useful information. "She's been there, paid her dues, earned her stripes": These are expressions of confidence in leaders that can be uttered only if people know something about your abilities and experience.

While leaders rarely have a monopoly on knowing what it takes to get a job done, they still need to be proactive about sharing their experience and their understanding, both to instill confidence and to expedite support for decisions. As we mentioned earlier, it can be counterproductive to hide leadership expertise where it exists. You need to make your expertise known. You also need to be candid about what you don't know.

Leaders' values and motives come through in how they communicate goals, plans, and decisions, and how they deal with people in the organization. For instance, ambiguous statements are often thought to indicate hidden motives. The more leaders openly discuss their motives and intentions, and explain their reasons for mak-ing certain decisions, the more their employees will see them as open, honest, and trustworthy. The opposite is also true: When people can't read you because you're overly circumspect and always keep your cards close to your vest, there's a greater likelihood for mistrust. When people find your remarks confusing, they might understandably feel that you are withholding information to keep them in the dark.

Leaders who can create trust in their decisions, and whose direc-tions are regarded as reliable and sure, are often the ones who take time to *explain themselves and their thinking.* They don't just say what they're going to do: They tell why they believe it's the right thing to do and what facts they based their decisions on. They don't just tell their plans; they reveal their intentions before plans are de-scribed and remind people during plan implementation. In short, good leaders don't ask you to read their minds: They let you know as thoroughly as they can the thinking behind their decisions. By making an effort to consistently communicate their thinking, lead-ers make themselves more *predictable* to their employees. Figure 5-2 lists ways leaders can make themselves better understood and more predictable.

Running through this checklist can be done either casually or more systematically. It's often worth the effort to be systematic, in-cluding consideration of how best to make your reasoning intelligi-ble and clear to each audience.

"FAIR PROCESS"

Leaders are regarded as trustworthy when people can rely on the logic and reasoning behind their decisions and direction. By sharing that reasoning, leaders make it easier for people to buy into direc-tions and decisions, even if those decisions later fail to meet expec-tations! Research on employee trust in leadership confirms this: "Individuals are most likely to trust and cooperate freely with sys-tems—whether they themselves win or lose by those systems—when fair process is observed."[8] *Fair process,* we would argue, is a leadership communication routine that consists of three elements:

Figure 5-2. Ways to explain your thinking.

A few things you might say . . .

❏ "Here's what I know about the situation."
❏ "These are my assumptions."
❏ "Here's the reasoning behind my decision."
❏ "Here's the data that supports my idea/position."
❏ "Here's the logic I used to arrive at this recommendation."
❏ "This is what I think my idea/position means."
❏ "Here are the criteria I used."
❏ "These were the deciding factors."
❏ "Here are some other options we considered (and why we didn't choose them)."
❏ "Here's what I think will happen if we go this way (or if we don't)."
❏ "Here's how I think it will affect the organization—and you."
❏ "Here's why I think it's the best way to go."

. . . And a Few Things You Might Want to Ask Yourself—Then Others

❏ "Are my assumptions reasonable and well founded?"
❏ "Have I missed anything; is there data I've overlooked?"
❏ "Are there gaps in my logic, flaws in my reasoning?"
❏ "Are there aspects of this decision that I cannot divulge, and, if so, how can I acknowledge that fact in a forthright way?"
❏ "Are there other conclusions that can be drawn besides the ones I've offered?"

---

1. Helping everyone involved and affected understand the reasoning behind decisions
2. Allowing individuals who are affected by decisions to question and challenge key ideas and assumptions
3. Clearly stating expectations for decision implementation and follow-through (which is discussed in more detail in chapter 6)

If colleagues and subordinates understand and accept your reasoning, they'll be able to support decisions and commit to carrying them out. If they understand your reasoning but offer corrections or worthy alternatives, additional benefits can result. Both of these positive organizational consequences depend on working to make your thinking visible, by telling more than you might normally do and by asking for feedback on what you have said.

Being Open

One of the unwritten rules of information sharing in organizations has always been the "need-to-know" policy, which, of course, can be interpreted strictly or loosely. How leaders actually interpret it can be determined by several things, but one important factor is the issue of leadership credibility and trust. *Openness* has become increasingly valued in leadership communications over the past few decades. For Donald Schon, openness is a characteristic of a wide range of leadership interactions, which "emphasize surfacing private attributions for public testing, giving directly observable data for one's judgments, revealing the private dilemmas with which one is grappling, actively exploring the other's meaning, and inviting the other's confrontation of one's own."[9]

Conversely, when leaders withhold information, or when people find out indirectly and after the fact what leaders could have told them directly and sooner, trust is weakened. Being open with people takes on several dimensions:

❏ What you say
❏ What you said previously, and what you will say in future (consistency)
❏ How much you say, and what you leave out
❏ When you say it
❏ Whom you say it to

When you speak as a leader, people *want* to believe you. In a sense, your leadership communication constitutes a promise. It describes a compact, and sets expectations of mutual trust and integrity.

"You Can Fool Some of the People . . ."

One of the things leaders learned during the 1980s and 1990s (especially in organization crises), and now in the first decade of the new century (with respect to public calamities), is this: People want to hear the bad news straight, without sugarcoating or garnishing. Take the 2001 "anthrax scare," for example. In the weeks after the

first incidents were discovered, various public officials "made confident statements that later proved false, tried simultaneously to in-
form and reassure, and limited the flow of information to the
public. . . . [They] speculated about what had happened or what
might happen. And they simultaneously warned Americans about
vague dangers while urging them to go about their lives."[10]

The result was an erosion of public trust in leaders who clearly
weren't sure about their facts, and whose motives were not always
clear either. In contrast, New York City's mayor Rudolph Giuliani
seemed a paragon of straightforwardness. He held daily press conferences about the city's anthrax exposures, provided audiences with
no more information than they actually could substantiate, and
begged their patience while promising that he and his staff would
try to keep them as up-to-date and well informed as possible.[11]

Lessons learned in both business and public spheres regarding
how leaders should talk about tough topics are summed up in Figure 5-3.

BEING IN CONTROL

> *Four fellows were playing a round of golf. After three of
> them had hit off the first tee, the fourth swung at his ball
> and missed it totally. "Whew," he said. "Tough course."*

Leaders don't always tell it like it is when the news is bad. In most
instances, this tendency can be explained by a couple of commonly
held leadership "values," identified by organizational researcher
Chris Argyris, who labels them as the desire "to remain in unilateral
control" and "to suppress negative feelings."[12]

Being in control is an obvious virtue in organizations. All leaders want work to go according to plan. Deviations and disruptions
cost money. Leaders manage against disruption; it's what they get
paid for. In addition, there's an element of "face" in the desire to
be in control; leaders want to be respected by their bosses and peers
for being "in charge," for keeping things in order. It's a matter of

Figure 5-3. Straight talk in tough times: eight *don'ts* and one *do*.

1. *Don't just tell half the story (or hold back on special contingencies):* People will pick up sooner or later on the fact you haven't told everything, speculate about the reasons you didn't, and lead themselves to generally negative conclusions.
2. *Don't whitewash:* People will feel you're afraid of the truth, or actually hiding something worse.
3. *Don't delay bad news:* People will see it as a breach of faith, and may feel (justifiably) compromised as a result.
4. *Don't equivocate:* If you're always saying "maybe," people may see you as incapable of making a decision. If you are in fact uncertain, tell people why.
5. *Don't speculate or express opinions you can't substantiate:* If you have to change your story later, people will hold you accountable for the change, and might not trust you later when you do have something they need to believe.
6. *Don't hide any special conditions or contingencies:* People may think you're trying to manipulate them, or that you're simply being devious.
7. *Don't try to spin your way out of trouble:* People are capable of dealing with most facts, and will respect you for being honest with them.
8. *Don't patronize your audience:* It's disrespectful, and creates a distance between you and them.
                                    But—
9. *Do treat people as stakeholders in a shared future:* Your basic communication objective during times of stress and turmoil should be to help people build sensible, well-informed opinions—and make good decisions—on their own.

reputation. In communicating this bias (sometimes without realizing it), leaders will say things like:

- ❐ "We run a tight ship around here."
- ❐ "I'm on top of the situation."
- ❐ "We know what's going on."
- ❐ "Everything's under control."

Contrast this picture with some recent research on leadership attributes that subordinates like and that lead to higher levels of trust and commitment.

Leadership Attributes That Strengthen Trust and Commitment

❐ Admitting uncertainty when leaders are not fully informed, or just don't know
❐ Selectively exposing weaknesses—areas where they can't claim expertise
❐ Expressing interest in analyzing failure, rather than ignoring it[13]

Leaders who are not afraid to appear vulnerable, and who can balance the need to seem in control with the ability to share doubt and uncertainty when they exist, are leaders who command more respect. Their words are listened to with more, rather than less, credulity. They are seen as more approachable, and more reliable, by people who work with them.

Leaders who maintain this less than totally rigid posture regarding the need to appear in control will say things like:

❐ "I may not have a full view of the picture yet."
❐ "I can't tell you right now that I have enough information to say anything useful."
❐ "I don't have a complete understanding of the situation."
❐ "I can't answer that question; I just don't know."
❐ "I'm not sure right now, and we're not going to make a decision until we're sure."
❐ "Don't count on me to be an expert in this area."
❐ "I may have made a bad call here."
❐ "We screwed up; let's acknowledge it, and move on."

It might seem uncomfortable (even "New Age") to traditional leaders to make statements like these, but the research and our own experience suggest that leaders have much more to gain than lose in backing off the tendency to always appear in tight control of the game.

Walking a Tightrope

Leaders probably most want to seem on top of the situation during times of major organizational shifts or crises. And it is during these times that assertions about the future and being in control are most likely to blow up in leaders' faces. To be sure, change situations can turn leadership communication into a tightrope walk. If leaders say too little, or confess ignorance about where the organization is going, their people are likely to lose confidence in them. In one large health-care organization that had gone through several mergers, employees indicated in a survey that they doubted their leadership even had a plan, because communication was either inconsistent or nonexistent. Leadership was generally thought to be asleep at the wheel.

Sometimes, leaders can wait too long to deliver important news. In one such instance, a big communication company embarked upon a major rebranding effort, backed by substantial research on their present market positioning and where it needed to go. The company actually ran a series of full-page ads in the *Wall Street Journal* to usher in its new identity before someone thought to formally communicate this shift to the workforce. Employees felt that leaders had shown them considerable disrespect in not informing them until after the general public. And it's not uncommon for us to find employees in different companies complaining that the way they hear important news about their organization is on Yahoo or some other public source.

Clearly there's a disconnect here. If leadership wants to increase employee commitment to the company and its goals, but informs them about significant developments only after the fact, the commitment will not come. To avoid falling off the communication tightrope, leaders need to err on the side of disclosure, while not being afraid to identify those aspects of change and the future, where they're legally constrained or just aren't sure about. In the final analysis, conceding vulnerability can be read as a strength.

Do What You Say

One of the most reliable indicators of trustworthiness in leadership is of course their ability to "walk the talk." Earlier we equated certain kinds of leadership communication with the making of a compact, a compact that commits leaders to make good on their word. Several companies we've worked with regularly survey their employees on how well leaders are delivering on this compact. Figure 5-4 lists tactics leaders can use to good advantage in doing what they said they would do.

There's another disconnect that has grave consequences for leadership reputation. It involves leadership touting values like teamwork and trust, but then sending a different message through their recognition and promotion practices. Organizations communicate to their members in many ways, but "who gets rewarded" is in itself one of the most telling communications, even if we don't think about job promotions, say, as a communications issue. Employees do, and they're typically quite attentive to this kind of organization communication.

Jack Welch's comments on not promoting those who made their numbers "on the backs of people" (cited in chapter 3) address this concern directly. Welch came back to this communication issue

Figure 5-4. Communication tactics for walking the talk.

❏ Consider statements of action to be promises—promises you're willing and able to keep.

❏ Leaders like to be action oriented, but if you're not sure you'll be able to pull something off, then bite your tongue and don't create expectations you can't meet.

❏ Don't leave loopholes; be as specific as you can about what you'll do and where and when you'll do it (otherwise, you risk letting others set expectations for you which you can't, or have no intention to, meet).

❏ Convey the impression of consistency by making the same points to different people: Copy remarks or correspondence to other stakeholders as appropriate; use a variety of communication vehicles to deliver the same message.

❏ Don't ask for opinions or advice unless you'll give them due consideration. Then, be sure to communicate what you heard and how you've considered it. "Empowerment" became the "E-word" in part because leaders went around inviting ideas and suggestions they had no intention of giving serious attention to.

❏ Talk the walk! Help people notice that you're walking the talk by putting yourself "on stage" (Example: the signs we mentioned earlier in this chapter outside the meeting room doors announcing that evaluation committees were in session).

❏ If they're not obvious, don't be afraid to "publicize" those actions that fulfill expectations: Use your in-house communication media to share accounts of who's doing what.

in an interview when he was asked by an audience member about GE's well-known practice of moving out the bottom 10 percent of performers. The questioner considered the practice a little harsh and unfair. Welch replied that the real unfairness occurred when employees were told in performance reviews that their work was satisfactory when it wasn't. Holding back poor evaluations and failing to point out specific performance deficiencies was, in Welch's view, an example of "false kindness." It represented an essentially dishonest communication to an employee, which ultimately rendered a disservice to employee and organization alike.[14]

CLOSING THE GAPS, STRENGTHENING THE PARTNERSHIP

One of the primary barriers to creating a community of trust is the perceived distance between people in bureaucratic organizations. Organizational hierarchy by its nature creates social distance that in turn can inhibit candor and openness. Just think about the almost ritual differences between your boss entering your office (or cubicle) and your entering hers. In the first case, there may or not be a courtesy knock before she enters, and in most instances, she'll seem like she's walking into territory she "owns," with free roaming privileges. In the second case, *you* will typically knock and wait outside to be invited into what is clearly not "your turf." Neither situation cultivates the open, candid conversation that is needed.

If you sincerely want to work against "caste" distinctions in the workplace, at least insofar as they inhibit productive communication, there are several communication strategies that can help. One of them has been well explored in the book *Communicating Change* by T. J. Larkin and Sandar Larkin. The Larkins make a strong case for getting frontline leadership involved in communicating change efforts in an organization. They argue, though, that it's not enough to simply insert supervisors into the communication loop. Rather, there's a need to reach out to frontline leaders in some special way, to create the basis for new trust levels at a time when senior leadership seeks their help and allegiance.[15]

One way to do this is "by ensuring that the supervisor has a voice in decision making, and making sure the supervisor has something to say, that she or he has privileged access to information."[16]

In sharing privileged information, senior leaders communicate a degree of trust that perhaps had not been previously extended. In asking sincerely for frontline managers' help at a critical time, senior leadership is communicating how valuable they are to the enterprise.

Building a stronger sense of partnership, where everyone has a common stake in success, works both ways. From a communication standpoint, leaders want to be able to share information reasonably openly. But they also want to be confident that everyone in the organization assumes the same regard for the value of information and becomes, if you will, a partner in protecting it as well. Organizational *stewardship* is about being a good custodian of organizational assets. Where communication is concerned, everyone needs to assume this role so that knowledge assets aren't leaked, squandered, or lost.

Internal communication within any organization becomes more critical as we gravitate to more knowledge-based enterprise. While increased access to information is becoming a hallmark of greater efficiency, it is also an important dimension of enhanced relationship building and higher levels of trust within the organization. In addition to emphasizing information stewardship and opening up new lines of communication with frontline managers, there are some other basic strategies for reducing distance, real or imagined, between organizational leaders and subordinates (see Figure 5-5).

Figure 5-5. Communication tactics for closing the gap.

☐ *Emphasize face-to-face communication as often as possible:* It's the ultimate strategy for humanizing relationships in a bureaucracy.

☐ *Share airtime:* Be seen as a listener as well as a direction giver.

☐ *Position yourself as a colleague:* Talk "common stake, common fate."

☐ *Invite criticism and push-back (and then be prepared to use it):* If you can take it as well as give it, communication roles can be leveled and better dialogue can occur.

☐ *Empathize:* Listen to people's stories and tell them you can understand how they feel.

☐ *Show employees you care about them as people:* Sincerely asked questions about nonwork matters, as well as expressions of interest in their careers, go a long way.

☐ *Don't be afraid to share a personal side of yourself:* It's about opening up to others and showing them it's okay for them to do likewise.

Habits of Attentive People

You've heard the one about the horse who said to his rider, after the rider kept patting his neck and saying what a good horse he was, "No, stupid. I said 'feedbag,' not 'feedback' "? Well, nobody can be expected to hear it right every time. But listening is still the too often ignored other side of the leadership communications coin. Being a good listener is a wonderful way to convey respect; strengthen relationships; and, ultimately, to reinforce trust.

Listening Skills

Many organizations address the need to improve listening effectiveness by having leaders (and perhaps others) polish up their "listening skills." Our take on effective listening is that it's not so much a matter of skills and their application as it is of forming habits and then sticking with them. Some of the habits are fairly intuitive and obvious: Pay attention to the speaker; tune out distractions. Others are less obvious and less frequently demonstrated.

A few years ago, AlliedSignal Aerospace wanted to move toward more team-centered work processes. Middle managers serving as team leaders would be critical to the success of this shift. As CEO Dan Burnham acknowledged in a message to them, "It's not enough to know only what *you* are doing. You have to know what *everyone* is doing too."[17] AlliedSignal accordingly placed internal communication among its highest priorities and made available to all leadership ranks a series of workshops and support materials on subjects like delivering effective messages, handling difficult situations, and leading a meeting.

The thread that linked all of these tasks was effective listening. A few years after this initiative, one of the authors encountered some AlliedSignal middle managers at a conference, where they acknowledged that one of the most significant consequences of making communication a priority was that people felt more connected to their managers; managers had become more accessible and more approachable. It's what can happen when leaders develop habits of listening more attentively. Figure 5-6 describes five good listening habits.

Figure 5-6. Habits to enhance listening effectiveness.

1. *Focus on the words (because it's easy to get distracted).* When we're listening to someone, we're typically processing several things more or less at once: body language, tone, what we already know about the person (and what we may expect to hear), etc. But because we're taking in all these "messages" simultaneously, the speaker's actual words are in competition for our attention. Often, they are losers in that competition, especially when the body language and the words seem to contradict one another. You cannot ignore the body language and other nonverbals, but you can work hard to keep them in perspective and pay more attention rather than less attention to the words. And for those times when the body language and the words contradict each other, simply use an opportunity in the conversation to note that, "I'm getting an unclear message, because I'm reading your body language one way and hearing your words another way."

2. *Resist trying to complete a speaker's thought.* We're all programmed to take shortcuts, and leaders are perhaps even more likely than others to want to "get to the point" quickly. One of the ways the mind helps this happen is by sensing where a speaker is going to wind up and then getting there before him or her. And sometimes we're in such a hurry that we complete the sentence for the speaker! This is also a habit, but not one that suggests to a speaker that you really care to listen to all she or he has to say. The habit to substitute—and it might take some deliberate effort—is to resist trying to complete the thought (and never to complete someone else's sentence).

3. *Withhold judgment until the speaker has finished.* This is obviously related to the previous habit, and in truth, it's connected to our natural impatience and our wanting to "get on with it." All communication is really about dialogue, speaking and listening and speaking again, and we can rush our turn as speaker at the expense of giving a fair hearing, particularly if we feel strongly about something that's just been said. Once again, this is a situation where one habit, one that can easily convey disrespect, begs to be replaced with another.

4. *Probe for a speaker's reasoning and assumptions.* Apart from the benefit to be gained from understanding better the point of view and argument you're trying to grasp, such probing can register positively as a gesture of interest and offer evidence that you've been listening. What you're conveying here is your concern to fully understand the points being made and how they're significant. This is a habit that can also strengthen a relationship based on mutual interest and respect.

Figure 5-6. (Continued).

5. *Paraphrase.* Often presented as a "listening skill," pa.
really nothing more than saying aloud what you th.
heard. Paraphrasing is a very natural act: it's actually th   we
listen and process what is being said. By saying something aloud,
we understand and remember better. Developing a habit of offering a paraphrase as an attempt to confirm understanding also carries
the same relationship-building benefits as the habit described in
no. 4. To improve the effectiveness of paraphrasing, you might
consider taking notes, as both a memory enhancer and a visual
confirmation of your listening. And when paraphrasing, you need
to be sure you got it right: "Is this the point you were making?"
"Did I understand you correctly?"

"How Are We Doing?"

More and more organizations appear to be formally assessing the
impact and effectiveness of their internal communications. Leadership communication is a big part of that and as such needs to be a
part of the research. Employee attitude surveys and performance
evaluations are two of the most common places to check on how
well you keep people informed, how you show respect, how you
solicit input and feedback from your people, and so on. We share
some assessment tools for strengthening leadership communication
in chapter 13.

If as leaders you understand that your communication is a critical element in creating a healthy, desirable work environment, in
which trust and openness are "values in use," you will welcome
assessment of how well you're doing. You will want to periodically
review the "leadership dialogue" across the organization and ask
how well it's working. Generally, this can be done through the
survey strategies mentioned above. But it's also worth noting that if
leadership senses any significant indications of mistrust in leadership,
then other measures can be taken.

Focus groups led by a skilled facilitator are one of the best ways
to learn more about such problems and how to fix them. These
discussions can get inside issues of weak leadership communication
and also suggest remedies. Because mistrust in leadership is generally
harmful to morale and a source of much misunderstanding, any red
flags here are well worth prompt attention.

In his elegant little book *The Magic of Dialogue*, Daniel Yankelovich lists three core requirements for effective dialogue in organizations: "empathic listening, equality of standing, and nonjudgmental surfacing of assumptions."[18] We think this list highlights much of what we've tried to say about the trust-building role of organizational leaders. It also suggests a starting point for organizing assessment initiatives. Being an effective, empathic listener; communicating as a colleague and "partner" as often as possible; and bringing ideas, beliefs, assumptions, and information, yours as well as theirs, out into the open, are all important leadership attributes and are all worth keeping track of so leaders can continuously work on developing them as personal and organizational assets.

NOTES

1. John A. Byrne, "How Jack Welch Runs GE," *Business Week* (June 3, 1998), 12.
2. Jack Welch, "Jack Welch: Icon of Leadership," interviewed by Stuart Varney at Fairfield University, *CEO Exchange*, WTTW Chicago (December 30, 2001).
3. U.S. Securities and Exchange Commission (Office of Investor Education and Assistance), *A Plain English Handbook: How to Create Clear SEC Disclosure Documents* (U.S. Securities and Exchange Commission, 1997), 12–17.
4. Ibid.
5. Jeffrey Pfeffer and Robert Sutton, *The Knowledge-Doing Gap: How Smart Companies Turn Knowledge Into Action* (Boston: Harvard Business School Press, 2000), 247.
6. Ronald A. Heifetz and Donald L. Laurie, "The Work of Leadership," *Harvard Business Review* (January–February 1997), 129.
7. Edward Wong, "A Stinging Office Memo Boomerangs: Chief Executive Is Criticized After Upbraiding Workers by E-Mail," *New York Times* (April 5, 2001), C1, 13.
8. W. Chan Kim and Renee Mauborgne, "Fair Process: Managing in the Knowledge Economy," *Harvard Business Review* (July–August 1997), 69.
9. Donald Schon, *Educating the Reflective Practitioner* (San Francisco: Jossey-Bass, 1987), 141.
10. Erica Goode, "Anthrax Offers Lessons in How to Handle Bad News," *New York Times* (October 23, 2001), D1.
11. Ibid., D6.
12. Chris Argyris, "Teaching Smart People How to Learn," *Harvard Business Review* (May–June, 1991), 103.
13. See Robert Goffee and Gareth Jones, "Why Should Anyone Be Led by You?" *Harvard Business Review* (September–October 2000), 64.
14. Welch, "Jack Welch: Icon of Leadership."
15. See chapters 1 and 9 in T. J. Larkin and Sandar Larkin, *Communicating Change: Winning Employee Support for New Business Goals* (New York: McGraw-Hill, 1994).
16. Ibid., 17.
17. "Exhibit 5: AlliedSignal Aerospace: A Message to Middle Managers," in Kathryn Troy, *Change Management: Communication's Pivotal Role* (New York: The Conference Board, 1995), 25.
18. Daniel Yankelovich, *The Magic of Dialogue: Transforming Conflict Into Cooperation* (New York: Simon & Schuster, 1999), 168.

III

The Leader as Navigator

> "For as knowledges are now delivered, there is
> a kind of contract of error between the deliverer
> and the receiver; for he that delivereth
> knowledge desireth to deliver it in such form as
> may be best believed, and not as may be best
> examined; and he that receiveth knowledge
> desireth rather present satisfaction than
> expectant inquiry."
>
> —SIR FRANCIS BACON, IN STEPHEN JAY GOULD,
> BEST AMERICAN ESSAYS 1994

The most basic function of leadership communication is to tell people what needs to be done and help them do it. In this sense, leaders serve as navigators for their organizations, assisting others in charting the right course, steering toward. it, and staying on it, no matter what the weather. This function has never been quite so easy and straightforward in its execution as leaders would like it to be, and that situation probably hasn't changed much in the four hundred years since Francis Bacon offered his observations in *The Advancement of Learning.*

In Part 3 we look at how leaders handle three navigator communication roles: *direction setter*—clearly identifying "true north" (chapter 6), *transition pilot*—keeping a steady course in times of transition and change (chapter 7), and *linking agent*—crossing organizational boundaries to keep all stakeholders moving and working together (chapter 8).

These chapters address issues of effective delivery and dissemination of key information. They cover some of the special challenges inherent in persuading people in organizations to make changes and in dealing with wholesale organizational change. They also examine the attributes of leadership communication that successfully connect different groups and different stakeholders in increasingly global enterprises.

Throughout, we take pains to be cognizant of the difficulty, even in the best of times and conditions, for communication to be truly successful: for leadership messages to be received, interpreted in the ways the speakers intended, and responded to appropriately.

6

Direction Setter

"Yesterday we stood on the precipice of a great abyss, and today we've taken a giant step forward."

—Unnamed Italian political leader, in

Keith E. Ferrazzi, *Across the Board*

Setting direction is a fundamental task of leadership, and communicating direction can be accomplished with varying degrees of effectiveness. We see the task as having three critical components. The strategies we discuss here and the illustrations we provide are all about dealing effectively with one or more of these three components:

1. Getting (and keeping) people's attention
2. Building awareness and understanding
3. Persuading people to act

Component 1. Getting (and Keeping) People's Attention

She: "You don't listen to half of what I say."
He: "Yes I do."

Let's face it. It's not easy to get people's attention amid all the other messages flowing out to employees in an endless stream. Leaders often have to elbow their way through this communication traffic to be heard. How then do leaders get people's attention?

In a survey of business executives, Thomas H. Davenport and John C. Beck tried to determine the attributes of those messages that attracted the highest levels of attention. Overall, the attributes, "in rank order, were:

- ❐ "The message was personalized.
- ❐ "It evoked an emotional response.
- ❐ "It came from a trustworthy or respected sender.
- ❐ "It was concise.

"The messages that both evoked emotion and were personalized were more than twice as likely to be attended to as the messages without those attributes."[1]

In a study we conducted of the relative effectiveness of various internal communication vehicles conducted for a large printing company, employees said they most regularly attended to e-mail messages sent by the CEO. Those e-mails were intermittent, but reasonably frequent, and sent to everyone in the company. Typically prompted by some important company decisions or significant industry developments, they were always short and to the point and "sounded like" the CEO. Employees said they felt like they were being spoken to directly by their leader and appreciated this as much for the gesture as for the information the e-mails conveyed.

Interestingly, the Davenport and Beck study reported that "almost half the messages that got high levels of attention were e-mails, while only 16 percent were voice mail messages. Messages in other media grabbed even less attention."[2] E-mails clearly lend themselves to being personalized, and when they embody the other attributes noted above, they can be an effective and inexpensive way to get the attention of large audiences. Leaders should be careful not to overuse them. For example, respondents in the printing industry study discussed above said that if the e-mails had been sent out on a scheduled basis, they would not have been nearly so appreciated as when they were perceived to be impromptu.

Several years ago we worked with a new spin-off company, one that was separating from a well-known blue chip corporation. Suffice it to say that employees tapped to go with the new organization were not ecstatic. Their most pronounced feeling was one of being a castoff from the mother ship. Enter the CEO-designate of the new organization, an upbeat, shirtsleeve, down-to-earth guy. He regularly sent out general e-mails to the workforce. He was also known for personally answering e-mails from individual employees. Despite the inevitable job reductions that came along with the spin-off, he received a rousing ovation from the workforce at the first headquarters employee meeting. People felt they could trust him to be on their side.

For leaders at all levels (not just CEOs), see Figure 6-1 for tactics for getting the attention of those you want to be listening.

Component 2: Building Awareness and Understanding

Once upon a time, Sherlock Holmes and Dr. Watson went camping. During the night, Holmes woke up, and he could see the stars

Figure 6-1. Communication tactics to get attention.

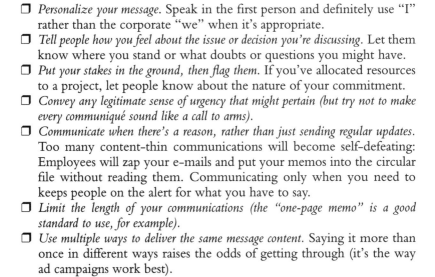

☐ *Personalize your message.* Speak in the first person and definitely use "I" rather than the corporate "we" when it's appropriate.

☐ *Tell people how you feel about the issue or decision you're discussing.* Let them know where you stand or what doubts or questions you might have.

☐ *Put your stakes in the ground, then flag them.* If you've allocated resources to a project, let people know about the nature of your commitment.

☐ *Convey any legitimate sense of urgency that might pertain (but try not to make every communiqué sound like a call to arms).*

☐ *Communicate when there's a reason, rather than just sending regular updates.* Too many content-thin communications will become self-defeating: Employees will zap your e-mails and put your memos into the circular file without reading them. Communicating only when you need to keeps people on the alert for what you have to say.

☐ *Limit the length of your communications (the "one-page memo" is a good standard to use, for example).*

☐ *Use multiple ways to deliver the same message content.* Saying it more than once in different ways raises the odds of getting through (it's the way ad campaigns work best).

shining brightly. He called over to his companion: "Watson, what does seeing the stars in the middle of the night mean to you?" Watson awoke, looked up and gazed at the sky for a moment, then said, "Infinity is sometimes incomprehensible and sometimes comprehensible. We are but a speck in the universe, yet we are blessed with a thing called consciousness. . . ." "Watson, you idiot," interrupted Holmes, "it means that someone stole our tent."

People in organizations are perpetually trying to figure out what their leaders *really* mean when they make pronouncements, state goals and priorities, or even when they merely make an observation or deliver some offhand news. One reason, to be sure, is that leadership isn't always adept at delivering messages in ways that are clear, complete, and consistent.

In our experience, all too many organizations discover, especially through internal surveys, that employees are often confused about what's important, what customers really want, and what they should be attending to. Research confirms this. In a Conference Board study, barely more than half the respondents rated their executive teams very effective at communicating direction; just 21 percent felt that senior management was very effective, and only 5 percent regarded middle managers as very effective.[3]

But let's be honest. Making sense in organizations can be a complicated task, where problems aren't always well defined, where issues are many sided, and where directives and directions are likely to come from several different sources at once. Employees look to their leaders to bring order to complexity, but the order is not always apparent. We would argue that coping with complexity is a challenge for *everyone* in an organization, and that imposing order over that complexity is what effective leadership communication aims to achieve.

Communication Filters

Here's what leadership communication is up against. In any organization, people are likely to *filter* the communications they receive according to:

❒ What they've heard before on the subject, and what they think they already know

❑ What they're hearing from other sources, including the grapevine (typically thought to be more credible and reliable than you!)

❑ What they think you want them to hear (versus the "real, hidden" agenda)

Leaders tend to think in the same terms and filter their messages through their own assumptions as to how people think, what they want to hear, how informed they already are, and how much understanding they have on the subject. People if asked would say they want communication to be simple and straightforward. But no matter how straightforward the outgoing communication, they will want to interpret it in complex and roundabout ways, using those ever-present filters. In fact, we can't help ourselves: We're programmed through evolution to have doubts and to screen for hidden meaning, and often, especially in organizations, such filtering helps us to cope and survive, and succeed.

Giving Clear Direction

Former CEO of SAS Jan Carlzon once said that "the leader's most important role is to instill confidence in people."[4] One way in which leaders instill confidence is by being clear and understandable when they talk about what's important to the organization. If people can't understand their leaders' directions and why those directions are worth following, they'll lack confidence in their leaders and in their own ability to carry the directions out. The strategies we discuss are all about delivering messages that are understood, both directly on their own terms and more broadly as part of the organization's mission and work.

To begin with, the "tactics for keeping it simple," outlined in chapter 5, work not only to enhance trust levels, but also to make communications more actionable. Figure 6-2 contains a set of tactics for leadership communication, spoken or written, to nurture clearer understanding regarding actions to be taken.

Using Data to Clarify Direction

All too often in presentations, leaders resort to using data in ways that shut down communication. Rolled up, interim performance

Figure 6–2. Tactics for setting clear direction.

❑ *Focus on a single objective whenever possible but make sure you show clearly how it fits in with everything else.* Discussing multiple objectives can be distracting and cause one objective to compete for attention with another.

❑ *Limit your discussion to two to three key points.* More than that, and people simply will not remember what you said. Multiple message points dilute the impact of the really important things you want to get across.

❑ *Prioritize your key points.* If you make it sound as if everything is of equal importance, you could well leave employees wondering which direction they should run in first. And since there doubtless is some sense of priority, don't assume your audience will be reading them in the same order you do; tell them.

❑ *Translate strategy to operating terminology.* The closer you can get to language that describes what people will need to *do,* the better they'll understand what the action implications are. If you don't talk about the actions you want, people will tend to do the same things in the same ways as before.

❑ *Repeat yourself.* The old adage "tell them what you're going to tell them, tell them, and then tell them what you told them" is still a useful organizing principle that contributes to better understanding and remembering.

❑ *Expose your reasoning.* If you tell people what's behind your directions, what your assumptions are, even what alternatives you might have rejected, you can count on two things happening. People will understand your directions better, and they'll see that you have confidence in them (we address this tactic on a larger scale in the next section when we deal with enhancing "business literacy").

❑ *Invite questions—and wait for them.* All too often the tag line "Are there any questions?" is spoken automatically, with no expectation that there will be any (we've actually witnessed speakers ask the question with their eyes still focused on their notes, making it impossible to see if any hands might be raised). The best tactic here is to make a point of waiting for at least five seconds, while you deliberately scan the room, so that you show your audience your invitation is sincerely made. (In large staff meetings at our former company, the CEO would ask for questions after his remarks; if none came, he started questioning himself, and he didn't just ask the softball questions.)

❑ *Summarize.* Hit the key points one last time. They become the "take-aways" that people will retain.

results expressed as various financial ratios (and for extra points, with the formulas that generated this stuff) can make audiences' eyes glaze over. When shown to an audience that has no real control over the numbers, your data simply doesn't communicate. Other times, data becomes a stick used to threaten or punish.

Yet data presented well can improve the clarity and impact of leadership communication. Data can be used to raise questions, make a point, draw a conclusion, or substantiate a decision, just to mention a few applications. Feeding data into a presentation can bring concreteness to an otherwise abstract message and specificity to an otherwise vague or unclear one. Figure 6-3 contains ideas for using data to enhance a presentation.

One potential "plot" structure for integrating different data to good advantage with employees is the *balanced scorecard*. In recent years, the concept of a balanced scorecard using a "family of measures" to define goals and provide performance feedback has gained a considerable following.[5] To our mind, this approach provides a way to effectively *bring measurement data into a conversation* about organizational goal setting, strategy building, and performance evaluation. In storytelling terms, it's about defining the quest, mapping the journey, and recounting the adventures along the way.

Balanced scorecards help make direction setting more disci-

Figure 6-3. Communicating with data.

☐ *Use data only if your audience will understand it.* Consider your audience before you consider the data—its needs, backgrounds, perspectives. If data is there mainly because *you* like it, consider dumping it and make your points in other ways.

☐ *Use data to help tell a story; don't make it* the *story.* Incorporate data into story plots that tell of organizational quests, journeys, victories, and defeats. This is the best way to help your audience make sense of data.

☐ *Use graphs and charts to present a lot of information and make it quickly and more completely understood.* They can help an audience *read* data and make numbers come alive in ways that columns and rows of figures will not. They can also fit data into basic plotlines.

☐ *Avoid the "scoreboard syndrome."* If people haven't seen the numbers yet and could use the feedback to guide further action, then telling them the score is important. Otherwise, leaders fool themselves in thinking that numbers by themselves can inspire, motivate, or otherwise communicate reasons for action. The numbers need to tell a story.

plined, while inviting several different "story lines" to play out simultaneously, much as they do in the real life of organizations. They also allow leaders to tell a story serially, based on regularly measured performance against goals. Perhaps most important, they bring greater clarity and specificity to the way in which leaders define goals and strategy. When leaders use a balanced scorecard, they can rely on more concrete indicators to communicate progress toward a goal.

A Scorecard for Communicating Goals and Strategy

The agricultural division of a major chemical company used a balanced scorecard to set the stage for a conversation about priority goals between its leadership and the rest of the company. A group of chemists and formulators first became interested in a balanced scorecard because they felt it might create a more comprehensive way to set and communicate direction across a diverse population of professional employees. The group proposed to senior management that a balanced scorecard approach to goal setting and strategy building be considered.

Senior leadership expressed a willingness to try it and developed its own set of balanced goals for the organization (in a session facilitated by the CEO!). In a series of workshops, company managers then plowed through their own goal and indicator development exercise. The outcome was a platform that leaders could talk from when they met with their own teams to set direction for team priorities. The company also chose to tie its performance appraisal process to the balanced scorecard platform, so that a truly unified communication could be made to all employees about what was important and how performance would be measured.

Clarifying Context

In chapter 3, on meaning-making, we mentioned that many organizations have made significant attempts to enhance the "business literacy" of their workforce, the fundamental understanding people have about the nature of the organization's business and how the organization actually functions. The assumption behind improving business literacy is simple: Employees will make more sense of organizational goals and objectives when they have a better understanding of the environment in which the organization works.

Leaders function as *direction setters* by helping employees understand better the territory in which the organization moves and operates. This territory can have several distinctive features, environmental markers that leaders can include in their discussions about organizational challenges and the journey toward organizational goals (see Figure 6-4).

If your workforce isn't reasonably knowledgeable about these topics, the directions you set to guide future performance will not be as clearly understood as they could be. It's that simple.

Putting the Facts into Play

Like many energy companies, MidAmerican Energy Corporation (MEC) was worried about the future.[6] A regional company serving customers in several states and overseas, MEC was concerned about the trend toward deregulation and the entrance into the marketplace of real competition. MEC knew that future prosperity, even survival, depended on its ability to win and keep customers who would soon have energy options to choose from. The organization would need to become, from top to bottom, a more competitive enterprise with a different outlook on its clientele.

Figure 6-4. Getting to know the territory: topics to address.

❏ *Customer Profiles and Customer Requirements.* Who are they, what do they want, what do they value, what disappoints them, and how might things change in the future?

❏ *The Playing Field.* What market, regulatory, and technological factors significantly affect the way the game is played? (For publicly traded companies, what's the role of the stock market and our relationship to it?)

❏ *Competition.* Who are they, and what do they offer that's different, now and in the future (also, how do we fare against them)?

❏ *How Work Gets Done.* Who does what in the organization, and how are various operations organized and coordinated? How does the business work, and what are the costs of doing business?

❏ *Information Sources.* Where do I go to find out more, and whom do I talk to?

The initial challenge to leadership was how to rally a workforce that had known only the environment of a regulated industry, where MEC, dealing in both gas and electric power, was practically a monopoly. MEC leadership felt one thing was obvious: Everyone would need to become more aware of a different competitive landscape already beginning to take shape. To set the stage, company leadership held an unusual kickoff at its annual management meeting, featuring groups of leaders discussing questions raised by a "planning worksheet" process.

Worksheets were big, measuring 3 feet by 4 feet. At the management meeting, cross-functional groups of corporate leaders, including the senior leadership team, had their own sheets spread across a table. The worksheet had the look of a game board, with different graphically displayed data fields arrayed around the sheet and cartoon drawings to "punch up" messages contained in the data fields. One field presented snapshots of other industries that had undergone deregulation; another, comparative statistics from other energy providers showing customers per employee and profit per employee; a third, maps displaying the new configurations involving power generation, marketing, and transmission made possible by new laws.

The worksheet was produced inexpensively, black and white on regular-grade paper. Armed with colored markers, participants could scribble, underline, and otherwise "customize" the worksheet as they talked. Worksheet discussions were prompted by a series of questions, contained in a booklet given to each participant. The booklets referred table groups to different data fields, asking them to consider possible implications for the company. Participants could also highlight key points, record notes, connect data fields they felt held implications for one another, and so on.

The sessions quickly became animated. They began with groups of five to six people seated at each of thirty or so tables. But that soon changed. People who had been quietly seated around the worksheets just a few minutes earlier now were standing, debating, gesturing, taking notes, marking up the worksheets, and in general figuring out where the company should go with an intensity that was remarkable. Each table typically had more than one conversation going on, as different participants were drawn to different data fields. This particular worksheet was called "The New Playing

Field" and was meant to engage a variety of leadership perspectives on key issues for which MEC would need to build strategy and set some new direction.

Expanding the Conversation After the meeting, leaders received their own discussion "kit," consisting of more worksheets and booklets for use in their own team meetings. In this way the conversation was carried across the company, with the intention to engage practically everyone in thinking about how MEC might best compete in a changing environment. Everyone was asked to consider the same data sets, the same issues and challenges. Thus, virtually all parts of the company drew not only a more accurate picture of the company's business context but also a remarkably consistent one.

The work unit and team conversations also allowed leaders and their people to draw their own conclusions regarding specific action implications for their respective functions and responsibilities. MEC later incorporated a version of the worksheet exercise into its new employee orientation program and regularly provides new data on how the organization is coping in its weekly employee publication.

Bringing Understanding to Complexity These worksheets are communication tools that help leaders not only present information in a compelling way but also engage their people to think and talk about organizational priorities and directions. They are good context builders for complex subjects, like the "future of the industry" or the "changing client profile." They also trade on a leadership communication technique as old as Socrates: the use of questioning to help someone arrive at a conclusion, or bring out a latent idea. The dialogue that MEC leaders facilitated with their own teams as part of a learning worksheet exercise might include questions like these:

- ☐ What could we do to minimize or prevent such problems in the future?
- ☐ If we tried to solve the problem this way, what might happen?
- ☐ What might success look like if we solved the problem?
- ☐ What could I help you do?

Communicating as a Mentor

Coach and mentor are two leadership communication roles that help employees navigate effectively through organizational life. Each role carries with it several critical communication attributes. Leaders communicate like a coach when they incorporate specific goals in their direction setting, as well as inspiration and instruction for achieving those goals. When leaders acts as mentors, on the other hand, they are less concerned with reaching a specific destination as they are with making the journey easier and more rewarding for the persons being mentored. Mentors have both a personal and an organizational interest in the success of their charges. They offer how-to advice, organizational shortcuts, personalized feedback, and moral support, among other things. They also communicate a valuable perspective for understanding organizational direction by:

❐ Distinguishing between "official explanations" and what actually happens in the organization
❐ Translating corporate communications into news the person can use
❐ Providing practical counsel for getting around organizational roadblocks

Communicating as a mentor might involve the tactics of Figure 6-5 to support direction setting.

Mentors succeed when they create and sustain a nonjudgmental, collegial relationship. Their communication strategy needs to be less directive and more facilitative, delivered in the manner of a concerned ally and trusted friend.

COMPONENT 3. PERSUADING PEOPLE TO ACT

"Leadership is the art of getting others to do something you want done because they want to do it."

—ANONYMOUS

Figure 6-5. Tactics for effective mentor communications.

- ❐ Be a respectful, attentive listener for those you mentor.
- ❐ Express clear bias toward their success.
- ❐ Establish their "readiness" for advice before you give it.
- ❐ Offer advice that's relevant to their agendas, not yours.
- ❐ Couch advice in the first person: "What's worked for me in the past . . ." (offered gently, modestly, and anecdotally).
- ❐ Illustrate advice with both personal successes and personal failures.
- ❐ Use the Socratic method discussed earlier: It's often the best way to deliver advice.
- ❐ Preface your feedback with your intentions for giving it: What's its potential for use? How might it benefit the user?
- ❐ Invite *any* kind of question (even those labeled by one mentor as "those silly-ass questions you know better than to ask").
- ❐ Be an "open channel" sounding board for hypotheses, guesses, trial balloons, anything they want to try.

Persuasion as Fair Process

Trying to explain his refusal to finance foreign language courses in schools, Texas Governor James "Pa" Ferguson in 1917 argued, "If English was good enough for Jesus, it's good enough for the school-children of Texas."[7] We think Governor Ferguson was onto something here, even though Jesus, of course, didn't speak English. Ferguson wanted to win the support of his constituents by explaining the reasoning behind his actions, and he wanted to make his explanation a compelling, if inaccurate, one.

W. Chan Kim and Renee Mauborgne, in their study of perceptions of "fair process" among managers and employees in knowledge economy companies, concluded that sharing a full explanation behind the reasons for decisions, as well as asking for input and feedback, are critical to the perception that fairness has been exercised. Leaders need to make sure that everyone with a stake in a decision and its outcomes should feel well briefed on how the decision was made. "An explanation of the thinking that underlies decisions makes people confident that managers have considered their opinions and have made those decisions impartially in the overall interests of the company. An explanation allows employees to trust managers' intentions even if their own ideas have been rejected."[8]

In chapter 5 we offered ideas for how leaders might best communicate the reasoning behind their thinking and decision making. Explaining underlying reasons and assumptions is an equally important leadership tactic when they want to be persuasive, steering people in the right directions. Chapters 9 and 10 include some thoughts on how leaders might uncover the reasoning of people who don't agree with them.

The first challenge in winning agreement and support for decisions that lead to significant work (and work life) consequences is forging a good understanding about those decisions with employees. Understanding includes both how the organization stands to benefit and how individuals are affected. Using data thoughtfully can also be an effective means to persuade. Being as specific as possible about individual consequences, both positive and negative, can also make an argument more convincing (at the risk of making HR and legal staffs uncomfortable).

Management professor Jay Conger has suggested that there are at least four ways in which leaders commonly *fail* to be persuasive:

1. "They attempt to make their case with an up-front, hard sell, "the "slam-dunk" approach that can trigger an instinctive push-back from others who might have been prepared to listen to a more collaborative approach.
2. "They resist compromise," when even a modest compromise might buy agreement, while stubbornness sends a message that forestalls future cooperation.
3. "They think the secret of persuasion lies in presenting great arguments," while sidestepping the importance of context, credibility, and mutual benefit.
4. "They assume persuasion is a one-shot effort," ignoring the importance of engagement as a key to fair process, and the time required for real buy-in.[9]

Each of these failures runs aground on the principles of fair process articulated by Kim and Mauborgne. To be persuasive, especially with more mobile and better educated employees, leaders must provide thorough explanations that connect with big-picture understandings. They must find ways to make common cause and to build win-win propositions. And they should try throughout to be open to questions, feedback, and ideas for alternative solutions.

In a study of American elections, researchers found that voters are influenced by language that is "highly certain, highly optimistic, highly realistic, and highly active."[10] So are American consumers, we would hasten to add, and people in organizations. The implications for leadership communication that aim to establish employee consensus and buy-in to a particular decision or initiative might therefore look like those in Figure 6-6.

In most organizations that work hard at building consensus around key decisions, leadership communications makes two things especially clear: what's best for the organization and what's best for its people. When the organization must take action that might compromise the immediate interests of some employees for the sake of the wider organization, leaders can still be persuasive if they explain thoroughly and listen to employee concerns.

Psychologist Robert Cialdini suggests an additional strategy here, based upon research indicating that most of us are more inclined to prevent lost opportunities than to reap potential gain.[11] Without resorting to fear mongering, leaders add an important dimension to any direction-setting communication by pointing out what the organization and its people stand to lose by not following a given plan.

Sustained Persuasion: Recognition of Effort and Accomplishment

Dilbert's manager is forever looking around for someone to pin a special achievement award on, while Dilbert and his colleagues are usually equal to the task of deflecting such recognition, because it's

Figure 6-6. Communication tactics to win buy-in to goals.

❑ Be realistic in setting goals, and what's needed to reach them.
❑ Express optimism about goal attainment.
❑ Use action verbs that convey energy and momentum to describe the means to goal attainment: *stretch, push, exceed, drive, win,* etc.
❑ Emphasize consequences and make it clear that success will be rewarded: People are motivated to work toward a goal when goal attainment carries positive and certain outcomes for them and for the organization.

essentially a meaningless ritual. And so are the numerous related gestures in organizations that routinely name an employee of the month, without specifying why he or she is so designated or what performance led to such mention (it may simply have been Jane's turn).

But when performance recognition is communicated effectively, it serves a solid purpose: reinforcing the continuation of desired behavior. There's a growing literature on reward and recognition strategies for organizations that highlights the importance of leader recognition of employee performance, both individual and team.[12] We think recognition is indeed a critical dimension of persuasive communication when it's focused on reinforcing goal-directed behavior, as well as solidarity with the organization.

So how can leaders avoid issuing just another jaded recognition communication? First, simply by tying recognition not to the calendar but to an activity or achievement. The phrase "catching employees (or colleagues) doing something right" probably captures this strategy best. Spontaneity equates with sincerity in acknowledging worthy performance, and doing it directly, face-to-face, is the most powerful way of all. But leaders can't always catch people in the act of doing something right, so the next best thing is to offer delayed recognition ASAP.

Letting Them Know You Know

Employee recognition is about leaders communicating two things: *awareness* ("I know you did a great job on that project") and *appreciation* ("Thanks for getting us out of this predicament"). That's it. Anything else is of secondary importance at best. The Gallup research discussed in chapter 2 clearly confirms the critical importance of leadership awareness and appreciation of work done. Hearing expressions of both are among the twelve elements "needed to attract, focus, and keep the most talented employees."[13] When neither occurs, ever, employees often look for another place to work.

Communicating awareness of employee performance fills a profound need that we all have to be acknowledged for the good things we do. We want others, especially our bosses, to know about the effort we make and the things we achieve. We want to be *visible* contributors to the organizations of which we are members. When we deliver value to our organization, our organizational identity, our sense of affiliation, is strengthened.

In the 2002 Winter Olympics, a Canadian figure-skating couple was at first awarded a silver medal, but then, after some alleged collusion among the judges, shared the gold. When asked how they felt about this attempt at restitution, they admitted the gold medal was nice, but what they really missed was being able to stand on the podium and watch their flag being raised while their national anthem was played (a wish that was, in fact, granted them a few days later). What they wanted was to *feel* the recognition of their countrymen at an important occasion.

Expressing appreciation for work done well provides a way for leaders to validate employee efforts, to acknowledge their value to the organization, and to reinforce employees' sense of self-worth as well. As your mother probably told you many times, "Don't forget to say *thank you!*" These two little words reinforce on-target behavior and ensure its continuance better than just about any other force known to managers.

Let us share a few of the ways organizations we know work at communicating awareness and appreciation to their people, although our lists are just meant as a sampler. Basically, recognition communications are made either individually (manager talking or writing to employee) or publicly. Opportunities to recognize employee performance occur along a continuum from totally spontaneous ("Gotcha!") to highly ceremonial (the annual "President's Medal" or some such award). In between, there are a lot of ingenious, as well as pretty simple (but effective), ways to get the message across. We offer ideas for individual and for group communications in Figures 6-7 and 6-8, respectively.

DELIVERING THE MESSAGE

When leaders want to communicate with the entire organization, they need to choose an appropriate medium. Some organizations schedule all hands "town meetings" via telephone to announce and discuss major developments. Participants typically gather in conference rooms or offices with speakerphones. The power of these

---

Figure 6-7. Communication ideas for individual recognition.

❐ *Spoken Acknowledgments:* They're most effective as communication when they
  ○ *Are personalized:* "I would really like to thank you . . .".
  ○ *Sound sincere and unforced:* A lot of leaders still feel uncomfortable in bestowing praise and wind up saying their thank-you's somewhat begrudgingly ("Well, I guess I should show my appreciation for. . . .").
  ○ *Are immediate* (rather than delayed or scheduled—"It's time to pick the employee of the month").
  ○ *Pinpoint a specific behavior or achievement:* Conveying real awareness of exactly what was done, rather than focusing on the person per se (also raising the likelihood that the behavior will be repeated).
  ○ *Don't sound patronizing:* "We think you did some pretty smart thinking on this job."
❐ *Written Notes:* Short and hand-written are best; they seem more personal and can carry the same value as a one-on-one conversation Many leaders use a smaller, cardlike stationery to distinguish their notes from more formal memos and letters.

---

meetings lies in the personal tone and immediacy that a leader can achieve through this everyday medium: the leader chatting with colleagues about matters of common interest, and it's all live and in real time.

The major print communication company discussed earlier relies, somewhat ironically, on an e-mail "letter," sent to all employees by the CEO, to get the word out about important business news. The CEO of a transportation organization that was facing stiff marketplace challenges held weekly teleconferences with several hundred managers on the line at the same time. The links that the CEO forged directly to his frontline leaders were invaluable to the company's ability to pull together and meet their challenge.

Consistency with a Personal Touch

Especially when presenting goals or launching a major planning process, you need to use a consistent set of messages across the organization. Naturally, these messages are carefully crafted beforehand to pack a lot of meaning into a few words and do it with just the right tone. Key messages are not an opportunity for ad-libbing.

Figure 6-8. Communication ideas for public recognition.

❏ *Bulletin Board or Web Site Postings of Projects Completed, Honors Won, Etc.* Leaders can add personal comments on these to make them really mean something; otherwise, they remain just another HR or corporate communications gesture.

❏ *Kudos and "Bouquets" from Clients and Colleagues.* Many leaders who receive these about their employees are good about letting the employee know. But they miss the opportunity to circulate them, with their own comments and thanks attached. In one agency we know, leaders post notes from customers that compliment employees on their office doors for passers-by to read.

❏ *Meetings.* Honor and recognition elements in staff meetings can be wonderful ways to manage peer recognition and acclaim, while delivering thanks for good work. If this is done frequently, and rather informally, leaders can add a valuable dimension to meetings. While some individuals might be embarrassed by being called out, they're more typically ambivalent about public recognition; they might feel awkward, but they also feel good. Sometimes, recognition of *teams* rather than individuals is easier for participants to accept and manage.

❏ *Special Events.* Many organizations recognize achievement at a special scheduled event, where leaders can deliver their appreciation before a larger audience, sometimes including members of honorees' families. As with all such occasions to express appreciation, the more knowledgeable the leaders sound about the details of performance, the more valued their comments will be. Arranging for "off-stage" opportunities, especially ones where leaders can let their hair down, perhaps with a drink in their hands, is another way to make such communication more memorable and more powerful.

So how can leaders balance the need for clarity, accuracy, and consistency with the parallel need to maintain a personal touch in these communications? One effective balancing act involves packaging key messages in a video, typically featuring the CEO, along with a set of briefing sheets and discussion guides to be used by onsite managers with employee teams. The video delivers the key message points consistently across the organization; local leaders put a local spin on them and talk about action implications for their groups.

Videos are not the medium of choice for employees, but incorporating a short video presentation into a larger, more personal communication puts it to good use. When senior leadership of a Big Three Detroit automaker met in retreat to develop a major quality improvement initiative, a documentary-style video of leaders in their shirtsleeves discussing key company issues was created. Because the video was not overproduced, it captured a degree of informality and honesty in their meeting that helped position the issues and their complexity for colleagues around the world. The video was then included in a communication kit with some basic discussion guidelines for managers around the company.

Who Speaks for the Organization?

"Unquestionably, the employee's immediate supervisor has more influence over whether or not a communication passes through the system accurately than does anyone or anything else."
—Jac Fitz-enz, *Eight Practices of Exceptional Companies*

No leader carries out the direction-setting role alone. It's a shared responsibility, and it has to be. Most organizations have a multitier communication "distribution system." Key messages originating at the corporate level typically are translated by various levels of management before they take on any real meaning for frontline employees. If this sounds like a paradox, it is.

In a similar way, value is delivered to customers only after employees translate broad organizational goals into specific behaviors that yield things customers want. At each management level, as well as at each divisional boundary, critical communications occur as *information handoffs*. Certain key message content needs to be preserved in each handoff, while new details need to be added to make the communication actionable by different functional groups. Inevitably, leaders in many different organizational roles, at all levels, play important navigational roles.

To manage a smooth flow of information handoffs, middle and frontline managers must be fully functioning, two-way communicators. They need to be well informed and up-to-date if they are to serve as credible, trustworthy interpreters of signals from the top of the organization. They also need to know what signals from the operational side of the organization are important to pass up. There are clear business literacy implications for managers in the middle, as well as implications for quick and timely information exchange (we treat this topic in our discussion of change communications in the next section).

The communication versatility that technology affords most organizational leadership in theory allows top leaders to reach everyone in the organization directly. But most employees still want to receive certain kinds of communication, especially nuanced messages that have potential job and career consequences, directly from their boss. So long as certain kinds of organizational communication require a dimension of personal trust, along with the ability to engage in real and immediate dialogue, employees will prefer supervisors to CEOs as communication sources and conduits.

Getting Back on the Same Page

Over the past decade, a major not-for-profit service organization has faced real competition for the first time. The competition, several privately owned firms, does not have the same public service mandate and can therefore choose customers and operate differently.

Several years ago, this organization realized it was time to revamp some administrative practices and to become more "business-like" in its operation. In planning these changes, agency leadership discovered two communication issues that required attention. One was the need to help two different operating divisions work more collaboratively. The other was to build employee understanding for why the agency needed to streamline some of its operating practices.

The organization had learned through surveys that "becoming more business-like" had been interpreted by some employees as "becoming more of a business." For many employees and volunteers, this attitude came out with the oft-heard comment, "That's not why we joined the organization!"

In fact, the agency had no intention of changing either its traditional mandate or its charter. Senior leadership was instead intent on improving productivity within a long and proud heritage of service. The leadership team was especially concerned about continuing to recognize the employees and volunteers who make the organization successful. Accordingly, the leadership team identified its challenge as a broad-based communication task to reaffirm the organization's mission and make intraorganization communications a top priority for development.

The team set about its task by holding an all-day meeting to systematically develop communication strategies that could respond to identified issues and goals. The strategies were built on a set of four key statements, or "core messages," which the agency would use to clearly articulate its mission and strategy across the organization.

The next step was probably the most important one. The headquarters team declared that improving organizational communications would be a top leadership priority during the coming year. Region and district managers were invited to take up the challenge to both share the four core messages with their colleagues and to shape them out further so they'd be well heard and understood. In a workshop setting, middle and frontline management were asked to think about, then discuss, the following questions:

- ❐ What does this core message say to you? How would you paraphrase the message in your own words?
- ❐ Do you believe it? Why or why not?
- ❐ What examples in your area would back up or validate the message?
- ❐ Does this message serve as a foundation for something you are currently stressing in your area, or that you would like to?

Agency leadership acted in concert on this initiative. They respected the importance of having leaders at all levels working to connect and reconnect people to the larger mission of the organization. They also committed to making communication within the organization more of a two-way street, allowing for real dialogue about issues facing the organization and the people in it.

In our experience working with organizations to improve communication *flow*, those that recognize middle and frontline managers as *the* critical conduits, are likely to be more successful. See Figure 6-9 for ways to support effective two-way message transmission within an organization.

Figure 6-9. Tactics to support message delivery.

❏ *Establish direct lines of communication with middle and frontline managers:* Set up discussion forums, "skip-level" interviews (interviews with the boss's boss), hotlines, etc.

❏ *Deliver regular briefings to middle and frontline managers:* Keep them in the loop and never bypass them.

❏ *Feed them "privileged information":* It reinforces their value and credibility to their direct reports.

❏ *Emphasize their importance as two-way conduits:* Clear paths for "upward communication" are critical for capturing the latest field intelligence and for sending up ideas for process improvement.

❏ *Listen to them and tell them that you're listening:* Feedback and positive reinforcement can stimulate continued upward communication that might otherwise be stifled by the perceived *indifference* of senior leadership.

❏ *Ask them to be interpreters and translators of key message points:* Encourage them to paraphrase and to "tell it in their own words." They're going to be asked to do it anyway by their direct reports; better that you recognize and endorse their role.

❏ *Use them to test-drive new plans and ideas and to offer feedback:* Many a bad move could have been avoided by simply checking with people who know better.

❏ *Give them a platform to speak from:* Use guest columns, management hotlines, focus groups, etc.

SURROGATE COMMUNICATORS

Sometimes the best, most trusted conveyors of critical information are influential nonmanagers. When a major office products company launched a new benefits program that involved employees customizing the program to suit individual needs, it realized employees might see the replacement of the old program as a loss. In order to be as clear and persuasive as it could, the company decided to offer two communication resources to employees who wanted information and answers.

The first was a detailed information site, featuring a kind of expert system that people could use as a tutor in building a program that was right for them. But the resource that was in fact most used was a group of employees identified as "key influencers" in the organization, most of them nonmanagers. Trained to give accurate information and some limited advice about the new program, these employees were turned to because they were seen as trustworthy and could empathize more readily with the situations of other employees trying to sort out what was in their best interests.

Communicating through employee peers can be both effective and powerful. The implications for leadership range from soliciting and using peer testimony to underpin decisions and plans, to understanding and deploying peer reasoning to better communicate how a decision might benefit all. Leaders need to build clear communication channels both to catch what people are saying and to deliver messages to key influencers. The use of employee councils, discussion circles, focus groups, and the like, regularly scheduled or prompted by special developments, can serve this purpose well.

Former CEO Bill Maritz, of Maritz, Inc., for example, held a monthly breakfast meeting with nonmanagement delegates from each operating company and from various corporate divisions. Delegates came with questions, Bill fielded them or promised to refer them to others, and the entire give-and-take was then edited and published for all Maritz employees. When leaders provide *forums* for people to ask questions, get answers, and offer input, organizational goals are better understood and more widely subscribed to.

In chapter 7, we continue the discussion of leadership's navigation role, but in a special context: the challenge of managing change and transitions.

NOTES

1. Thomas H. Davenport and John C. Beck, "Getting the Attention You Need," *Harvard Business Review* (September–October 2000), 124.
2. Ibid.
3. Kathryn Troy, *Change Management: Communication's Pivotal Role*, Report No. 1122-95-RR (New York: The Conference Board, 1995), 23.
4. Ronald A. Heifetz and Donald L. Laurie, "The Work of Leadership," *Harvard Business Review* (January–February 1997), 129.
5. See especially the work of Robert S. Kaplan and David P. Norton, the most well-known proponents of balanced scorecards; for example, *The Strategy-Focused Organization: How Balanced Scorecard Companies Thrive in the New Business Environment* (Boston: Harvard Business School Press, 2001).
6. See Robert Mai, "Branding Begins at Home," *Journal of Employee Communication Management* (September–October 1999), 31–34.
7. Nicholas Kristof, "Fortune Cookie: Your Ignorance Clouds Asian Joy," *New York Times* (August 13, 1995), E5.
8. W. Chan Kim and Renee Mauborgne, "Fair Process: Managing in the Knowledge Economy," *Harvard Business Review* (July–August 1997), 69.

9. Jay A. Conger, "The Necessary Art of Persuasion," *Harvard Business Review* (May–June 1998), 87.

10. James S. Kouzes and Barry Z. Posner, *The Leadership Challenge: How to Get Extraordinary Things Done in Organizations* (San Francisco: Jossey-Bass, 1991), 121.

11. Robert Cialdini, "Harnessing the Science of Persuasion," *Harvard Business Review* (October 2001), 78.

12. Glenn Parker, Jerry McAdams, and David Zielinski, *Rewarding Teams: Lessons from the Trenches* (San Francisco: Jossey-Bass, 2000).

13. Marcus Buckingham and Curt Coffman, *First, Break All the Rules* (New York: Simon & Schuster, 1999), 28.

7

Transition Pilot

"Stability through change demands clarity about what you are trying to do."

—WILLIAM BRIDGES, *MANAGING TRANSITIONS*

For most organizations today, change is a constant occurrence, and major transitions—merger, restructuring, rebranding, spin-off—have become commonplace. A generation of American workers has now lived through the turbulence of these new terms and conditions of organizational life. For the next generation, at least, such experiences will be seen more as the norm, and transitions will, in all likelihood, be less traumatic, if only because our work life expectations will have been altered. But transitions will still present navigational problems for leaders as they work to relocate and reorient their people around "true north."

In 1995, a Conference Board study cited research showing how poorly most managers handled transition-related communication.[1] Since then, we have seen some progress in change management communication. Companies like Emerson, GE Capitol, and SBC, for example, which have grown considerably during this period by way of merger and acquisition, have developed transition management as a core competency. But for many organizations, managing transitions still poses some daunting communication challenges. Another Conference Board report titled *Employee Communication During Mergers* concluded some five years later that employee (as well as frontline and middle manager) communication needs were still not being met. As a consequence, "inaccurate and incomplete perceptions can form, and employee anxieties may continue to grow and fester."[2]

No matter how experienced they might be in orchestrating change, leaders who manage transitions must continually wrestle with a special set of communication tasks. At stake is the need for organizations to accomplish continuous and sometimes rapid change with a minimum of workforce dislocation and dysfunction. Failure to do so can result in a change operation that leaves the patient in worse, and weaker, shape than before.

This chapter focuses on a three-dimensional communications plan for managing transition and change effectively. The plan is drawn from lessons learned in working with more than a hundred organizations, plus some common sense about how to communicate with people. The three plan dimensions are:

1. Empathy and assurance
2. Focus and alignment
3. Ownership and involvement

EMPATHY AND ASSURANCE

"Most companies spend far too much time talking about change and not enough listening to how their employees really feel about it."

—PETER LILIENTHAL, "TUNE IN IF YOU WANT TO TURN ON EMPLOYEES"

Once upon a time (perhaps), leaders of organizations contemplating disruptive transitions usually approached employee communication through any or all of these assumptions:

❐ In this business, people should be happy to have a job.

❐ Those who aren't whining are probably okay; those who are would whine no matter what.

❐ Employees can wait for information until everything gets sorted out.

❐ My commitment and enthusiasm as a leader will be contagious.

❐ Employees take my words at face value.

❐ Our people will deal with ambiguity and uncertainty in a rational manner.

❐ They'll get the picture when we run a story in the monthly employee newsletter.

But that was long ago. We know better now. Today, employees want to know leadership is thinking about them as individuals at the same time that they're making plans for new organizational moves. Employees have good reason to fear transitions: Historically, organizational change has typically involved loss of jobs, reassignment, and restructuring. Thus, such fears are inevitable. What's not inevitable, however, is fear fanned by uncertainty due to unclear, delayed, inconsistent, and less than candid leadership communications. Leaders owe their employees:

❐ *As full a disclosure of plans and schedules as is legally possible:* We recommend strong pressure on the legal and financial advisers involved to maximize, not minimize, disclosure.

❐ *Minimum speculation:* Tell only what you know to be fact.

❐ *Review of career implications* brought on by change.

❐ *Discussion of steps people can take now* to plan for their future.

❐ *Complete alignment, both in content and timing,* between what you tell your employees and what you say to customers.

Countering Resistance to Change

Psychologist Robert Goldberg observes that employees can regard change as a threat to any number of things they value: feelings of control, sense of competence, relationships with other employees, and personal identity within the organization. "We on the outside," he suggests, "might view the expression of that core as resistance, but on the inside it is experienced as the need to preserve something precious and worthwhile."[3]

Organizational leaders expect some natural resistance to change, and their expectations are seldom disappointed. In building a communication strategy to overcome resistance, however, leaders often misconstrue their target. Usually, employees are not so resistant to going in new directions as they are to having the will of others forced upon them, or to being made vulnerable to forces they don't control.

In general, a message strategy designed to prevent resistance to change would focus *not so much on what people fear, but on what they want for themselves:*

- ❑ Some degree of security and control regarding their jobs and careers
- ❑ Connectedness to networks, resources, support systems
- ❑ Opportunities to be successful, and to advance their careers
- ❑ Recognition for their contributions and their talents

Doing Your Homework

Organizations that have learned through experience about change communication prepare by first doing their homework. Leaders put their ears to the ground to determine how people feel about proposed changes, and what kinds of questions they're asking. They interview people at all levels of the organization to become better acquainted with special sensitivities, potential pitfalls, and troublesome issues that need to be addressed that may have gone unnoticed otherwise.

This information-gathering process is a delicate and ongoing one. The best organizations have already built a track record of listening to employees. Thus, when they start their inquiries to prepare for a coming change, they raise fewer concerns. It's a fairly simple process to take the pulse of the workforce. It usually involves anonymous surveys, and focus groups conducted by third parties with reported comments separated from participants. So why do so few organizations undertake this homework assignment? There are two reasons, and they're closely related. The first is that they may be afraid to hear what employees have to say. The second is they fear raising employee expectations about fixing the problems flagged in the survey.

To prepare for their change initiative, MidAmerican Energy conducted separate one-on-one interviews with senior executives as well as with representative frontline management. They followed these up with the "worksheet" exercise described in chapter 6, which served to tease out additional issues and concerns. Countless other organizations have made similar efforts to systematically determine what's on employees' minds as they ready themselves for transition and change.

In creating a pretransition profile of the "state of mind" of the organization's workforce, leadership needs to raise questions like those in Figure 7-1.

Developing *empathy* for employee issues and concerns in advance of change is the key communication strategy for leadership. At SBC, the CEO of the Southwestern Bell Telephone subsidiary, prior to the installation of several new service operations, was asked what his priorities would be. He answered "Basically, my priorities for the next 100 days fall under two headings: look and learn."[4] In fact, the "look-and-learn" strategy needs to be adopted at all leadership levels. It needs to be acknowledged as an *ongoing communication priority* by leaders up and down the organization in their conversations with colleagues and reports: "What's the buzz about the transition this week?" "What are people saying, and what do they want to know?"

Figure 7-1. Questions to guide transition communications planning.

❏ What assumptions do people hold about the general need for change?
❏ What are they most concerned about?
❏ What do people most want to hold onto when changes are made?
❏ What do these things do for them, or mean to them?
❏ How might you provide suitable substitutes or trade-offs if necessary?
❏ How trustworthy has leadership been in the past (especially regarding change and transition)?
❏ How confident are they about the company's leadership for the future?
❏ What are the most reliable internal sources and media for change communication?

Asking such questions demonstrates leadership's interest in how people are feeling during stressful times. Repeating what they've heard through paraphrasing and feedback not only confirms leadership's interest but helps as well to clarify the definition of specific issues and concerns on organizational radar screens. Talking with people about what they're afraid of losing or reluctant to give up helps determine how best to assist them in making the right trade-offs for success in the future.

Peer Empathy

Sometimes the best people to communicate change messages are respected peers. They understand the difficulties involved in transitions because they're experiencing them in the same way. A large transportation company in a position to recruit former employees of a failed competitor chose to approach potential new hires through a team of middle managers. Dubbed "ambassadors," the group was made available to discuss not only job opportunities, but, more important, to talk about the work experience and work life conditions from a firsthand perspective.

Since the company had a reputation in the industry as a buttoned-down, business-like operation, ambassadors had a special agenda to create a balanced view of the corporate culture and an appreciation for what it contributed to the organization's performance. Three key message points became the foundation of all their communications with these new recruits:

- ❐ This is a good place to work.
- ❐ We look strong for the future.
- ❐ We respect your former company and value its people and the roles they can play.

Able to meet with recruits off campus, as well as to serve as hosts for family visits to the headquarters town, ambassadors were successful in convincing a significant number of prospects to sign on. Fittingly, the company followed up with a mentoring program that helped new hires affiliate quickly with their new colleagues.

FOCUS AND ALIGNMENT

> *"The beginning of wisdom is to call things by their right names."*
>
> —CHINESE PROVERB, IN WILLIAM BRIDGES,
> *MANAGING TRANSITIONS*

One of the most immediate communication challenges for leadership during a transition is to keep the organization moving forward. It's easy for operations to experience drops in productivity because employees aren't sure about new priorities or how to get things done in the new organization. People may be confused or simply paralyzed, waiting on the sidelines to see what will happen to them. A basic theme for leadership communications here is *"Don't stop!"* We're still in business, we still have customers, and we still have competition (which might be gaining on us if we slow down).

What Employees Want to Know

The "don't stop" theme cannot simply be an order or a directive. From countless studies on organizational change, we know that employees want to be put in the picture. They want to hear the latest plans, and they want explanations. In essence, they want their leaders to address five rather predictable questions in a timely, candid, and useful way (see Figure 7-2).

These are critical questions, and leaders need to work at responding to them throughout the transition period. The five questions need to frame much of the communication strategy and

Figure 7-2. Questions employees want to ask about change.

❏ What are the organization's change plans?
❏ Why are they important?
❏ What's going to happen to me? (And when will it happen?)
❏ What do you want me to do?
❏ What's in it for me?

provide content for a family of key messages that leaders will deliver continually.

Responding to these questions represents a critical make-or-break component of change communication. Too often the people at the top believe that the future vision they paint, exciting though it may be, will be as motivating and reassuring to employees as it is to them. But they're wrong. Senior leadership has to turn that thinking on its head. Leaders have to see the picture from the point of view of the employee. Counterintuitive though it may be to senior leadership, the communication works best when it starts not with the big picture, but with details that respond to the five questions and to the concerns that surfaced from the homework assignment.

Behavioral science offers leaders some useful tactics for making more effective presentations on change. For instance, research has shown that people prefer bad news before good news. So get the bad news out of the way and state the downsides early.[5] An honest statement of any plans to let people go, for example, should be made close to the beginning of a major change announcement.

While there is debate about when to announce potential job reductions (Does such an announcement merely cause unneeded tensions? Is it better to wait until you have all the specifics?), our experience has been that the rumor mill is already way ahead of management in this area. Better to get information out there than to allow the rumors to continue unchecked. Even with nothing more than general information to share, you are providing *something* to employees, and you're showing them respect and concern. It also signals that leadership is prepared to deliver the hard facts of change, rather than hiding or sugarcoating them. For most employees, this is the information they most urgently seek, and there's no point in postponing it.

Don't Lose Ground

Equally important to the need to sustain day-to-day work flow against the threat of slowdown or paralysis is clear guidance on how and when to regroup around shifting priorities (or around priorities still in place). The critical variable for any organization going through transition is *recovery,* adapting to changes so quickly and so seamlessly that the organization doesn't miss a beat or lose any ground. This means keeping everyone's head in the game, focused on the job at hand.

As a general strategy, leaders need to put stakes in the ground for all to see as early as possible: What's the new game plan, which action steps do we need to attend to, and what jobs do we need to get done now? There's another advantage to communicating an action bias when managing transition. Getting the workforce to jump on key tasks can alleviate some of the anxiety and discomfort inherent in major change. One way to reduce the pain of a toothache is to divert attention elsewhere. Changes to the management structure, reporting relationships, and any other decisions that potentially affect jobs should also be revealed sooner than later. Remember—people want their own little picture painted before they'll give more than passing attention to your larger agenda for change.

Getting One's Mind Off Change: The Parable of the GI Party

One of the most time-honored traditions in the U.S. military is that social event known as the GI Party, a euphemism for cleaning up the barracks to spit-and-polish perfection in advance of a visit from the dictatorial drill instructor. These little parties are about more than elevating an already pristine clean barracks into an even higher level of clean. They have to do with building teamwork and motivation, while at the same time making homesickness and the like fade into the back of the recruits' minds.

In the typical scenario, the new recruits have just arrived at their barracks after being issued Skivvies, uniforms, and the rest of their gear. They now feverishly hang the new clothing up and put everything else away in their footlockers. They make their beds. They move quickly, in anticipation of the arrival of the only god they know at the moment—the dreaded drill instructor. He has promised an inspection in one hour.

The hour passes, and Sgt. Creases-Up-His-Pants-and-Shirt struts in with evil on his face. And guess what, he is disappointed.

No, he is enraged. The place is a dump. He upends footlockers with stuff scattering across the floor. He rips uniforms off hangers because they are one-half inch too close to the next one. He screams, he yells, he rants. His voice is full of rage and loathing, his language sprinkled with profanity. Once he's through with his so-called inspection, the place looks like the aftermath of a full-contact pillow fight or a drunken slumber party.

Yet Sgt. Omnipotent is a benevolent tyrant. He announces grudgingly he will give them one more chance. He will return at midnight (yes, midnight) and reinspect. He leaves, and mayhem occurs, but the mayhem becomes organized and purposeful. Latrine teams are established; beds are remade, their sheets tested for tightness by bouncing a nickel off them; recruits' razors are dissembled and hidden in bedposts, while "show razors" assume their precise place in the footlocker. Meanwhile buffers are out on the floor, wax on, wax off. And so on, through dinner, through the evening. The recruits check and recheck everything.

Midnight comes around and so does Sgt. Spitshine. Stern and mean as ever, as he slowly struts and checks things. But this time he is not yelling or ranting. There are only the occasional harrumphs of satisfaction at the work or grunts of frustration that he cannot find anything wrong. Everyone is at attention, waiting for the first footlocker to be attacked, but miraculously, no footlockers take to the air. He storms out. The exhausted eighteen- and nineteen-year-olds are high-fiving, feeling good. They showed that jerk. They collapse in bed, tired beyond words, with absolutely no energy left to let the mind wander into homesickness. They sleep the sleep of a new team that accomplished the impossible. And they know the sergeant will be back tomorrow. The "action bias" of a GI party has taught them the first lessons of team in less than twelve hours.

Apart from fear, there are several ready topics leaders can use in their efforts to keep people focused and on task during transitions (see Figure 7-3).

It's especially important that communication channels are wide open at these times. Leaders can err on the side of too much talk here, because the opposite, silence, or the perception of silence, erodes credibility and causes needless anxiety among employees. Hands-on, shirtsleeves-rolled-up visibility is critically important for leaders at any level in the organization. Leaders need to be accessible

Figure 7-3. Communication topics to refocus and reengage employees.

❑ *The Business Challenge:* What prompted the change, and how does it answer the challenge?

❑ *The Customer:* Who are they now, and what do they require? How will we serve them better because of the change?

❑ *The Competition:* Who are they now, and how do we succeed against them?

❑ *Competitive Advantage:* How will change make us stronger? What could happen if we don't change?

❑ *Goals and Targets:* What are the priorities now? What near-term targets must we shoot for?

❑ *Resources and Support Systems:* What do we have now that we didn't have before, and how can we do our jobs better because of them?

---

face to face, open to questions, and ready with answers. Where they don't have answers, they need to be candid and, if possible, promise to get back to the questioner later.

CEO sightings are particularly important here: the more, the better. CEOs might not see this as a good use of their time, but consider the effectiveness of the employee grapevine in spreading any single personal communication to many other ears as well. Such informal, spontaneous exchanges with employees also enjoy a kind of offhand credibility that no memo, newsletter, or video ever could.

Hit the Ground Running

When 3M decided to spin off a part of its data and computer services, a new company, Imation, was born. But giving birth wasn't easy. Morale in a workforce containing people who had grown up with 3M had plummeted after plans involving the spin-off were first announced. Many employees were angry.

One of the first tasks that Imation leadership faced was to re-shape the operating units it inherited so they could hit the ground running. Reshaping would involve a reduction in staff, based on business analysis of both present and future requirements. Imation's leadership chose to make the situation as clear and plain as it could to the workforce in a series of face-to-face announcement meetings at seventy-four work sites around the world. Plans were presented and questions answered directly and honestly. Later, employees (and their families) received a "Welcome to Imation" information kit that had been sent to their homes. After the launch events, senior leadership continued to deliver updates, with feedback opportunities, to employees electronically.[6]

Do the Players Have the Playbook?

We've seen several instances in which business organizations planned a major shift in market positioning (a "rebranding" initiative) but neglected to tell frontline employees until the last minute, or later. The situation is akin to a quarterback calling a play from a playbook that only he has read. It's a design for a "busted play."

The rebranding strategy has attracted considerable interest since the 1990s, and organizations that succeeded with it did two things well. They described a new value proposition for customers and then they delivered on it. In other words, they made a promise, and their employees successfully kept that promise. Where rebranding has worked, it has involved leaders calling new signals that teammates understood and could execute.

Rewriting the Playbook for Everyone

In the late 1990s, MidAmerican Energy decided that the best strategy for enhancing its competitive status was to reenergize its focus on customers and customer service. "Putting a face" on an energy company is not an easy task, since most customers only consider their energy supplier when something goes wrong or when they have to pay a bill. MidAmerican launched an ambitious campaign built around a set of specific customer promises:

1. I'll do the job right . . . and then some.
2. I'll be here when you need me.
3. I'll respect your property, neighbor.
4. I'll respect your time and won't waste it.
5. I'll teach your kids about energy safety and help us all stay safe.

Simultaneously, MidAmerican leadership made a set of promises to its employees. Earlier, employee councils had cautioned leaders, "Don't go making another set of promises you can't keep. We've heard that before." Their advice to leadership was to think of this new set of "promises" as *commitments,* to be invested in seriously. And commitments they became, headed by the statement, "You support the customer. We'll support you."

1. We'll provide you a safe, rewarding work environment.
2. We'll get you the resources and support you need to best serve our customers.
3. We'll tell you clearly and reasonably what our expectations are and how you can meet them.
4. As the marketplace and our industry evolve, we'll tell you what we are doing to prepare and why.[7]

Top-to-Bottom Alignment

Planning for change typically does not yield a cleanly drawn blueprint, but rather a set of goals and ideas for how to achieve them. The extent to which leadership communication can create continuity and alignment with these goals is usually contingent on which and how many management levels are involved in the communication process. T. J. Larkin and Sandar Larkin cite years of research confirming the value of involving frontline supervisors in communicating change efforts. Given the reasonable potential for distrust in senior management's communications about change, Larkin and Larkin suggest a different course. Instead of using the traditional top-down methods, organizations should strongly consider letting frontline supervisors deliver the news.[8]

In the past five years or so, most companies we've worked with agree in principle with giving supervisors a key role in communicating new developments. What they don't all do, however, is carry out a communication plan to prepare supervisors to want and be able to deliver the news. There are indeed companies that have done this well. In our experience, these include AlliedSignal, American Red Cross Biomedical Services, Levi-Strauss, and SBC.

All provided special orientation sessions for various levels of leadership in advance of a major transition. These briefings often contained some presentation skills training for middle and frontline management. As a communication strategy to align the workforce with an organization's transition goals, using managers who are closer to the frontline operations of the organization and to the bulk of the workforce just makes sense. See Figure 7-4 for steps that senior leaders can take to maximize the effectiveness of these operations managers.

Change communication needs to be carried out as a shared responsibility among all levels of organizational leadership. It also should be both centralized and decentralized. Communication should be centralized (and broadcast) to reliably convey content and key messages. Communication should be decentralized to make it more understandable and credible and to allow employees to feel more comfortable in asking questions and offering feedback. Broadcast communication needs to reflect what the organization knows about people's issues and concerns. Decentralized, face-to-face communication needs to be accurate and consistent with key message points so that people don't get confused.

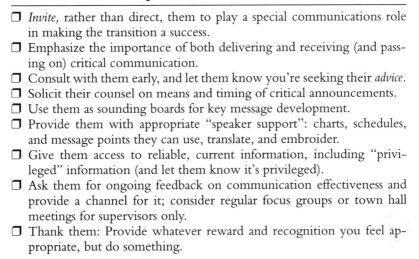

Figure 7-4. Ways to enhance change communication effectiveness for supervisors.

❏ *Invite,* rather than direct, them to play a special communications role in making the transition a success.

❏ Emphasize the importance of both delivering and receiving (and passing on) critical communication.

❏ Consult with them early, and let them know you're seeking their *advice.*

❏ Solicit their counsel on means and timing of critical announcements.

❏ Use them as sounding boards for key message development.

❏ Provide them with appropriate "speaker support": charts, schedules, and message points they can use, translate, and embroider.

❏ Give them access to reliable, current information, including "privileged" information (and let them know it's privileged).

❏ Ask them for ongoing feedback on communication effectiveness and provide a channel for it; consider regular focus groups or town hall meetings for supervisors only.

❏ Thank them: Provide whatever reward and recognition you feel appropriate, but do something.

OWNERSHIP AND INVOLVEMENT

> *"The lesson of systemic reform is to look for those strategies that are most likely to mobilize large numbers of people in new directions."*
>
> —MICHAEL FULLAN, "TURNING SYSTEMIC THINKING
> ON ITS HEAD"

An organization can get a jump start on building ownership in change goals if it involves a diverse array of people early on. When organizations create broad-based task forces to develop transition plans, they are hedging their bets on subsequent buy-in to the plans.

Many organizations choose to actively involve frontline managers and employees in taking the planning process to the operational level. The process provides a chance for employees to have a say in shaping the new organization.

Almost any major transition gives birth to a "new organization," and those assisting in the birth can take special pride in their roles. The best way to build ownership in the new organization is to get people working together to define what the new organization should look like.

The leadership challenge in asking for input from a broad range of employees is not to build unrealistic expectations that all their ideas will be used in the plan. This challenge can be met by clarifying expectations and by dealing with suggestions in a fair and thorough manner. Here are some steps to consider:

❒ In announcing the call for ideas, make it clear that while employee input is important to any organization, many ideas are never implemented, no matter where they come from.

❒ Set up a process for recording each suggestion received, along with the person submitting it. Be sure some sort of acknowledgment follows, either from the CEO or from the person in charge of the program. A hand-signed message, even if the message is canned, works best.

❒ Keep on communicating the invitation to participate and

give input, what's been adopted so far, and how important the effort is.

Presenting the Need for Change

How do leaders set the stage for winning employee commitment to change goals? Presentation strategies designed to show that change is both necessary and advantageous need to trade on some obvious, and some not so obvious, communication logic. For example, it makes perfect sense to start with the rationale behind the change because people throughout the organization want to know that there is indeed a well-considered "business case." But there's another reason to introduce the "business problem" early on: to clearly identify the negative consequences of *not* changing and to get audiences to project themselves into such a scenario. Just as you want to empathize with your people and their circumstances, you also want to foster empathy for the challenges to the organization as it looks to the future.

In this vein, leaders need to "unpack" the decision-making process that led to the transition plan, answering (before you are asked) such questions as, What were the deciding factors leading to the proposed change? What assumptions underlay these calculations? Who was consulted, and who took part in whatever "due diligence" exercise occurred? Did anyone consult with people at the frontline? What alternatives were considered, and why were they rejected?

When discussing how decisions were made, leaders should also avoid being defensive or apologetic. The "we had no choice" line rarely plays well here, begging more questions than it answers. Nor should decisions be presented as still open to debate (unless that is a real intention). The objective in shedding light on the decision-making process with fellow employees is to build awareness and understanding as the basis for commitment and support, not to keep deliberations open.

Change as Opportunity

Proposed change must be about opportunity, not just for the organization but for employees too. However, transitions often mean loss of opportunity, at least for people whose jobs will be lost or whose chances for advancement will shrink. Furthermore, it's not uncommon for those who still have jobs after a transition to feel guilty about it: Their "opportunity" comes on the backs of friends who were let go. Given these issues, leaders still must communicate the case for employee opportunity around the business case for change. Figure 7-5 contains message point ideas to consider in delivering this argument.

Behavioral research has found that ending an encounter on an upbeat note is likely to generate positive feelings. By "finishing strong," highlighting change as opportunity and supporting the likelihood that opportunity can be realized, for example, leaders stand a better chance of gaining stronger buy-in from their change presentation.[9]

Rosabeth Moss Kanter argues in *The Change Masters* that leaders need to continually describe the opportunity that change may afford. "In successful change efforts there is a continuing series of reinforcing messages from leaders, both explicit and symbolic. And individuals find that using the new practices clearly creates benefits for them; more of something they have always wished they could have or do."[10]

Figure 7-5. Conveying change as opportunity.

☐ *Clearly state the alternatives for employees and employment:* "If we stay on our present course, . . ."

☐ *Help people sort out what's most important to them in their jobs:* How might we best guard and preserve those things? What might we need to place at risk? What might have to be sacrificed? What kinds of trade-offs might be considered?

☐ *Acknowledge the contributions made by those leaving the organization and mention in a general way (if appropriate) how their futures are being staked by the company.*

☐ *State what employees might realistically expect from the transition:* What kind of growth potential might they enjoy (and why is it contingent upon transition)? What ways might they be able to contribute to success?

☐ *Identify the gaps between present reality and the organization's new goals:* Use game metaphors to challenge the "new team" to close the gaps.

☐ *Build commitment through choice:* Emphasize that we all have choices to make with respect to our future roles in a new organization.

☐ *Close on a message of common stake, common fate:* We need to learn, grow, and win *together.*

Talking Growth and Opportunity

The SBC–Pacific Telesis merger was an unprecedented and controversial move.[11] In addition to the anxiety expressed by business experts, financial analysts, consumer groups, and regulators, employees of both companies feared massive restructuring and a painful culture clash.

SBC leadership identified a clear internal communication objective: Focus employees on the merger's opportunities and on winning customers in an increasingly competitive environment. The communication strategy centered on a single message: The merger is about "growth and opportunity."

Strategy implementation started with announcement day, during which the two CEOs met with employees in person and via satellite to set the stage. Powerful slogans and visual symbols were created to communicate key merger messages: "*Our Future Is Growing Together*" became the banner for both internal and external audiences. A related strategy was to build support from the inside, among employees, to reassure customers and communities. SBC equipped a legion of employees with talking points and fact sheets to be used with chambers of commerce and other groups.

Announcement day was followed up with "town hall" meetings with Pacific Telesis employees in California. On the day the merger closed, employee events were held across the company, with people receiving a commemorative magazine and other mementos. All supervisors were given a "meeting in a box" with ideas and props to conduct effective roll-out meetings with their teams. Two years after the merger announcement, employee retention remained high, particularly with key managers. Employee focus groups throughout California showed strong support of SBC management and equally strong understanding of the company's priorities and growth strategies.

"We Are the Agents of Our Future"

> *"The objective is not to get people to support change but to give them responsibility for engendering change, some control over their destiny."*
> —GARY HAMEL, "STRATEGY AS REVOLUTION"

A key element in launching any major change initiative is to establish an understanding with employees that "we are the agents of our future." By acting rather than being acted on, organizational members can shape the contours of change to provide greater advantage, both individually and collectively.

Leadership communications can deliver this message both directly and indirectly. Challenging employees at all levels to take responsibility for determining how the work will get done, given changes in objectives, structures, or systems, is a direct invitation to take charge of change. Reminding employees that sitting back and waiting to see what will happen next is, conversely, a recipe for losing ground.

Helping employees understand the reasons for change can strengthen their willingness to assume responsibilities for managing transitions. But without sufficient levels of "business literacy," people are at a disadvantage in grasping the business case for change, let alone seeing how change might best take shape at operational levels. To ask them to assume key roles in implementing transition plans, leaders need first to communicate enough background information to provide *context* for further action.

Inviting employees to take charge of their future is at once an invitation to seize opportunity and to incur risk. To engage in redefining work practices, trying new approaches, and working with new colleagues can be both an exciting prospect and the cause of anxiety. One way leaders can position this invitation involves talking about the kinds of new responsibilities that they themselves will be undertaking and how they feel about it. Conversations on this subject could include talking points like:

- ❐ "I've been doing it this way for a long time; now I'll have to change."
- ❐ "I'm not sure what the changes will actually look like . . ."
- ❐ "What I'll most regret losing is . . ."
- ❐ "I don't think we can go on doing it the way we have because . . ."
- ❐ "I'll be making a commitment to:
  - ○ "give up . . ."
  - ○ "try a new . . ."
  - ○ "take a chance with . . ."

Through all these communications, you will want to sound a consistent note of *agency*: We are not going to let change *happen* to us; rather, we want to take charge of change and manage it to serve our best interests.

NOTES

1. Kathryn Troy, *Change Management: Communication's Pivotal Role*, Report No. 1122–95-RR (New York: The Conference Board, 1995), 22–23.
2. Nathan D. Ainspan and David Dell, *Employee Communication During Mergers,* Report No. 1270–00-RR (New York: The Conference Board, 2000), 12.
3. Robert Goldberg, "Talking About Change," *Issues & Observations* (Center for Creative Leadership newsletter), nos. 1–2.
4. "The First 100 Days: New Leadership Outlines Its Priorities," www.sbc.com (May 1998), 4.
5. See Richard Chase and Sriram Dasu, "Want to Perfect Your Company's Service? Use Behavioral Science," *Harvard Business Review* (June 2001), 79–84.
6. Information taken from "Launch of the Imation Spin-Off," 1996 PRSA Silver Anvil Award submission. Published material available from Public Relations Society of America (New York).
7. See Robert Mai, "Branding Begins at Home," *Journal of Employee Communication Management* (September–October 1999), 31–35.
8. T. J. Larkin and Sandar Larkin, *Communicating Change: Winning Employee Support for New Business Goals* (New York: McGraw-Hill, 1994), 102.
9. Chase and Dasu, "Want to Perfect Your Company's Service?"
10. Rosabeth Moss Kanter, *The Change Masters: Innovation for Productivity in the American Corporation* (New York: Simon & Schuster, 1983), 300.
11. Information taken from "Growth and Opportunity: The SBC-Pacific Telesis Merger," 1998 PRSA Silver Anvil Award submission. Published material available from Public Relations Society of America (New York).

8

Linking Agent

*"Birds that flock learn faster. So do
organizations that encourage flocking
behavior."*

—ARIE DE GEUS, "THE LIVING COMPANY"

People have to connect not just with their organization but with one another too. Helping them make and keep these connections represents yet another critical communication task for you as a leader. By establishing and supporting clear channels for people to maintain informal as well as informational links, leaders support an enterprise that is efficient; cooperative; and, above all, effective.

This chapter is not about information management per se, so we do not discuss information infrastructures or related systems issues that are more the province of information professionals. Instead, we concentrate on ways that leaders can help employees connect across hierarchical and functional lines. We also explore how you can get the most from staff and team meetings. Finally, we address ways leaders can effectively forge linkages with other stakeholders—customers, suppliers, distributors, et al.—who, though outside the organization, nevertheless have a big influence on the success of the enterprise.

Bottom-Up Communications

> *"The quality of information declines as it moves upward through bureaucracies."*
>
> —Anonymous

Within the so-called knowledge industries, there is little argument today about the value of employee knowledge and expertise. But employee knowledge and know-how are important in almost any kind of organization. What people know and how they share it with one another are more than ever critical factors in any organization's success.

We believe the communication work begins not with top-down talk, but with top-down *listening*. When you create the habit of listening to your employees, then the people who are closest to the marketplace, customers, suppliers, and partners, can add their unique point of view to your planning and strategy building. Lacking this input, leaders can often find themselves developing strategy in a vacuum or missing critical opportunities to make changes in strategy. By enabling people from all levels of the organization to report their observations and insights, you gain invaluable intelligence about how and where improvements can be made and advantages secured. (We take up the subject of improvement again in the next four chapters when we look at leadership communication for renewal and innovation.)

The "E" Word Revisited

For at least fifty years, management literature has acknowledged the merits of "employee involvement" and input in decision making. In the 1980s and 1990s, employee *empowerment* became a watchword. Today, most leaders would say they believe in the virtues of including employees, if only indirectly, in the planning process. They also express support of employees coming up with their own ideas and questions. Yet employee surveys conducted by organizations we know continue to document that in reality, employee input for strategy development is not regularly or systematically sought.

To be fair to leadership, employee involvement can be difficult to manage and may deliver uneven results. Employees may lack contextual information and fail to appreciate big-picture perspectives. They may often seem ambivalent about wanting to be included in the conversation, or they might want to give input to decision-making but not share responsibility for carrying decisions out. Or they simply might not believe speaking their mind is a safe and smart thing to do. In a way, managing such a dialogue is like running a three-legged race with the seven-foot-one NBA star Shaquille O'Neal: Allowances have to be made for the conversation to get anywhere.

Ultimately, most leaders opt for the three-legged race. It's the smart thing to do because there's too much potential value in workforce input and too much to lose in ignoring it. Managing bottom-up communication, then, is first of all a matter of *putting a value on what frontline employees know and hear.* You need to make it clear that your employees are encouraged and expected to bring forward any ideas, information, or intelligence they think should be shared, on the grounds that their experience and perspectives are vital to the organization's success. Second, speaking out needs to be perceived by employees as beneficial to them, as opposed to risky, self-compromising, or simply a waste of time.

Claiming a Seat at the Table

HOK is among the world's largest architectural firms. Its projects include sports stadiums, hospitals, colleges, museums, public buildings, and corporate headquarters. HOK project teams bring together architects, interior designers, planners, and engineers, among others, and they must work efficiently together over extended periods to deliver projects on time and within budget.

A key operative in supporting project team effectiveness is the marketing coordinator. Marketing coordinators are neither architects nor engineers. Their main responsibility is to manage the project team's schedule and keep everyone on track. This task can be a lot like herding cats, and marketing coordinators often feel ignored by their more highly credentialed colleagues.

For marketing coordinators to do their jobs well, they needed to regard themselves as full-fledged members of high-powered project teams. They needed to feel free to raise red flags when they see problems and make demands on colleagues in the name of the project and its success. To help them feel more comfortable speaking out and generally holding their own as team members, HOK leaders decided to collect some common sense guidelines for effective teamwork and create what would be called a "Marketing Coordinator Bill of Rights."

The "Bill of Rights" was introduced to marketing coordinators in a training session, where corporate training director Marsha Littell led discussions centered on how to exercise those rights and how best to remind project colleagues about their importance. Marketing coordinators were told that company leadership was clearly behind them when they needed to stand their ground with project team members. The "Bill of Rights" has improved morale and has helped marketing coordinators take a more active role as team contributors.

Communication Forums

> "What we need to create inside companies are forums wherein people can . . . talk about how they can best add value and then move on from there."
>
> —C. K. PRAHALAD, 1996 INTERVIEW

Sometimes, the most effective way to solicit and receive bottom-up communication is to arrange some kind of group meeting. The GE Workout sessions are probably the best known contemporary example and have been much emulated in recent years. These formal platforms for gathering employee input offer two critical advantages that more informal mechanisms may lack: clearly establishing the value of these conversations to the organization and protecting and reinforcing participants who speak out. One clear reinforcement is letting people know how the input from such discussions is later acted on. Another is a recognizable pattern of reward and promotion for employees whose input delivers value to the organization.

This is not to say that less regular forums aren't worthwhile. Prahalad prefaced the statement above with an acknowledgment that "there are no natural forums for focusing the energies of people who are waiting for change to happen and who understand that change needs to happen."[1] So leadership needs to invent such forums. In advance of planned transitions, many organizations are using internal focus groups as an ad hoc means to find out what people are thinking and to seek their advice on change strategies.

A more traditional version of the leader-sponsored forum is the annual sales leaders trip with the CEO and other top brass. Such meetings are positioned as a social reward for high performers, but they also give the headquarters staff an opportunity to put an ear to the ground and learn about what's happening in the field. Similarly, sales and other honorees can use the trip to swap how-to stories and techniques.

An even less structured link between leadership and employees is the "hotline" concept, where people have a direct line, typically via e-mail or a special Web site, to connect with specific organization leaders, often the CEO. Our experience so far with companies using leadership hotlines is that this means of bottom-up communication has not yet provided the same kind of value as group gatherings have in delivering employee intelligence to the decision-making process.

Frontline and Middle Managers as Linking Agents

"We often regard them as the problem instead of the solution, the roadblock to things getting done instead of the bridge between levels and functions in the company."

—DAN BURNHAM, "EXHIBIT 5: ALLIEDSIGNAL AEROSPACE"

Middle and frontline managers serve as a bridge for communications up and down the organization. In chapter 6 we talked about the importance of these leaders in relaying and translating organizational messages to their own reports. But as senior leadership from

AlliedSignal and other organizations attest, their role in moving messages back up the channels is equally vital.

In this regard, middle and frontline managers are communication conduits, helping messages get to the right parties at the right levels. They are also in a position to encourage and solicit input from their team members. Given the disposition of many organizations not to reinforce bottom-up communication in any significant way, the ability of middle and frontline managers to engage their people in larger organizational conversations can be critical. Opening the faucet and letting conversation flow is an important step in bringing the voice of the frontline employee into play. Priming the pump is even more important (see Figure 8-1).

STAFF MEETINGS

Practically every organizational leader holds staff meetings. Whether it's a group of UPS drivers gathering in a depot before their shift,

Figure 8-1. Tactics to encourage bottom-up communication.

❒ *Routinely ask for people's opinions:* "What do you hear?" "What can we pass up to division management?"

❒ *Emphasize the* value *of the frontline perspective:* close to the customer, close to product application, close to job aids and tools, etc.: "You guys know what customers are saying better than anyone else in the organization."

❒ *Build on received ideas and comments; spread the word:* "Arlen mentioned we're getting a lot of customer callbacks on this product. Who else has seen this?"

❒ *Dramatize your conduit role, then report back on what happened:* "I brought this idea up at my boss's staff meeting, and it looks like we're going to move on it."

❒ *Recognize communication initiative:* "These comments are going to make our team look good when we pass them up the line."

❒ *Tell as many stories as often as possible about "employee All Stars" who provided important intelligence, and about how the information was put to use:* "I know you've heard me say this before, but when I get an idea like the one Joan brought forward . . ."

❒ *Use staff meetings and gatherings as forums for employee input:* not just as information pass-down sessions.

or a sales team connecting on a conference call, or a traditional Monday morning departmental planning session, meetings are an ideal occasion to support bottom-up communication. But in more cases than not, most meeting time is taken up by leaders repeating messages handed down from above, reviewing progress reports, issuing directives, and so on. The potential in staff meetings for tapping into the collective thinking of participants is too often underused.

Unfortunately, staff meetings are often driven by convention. They are typically held hostage to the premise that the leader needs to hold the floor. Conversations are typically one-sided, and "there's never enough time to open it up" for discussion. At their worst (think *Dilbert* here), they're dominated by empty posturing and endless information dissemination. when that information could have been better presented through other more efficient and effective means. Even when an attempt to share airtime is made, it can often be so ritualized ("Who's giving the next report?") that participants wind up listening only so they don't miss their turn to recite.

We see the staff meeting as offering an undeniable opportunity for leaders to manage communication for organizational gain. The key here is to consider *the staff meeting as a two-way conversation,* involving a group of people who can all add value. Running a meeting as a conversation instead of a monologue involves being able to stimulate dialogue and to capture yield from the dialogue.

Driving Participation

> *"Rigid structure is the enemy of dialogue."*
>
> —DANIEL YANKELOVICH, *THE MAGIC OF DIALOGUE*

Getting people to participate actively in a meeting is a matter of habit formation: discarding old ones and adopting new ones. Habits of nonparticipation aren't changed overnight. New habits need to be learned, practiced, and reinforced.

There are a number of ways to turn traditional, leader-dominated staff meetings into open, collaborative dialogues. First, the agenda can be redesigned. Put the discussion and feedback sections at the start of the meeting, not the end. This shift in agenda announces a different ordering of priorities. If there is more value to be derived from such discussion than from listening to the contents of a memo you just got from above, then capture the value. Also, publishing an agenda that contains discussion topics or questions can allow people to gather their thoughts and ideas beforehand and feel better prepared to bring them forward.

Second, develop a looser meeting structure by being prepared to expand discussion as situations warrant. Flexibility in following an agenda allows meeting leaders to be more opportunistic in identifying and capturing value from unanticipated sources. Announcements and reports would typically be the agenda items that get bounced to allow for extended discussion (the reverse of what normally happens at staff meetings).

Third, consider how room arrangement might best facilitate open discussion. Sitting around a table is more conducive to conversation than classroom or theater-style layouts. U-shaped table arrangements can accommodate groups too big to fit around a single table. Where and how the meeting leaders position themselves (Are all participants facing them? Are leaders standing while others sit?) definitely influences the amount of participation that occurs.

Fourth, manage discussion by using good facilitation tactics, including the list in Figure 8-2.

Capturing Yield

The output from these meetings can be invaluable, but only if it's remembered and put to use. Whether or not a "product" from the meeting is clearly expected (beyond meeting minutes, say), taking notes or otherwise recording the meeting's key points is a step toward capturing value from discussion. Furthermore, by recording key output on a flip chart, white board, computer screen, or "Smart Board," meeting leaders can keep these items "in play" for others to add to, build on, or otherwise extend to increase the yield.

Michael Schrage calls these recording devices "collaborative media"—they help participants *see* their contributions to the con-

Figure 8-2. Tactics for running high-involvement meetings.

❏ *Ask for participation (politely and sincerely):* "Please offer your comments and ideas . . ."

❏ *Sell participants on the value of their input:* "If we don't tap your thinking, we're not working as smart as we need to."

❏ *Make a point of saying you want to hear from anyone who has a question or something to add:* Make it easy for people to jump in.

❏ *Insert a personal tone:* "How do you feel about that, Alice?" "Did that ever happen to you?"

❏ *Consider "going around the room," but state explicitly that people can "pass" if they want to, and don't impose equal-time requirements.*

❏ *Assume a nonjudgmental stance and a low profile as ideas get tabled, then debated:* Don't be in a rush to evaluate them.

❏ *Call a time-out if discussion seems stalled or debate slow to resolve:* Talk about process considerations, alternative paths to take, the will of the group to continue, etc.

❏ *Emphasize your role as a listener:* Ask questions, offer paraphrases, piggy-back on comments, and take notes.

❏ *When you need to close discussion, do so on behalf of the group as well as yourself:* "I know we could continue, but we need to move on."

❏ *Thank participants (politely and sincerely) for their involvement:* "I really appreciate your ideas and comments. We moved the needle today."

versation. "The focus is no longer on who said what but on what's on the screen. It's not that comments are anonymous, it's that presenting them on the screen physically decouples them from the speaker. The comment literally becomes a contribution to the meeting. . . . Participants aren't just speaking to be heard; they're speaking to be seen."[2]

Media that make dialogue visible also validate speakers' ideas and reinforce their participation. Meeting participants will be encouraged in knowing their input has a life beyond the immediate meeting. At the same time, capturing key points strengthens the collective memory of the group and makes these items available for continued discussion and elaboration.

CROSS-BOUNDARY COMMUNICATION

Connecting people who work in different locations or functional groups presents its own set of challenges for leaders. We've come to accept the inevitability of organizational "silos" or "chimneys," even as we deplore them as barriers to effective cooperation. Since silos are creations of both bureaucracy and professional orientation (engineering sees the world differently from sales), they're not something we can readily eliminate. Rather, we simply need to accept them as part of the territory, while working to reduce their negative impact on knowledge management, process handoffs, and general organizational solidarity. What leaders can do here is *build and maintain communication bridges* across silos, linking them more effectively to one another and to the organization as a whole.

Bridges People Can Cross

> *"We must find ways to communicate across the cultural boundaries, first, by establishing some communication that stimulates mutual understanding rather than mutual blame."*
>
> —EDGAR SCHEIN, "THREE CULTURES OF MANAGEMENT"

Because organizational boundaries are often drawn around different cultures (Schein talks about three basic occupational cultures of executives, engineers, and operators, for example),[3] leaders must serve as go-betweens or emissaries. From a communication standpoint, you are also a translator, helping different occupational groups make sense of what one another is saying. This interlocutor role means your success will depend in part on how well you can speak other languages and understand other cultural values and assumptions.

You can connect different parts of the organization and different players inside and outside the organization by helping *articulate* different perspectives and points of view. The more "cosmopolitan," rather than parochial, leaders are, the more effective they can be as linking agents. The leader as linking agent is a spokesperson for different parties, articulating their interests to others. The Latin cognate of "articulate"—*articulus*—"belongs to a large group of related terms preserving an ancient root, -ar, that originally meant 'to join,' 'to fit,' and 'to make.' Many words in Greek, Latin and modern languages come from this root, all of them having to do with joining in one sense or another."[4]

Sometimes, cross-boundary communication can be downright hostile. In manufacturing companies, different divisions can be in competition with one another, actually maintaining closer ties with their outside suppliers and distributors. We have heard hospitals described as housing three armed camps—doctors, nurses, and administrators—who are constantly at war with one another. In such organizational climates, cross-boundary communication is likely to feature, as Schein suggests, as much blame as cooperation. In our experience, building communication bridges that link disparate organizational groups involves three key tasks: making bridge building a leadership priority, emphasizing common goals and common stakes, and convening mixed-group task-oriented forums.

Making Bridge Building a Leadership Priority Organizations that benefit the most from the leader's role as linking agent are often those with many different operating units. Emerson, for example, has more than sixty business units and a need for close coordination to sustain business advantage in highly competitive manufacturing industries. Emerson clearly recognizes the value of cross-functional linkages and recently made *cooperation* one of three main criteria by which it evaluates leadership performance. Other companies offer promotions to the leaders of successful cross-functional project teams. Still others make sure to recognize leaders who successfully unite different operating groups to win battles and advance the organization.

Emphasizing Common Goals and Common Stakes As a leader you need to seize on what people have in common so as to knit groups together around shared interests and goals. Psychologist Robert Cialdini reminds us that people like those who like them, so leaders should work to identify common attributes among values, beliefs, interests, and motives, and then call attention to them. Communicating these similarities early on "creates a presumption of goodwill and trustworthiness in every subsequent encounter."[5] Leaders focusing on potential bonds to generate closer functional ties might use communication tactics like those in Figure 8-3.

Convening Mixed-Group Task-Oriented Forums

> *"The planner of a modern, humane city will overlay differences rather than segment them."*
> —RICHARD SENNETT, *THE CONSCIENCE OF THE EYE*

Leaders have a more formal recourse as linking agents. They can create functional overlaps on different teams to improve continuity and information sharing. They can also establish a variety of ad hoc or standing committees of representatives from different sides of the organization. These groups may have specific tasks or simply serve an ongoing advisory or monitoring function. Heterogeneous committees have three advantages in developing cross-boundary communications. They share the common focus of their committee's assignment, they are engaged as active participants rather than as passive recipients of news and updates, and they meet face-to-face (at least some of the time) with the potential to develop a personal, as well as a shared-task relationship.

Mixed groups can also play by different rules, thereby circumventing some of the hostility or noncooperation that might exist in more regular organizational exchanges. Special task forces, for

Figure 8-3. Communication tactics to connect across boundaries.

☐ *Emphasize the customer as the ultimate common focus:* We're all judged by how well we satisfy the customer.

☐ *Make a point about having respect for, and wanting to learn about, the ways that other divisions approach problems, understand challenges, etc.*

☐ *Ask often about others' views on specific issues:* "We see the situation this way, but how do you view it?"

☐ *Be a mediator, even if you have a dog in the fight:* A stance of neutrality will make you a more trusted bridge builder in general.

☐ *Look for ways to* translate *one side's views to other parties.*

☐ *Look for ways to* summarize *by combining (and reconciling) different views:* They might be closer together than they think, or want to think.

example, have a direct mandate to accomplish a specific job that will require smooth and open communication and good coordination. Task force members will typically behave differently, often with feelings of relief, as apt and willing colleagues in this kind of "multilingual" environment.

Discovering How Well We Work Together

A major financial services company was in the process of creating a new brand identity around a new approach to personal financial planning. Leadership decided to seek the counsel of key representatives from four functional areas (customer service, marketing and communications, product development, and sales and distribution) in determining how the new brand promise might best be implemented. These representatives were in turn drawn from several different operating companies, who had very little contact with one another in the past. In each of the four sessions, attendees from various operating companies were asked to address two questions: "Where do you see the best opportunities to deliver customer value?" and "Of those, which ones might be targeted for development so as to raise the bar on promise delivery?"

The several discussion forums produced a rich yield of strategies and improvement targets. In the closing moments, participants were asked for general observations and comments. Many of them volunteered that they were struck by how easy it had been for people from different companies and businesses to quickly establish a common picture and a shared understanding of brand delivery issues. Groups were able to identify many commonly held views about where the new brand promise could deliver value over the life of a customer relationship. They were then able to agree fairly easily on a set of improvement priorities for brand launch initiatives.

Mixed-group forums offer participants an opportunity to engage in real collaboration. One of the many useful legacies of the Total Quality Movement, which had widespread currency in the 1980s, is the use of process improvement task forces that blend people from different but related positions to solve a problem or improve work process. Michael Schrage suggests that such collaboration, especially when supported with interactive media, "means that people are less interested in displaying data than in creating a shared space to play collectively with ideas and information."[6] We visit other examples of cross-boundary forums in chapter 12 when we address the roles of leaders as renewal agents and as sponsors of creative collaboration.

CONNECTING WITH STAKEHOLDERS

> *"We almost never hear something really new through established channels. That's true almost by definition. . . . Truly new news comes from customers or competitors we don't know about. Outliers hear it first. If rapid change means there's more news than ever, it's vital to use the fringes of an organization better."*
>
> —THOMAS STEWART, "COMPANY VALUES THAT ADD VALUE"

Some years ago, American business coined the phrase "voice of the customer." Companies were interested in hearing that voice more clearly and commissioned research programs to learn what was on customers' minds. But as often as not, few outside the organization's marketing department, or whoever it was that commissioned the research, got to hear what customers had to say. Hence, a different challenge emerges for leaders as linking agents: How do you listen, then relay what you hear? How do you talk back to customers? How do you extend the conversation and make it truly interactive?

Forums for Customers

Creating opportunities for linking with customers is easier if you're in direct contact with them. But not everyone in an organization is. What leaders in companies like American Express Financial Advisers, Fort Sanders Health System, and Cadillac did was to find ways to capture conversations with customers and pull them back into the organization where they could prompt action.[7] In effect, leadership in these organizations was asking, "Who in the organization can best use this information?" "Where would it deliver the most value?"

Connecting Leaders to Customers At American Express Financial Advisors, leadership starts with the advisers in the field, who *are* the company to their customers. Customer research had been routinely aggregated on printouts and sent to advisers located in small offices around the country. As often as not, advisers found the printouts difficult to read and not all that relevant. But when the company decided to unbundle the data and send to all advisers the reactions their customers shared about their service, advisers' interest and usage both increased.

In the new plan, financial-planning customers were asked performance questions relating to seven attributes that described service priorities (determined through another customer research project). Advisers were rated in absolute terms and also against various region and company averages. Where they were rated low, they had the opportunity to seek attribute-specific help, from experts captured in an interactive video library or from other designated resources. Advisers were now linked to customers, colleagues, and expertise in a way that directly supported continuous growth and improvement.

Carrying the Conversation Forward Fort Sanders Health System, then a five-facility health-care agency in Kentucky, wanted to improve quality and productivity in an increasingly competitive environment. Fort Sanders knew that it really had two kinds of customers: its patients (and indirectly, their families and friends who visited them at a facility) and its physicians, who referred patients to Fort Sanders.

Leadership decided to engage customers, convening a series of focus groups with patients and family members, and physicians. From these conversations, leaders learned what each group of customers valued most in the way of service and support. Through additional focus groups with employees, they also learned that employees and physicians had different ideas about what patients valued most.

When leadership used this research to measure customer satisfaction levels against new service priorities, they were able to determine with some precision where to invest systematic improvement efforts and resources. Some of the targets were fairly obvious, and appropriate leaders could be assigned that responsibility. But in other cases, Fort Sanders commissioned Continuous Quality Improvement teams to investigate, then recommend solutions to problems that were a little more complex. In effect, they carried the conversation forward, connecting with more and more people, until they were able to deal with the situation satisfactorily.

Forums for Partners and Allies

"Information about customers is always the most valuable knowledge, but it might be worth most to somebody upstream."

—THOMAS STEWART, "THE INFORMATION WARS"

Or downstream. Cadillac, like all automotive manufactures, surveys customers about their satisfaction with the product and service. But they also convened focus groups with customers and "walk-aways" for specific dealerships, videotaped the proceedings, and then provided dealerships with the tapes. The effort had an impact. A dealer principal who might have shrugged off the latest statistical findings was hard pressed to ignore several customers on a tape complaining about the limited hours the dealership stayed open on weekends. These were issues that dealers needed to deal with. And when the solution wasn't so straightforward as expanding store hours, Cadillac helped dealerships organize employee teams to develop one.

Many dealer principals expressed surprise on two counts: what customers really thought of them and how well their employees could generate creative ways to improve the customer buying and service experience. And Cadillac's leaders won on two fronts: They strengthened relationships with dealerships and at the same time improved customer satisfaction levels. By creating open forums for people with vested interests and then sharing the yield with those who could do something about it, Cadillac got a greater return on its linkage investment.

Bridging Two Cultures

Just as a manufacturer can pass critical information to its dealers, so too can the linking work in the other direction. Leadership at Ford Motor Company saw an opportunity to improve customer satisfaction with its product line, by focusing on the dealer's cleaning and preparing of a new vehicle for delivery to a customer. The plan was to ask "dealer prep teams" who would normally spot any vehicle defects not caught at the plant (most defects found at the dealership are actually caused by vehicle transit from factory to dealership) to let the plant know within forty-eight hours of delivery. Dealer prep teams would also be invited to talk directly with Ford's quality engineers about suggestions they might have.

Normally, plant engineers don't talk with dealer service people. To facilitate this new kind of cooperation, Ford leadership needed to open up new lines of communication between the factory and the dealerships. Plant engineers and their associates would have to become comfortable accepting input from dealer prep teams. As one Ford project manager commented, "Most engineers are afraid to admit they have a problem. They fear people will think they don't know how to do their job, and they dread interference from others who think they know the answer."[8]

Ford leadership addressed the challenge by bringing dealer prep teams into the plants to establish a face-to-face relationship with key plant personnel and to agree on some new reporting protocols. In a two-day visit (followed up by another six months later), dealer service personnel learned about the manufacturing process, met their plant colleagues, and established the basis for a cooperative working relationship. With this procedure for "boundary crossing" in place, Ford plants reported more timely and accurate feedback from dealerships. Furthermore, plant engineers were actually able to make several major assembly improvements to reduce defects in delivered vehicles.

Linking the Widespread Network

When an organization goes to the trouble of convening a meeting of partners, board members, advisers, trade allies, or any other group of significant others, leadership will want to maximize the gain from such an occasion. There are many ways to organize disparate people attending a meeting so that every voice is heard. Some of the more traditional involve breaking large groups into smaller ones in which conversation can be more intimate and discussion more focused. But as linking agents, leaders also can use a tried-and-true technique that can yield stronger connections and commitment to the organization.

Going Around the Table The Association for Investment Management and Research (AIMR) is a fast-growing membership organization whose primary function is to advance the global investment profession, primarily through the Chartered Financial Analyst (CFA) Program. Because current growth is most dramatic outside the United States, AIMR's board sought new insight into a host of special growth-related issues as part of its planning process. To accomplish this objective, a board planning committee decided to hold a retreat for some fifty representatives of its various global constituencies and headquarters staff. The three-day retreat engaged participants in different breakout discussion topics, each of which addressed both issues and barriers and action recommendations. Board members and headquarters staffers served as discussion facilitators, and a healthy yield of ideas for the future was collected.

On the final morning, after the last round of breakout discussions had ended and reporting out was concluded, the meeting facilitator invited the participants to share what their takeaways would be as they prepared to leave the meeting. This "going around the table" routine can be a pleasant, albeit bland, laying on of hands, a nice closing ritual that ends on a feel-good note. But it can also provide a platform for each participant to speak his or her mind to the full assembly, to truly represent an individual point of view to the entire organization. The dynamic created by going around the table often challenges successive participants to dig a little deeper for something trenchant to say, rather than succumb to the old standby "I agree with everything that's been said."

The specific invitation to the AIMR retreat participants was to add some final value to the proceedings, to summarize or highlight what each member felt to be important in his eyes. The tone of the comments was predictably upbeat. But this last round of input also brought forth some sharp analysis, clear statements of interest, and strong signals for headquarters to hear and act on. The routine went way beyond its feel-good potential, providing a productive, substantive capstone to the weekend's discussion.

The Mighty Water Cooler

Intranets, Web sites, and broadcast e-mail are already creating new, productive linkages across organizations. But ultimately, these means for linking people within and without an organization fall short of face-to-face contact. Face-to-face communication is simply more effective than the other forms when delivering sensitive information, defending a position, or seeking support, as the Ford example above ably demonstrated.

Networks are built on social processes that link people and their needs, both occupational and personal. We will probably never replace the fabled water cooler conversation as the ultimate in free form, value-driving communication. So the challenge for leaders is to find ways to create more water coolers (and certainly not discourage water cooler conversations from taking place).

We end this chapter with a nice water cooler story about Xerox, related by Brown and Duguid. Xerox customer service reps are provided with documented repair processes for diagnosing and fixing copier problems. But these "maps" for fixing machines are sometimes inadequate: Reps regularly "fall off the map." What they did to hedge their bets, as well as to solicit direct consultation help, was to meet before their first call to have breakfast together. During these informal gatherings, conversation was invariably a mix of gossip and business. "They posed questions, raised problems, offered solutions, constructed answers, laughed at mistakes, and discussed changes in their work, the machines, and customer relations. Both directly and indirectly, they kept one another up to date about what they knew, what they'd learned, and what they were doing."[9]

Anthropologist Robin Dunbar's theory about the origin of human communication argued that we invented language as a means to make social bonding and community building more efficient: Our earliest "conversations" were about gossip, reputations, and where people stood with one another.[10] And so they still are.

As a leader you'll need to continually sponsor community-building conversations and to help functions and departments link with other functions and departments. In this sense, any large organization is a community of communities. Parochial communities fold into themselves (and in worst cases, become ghettoized). Cosmopolitan communities have open borders and reflect a mix of voices. Leaders need to insure that communication boundaries remain permeable, that dialogue is well integrated, and that each community sees itself as both distinct and also as part of a larger association.

NOTES

1. C. K. Prahalad, "An Interview With C. K. Prahalad," interviewed by Joel Kurtzman, *Strategy & Business* (3rd quarter 1996), 90.
2. Michael Schrage, *Shared Minds: The New Technologies of Collaboration* (New York: Random House, 1990), 127.
3. Edgar H. Schein, "Three Cultures of Management: The Key to Organizational Learning," *Sloan Management Review* (fall 1996), 9.
4. Lewis Hyde, *Trickster Makes This World: Mischief, Myth, and Art* (New York: Farrar, Straus & Giroux, 1999), 254.
5. Robert B. Cialdini, "Harnessing the Science of Persuasion," *Harvard Business Review* (October 2001), 74.
6. Schrage, *Shared Minds*, 31.
7. See Robert Mai, *Learning Partnerships: How Leading American Companies Implement Organizational Learning* (Chicago: Irwin/ASTD, 1996), chapters 7, 8, and 10.
8. Mai, *Learning Partnership*, 71.
9. John Seely Brown and Paul Duguid, "Balancing Act: How to Capture Knowledge Without Killing It," *Harvard Business Review* (May–June 2000), 76.
10. Robin Dunbar, *Grooming, Gossip, and the Evolution of Language* (Cambridge, Mass.: Harvard University Press, 1997), 202.

IV

The Leader as Renewal Champion

> *"If the West enjoys a moral advantage over other cultures, the advantage lies in placing a high value on the experience of being unsettled. It esteems self-criticism perhaps as much as self-confirmation. . . ."*
>
> —David Denby, *Best American Essays 1994*

Intel's Andy Grove stated the mandate (and the timing) for organizational renewal this way: "The more successful we are as a microprocessor company, the more difficult it will be to become something else. . . . We're going to have to transform ourselves again, and the time to do it is while our core business is so strong."[1] Leaders of organizations that need to stay nimble and flexible in the face of evolving competition and changes in the marketplace must assume a special communications responsibility. They need to embrace one of the most compelling paradoxes that organizations experience today: the importance of leveraging conventional wisdom while questioning that wisdom for its future suitability.

In most organizations, the path of least resistance is a road paved by conventional wisdom. By extension, the path of maximum advantage is less clearly marked, and bridges to be crossed may have "trolls" underneath. In the next four chapters, we examine communication roles that leaders can play as they try to *challenge conventional wisdom* and *pursue maximum advantage.*

CULTURE AND LEADERSHIP COMMUNICATIONS

When Andy Grove spoke of leadership needing to create an "environment that allows more strategic initiative and debate to emerge from below,"[2] he was describing a certain kind of organizational culture. The most powerful determinant of organizational culture, as perceived and experienced by employees, is the organization's *leadership,* at all levels. Leadership gives shape to a culture that either values or deters organizational learning and renewal. The four communication roles we see serving Grove's call for initiative and debate across the company are those of organizational *critic, provocateur, learning advocate,* and *innovation coach.* Leaders who sponsor debate and inquiry have an agenda to keep the organization vital, dynamic, and opportunistic. They are champions of organizational renewal.

We've chosen to describe the leader as Renewal Champion in four role dimensions to give each one proper emphasis. But in reality, they're part of the same key undertaking: The actions of these four roles typically blend and unite toward a common goal—to help the organization continuously adapt and evolve and thereby meet with continued success.

NOTES

1. Andy Grove, quoted in Sumantra Ghoshal and Christopher A. Bartlett, *The Individualized Corporation: A Fundamentally New Approach to Management* (New York: HarperBusiness, 1997), 128.
2. Ibid., 305.

9

Critic

> *"I know that most men, including those at ease with problems of the greatest complexity, can seldom accept even the simplest and most obvious truth if it be such as would oblige them to admit the falsity of conclusions which they have delighted in explaining to colleagues, which they have proudly taught to others, and which they have woven, thread by thread, into the fabric of their lives."*
>
> —LEO TOLSTOY, IN JAMES GLEICK, *CHAOS:*
> *MAKING A NEW SCIENCE*

L et's start by explaining exactly what we mean by the role of critic. We are referring to someone who continually questions and probes the status quo, whether the status happens to be good or bad at the moment. We are referring to the activity of seeing things from a distance and seeing them clearly and dispassionately. We are referring to someone who knows the value of the right question asked in the right way.

Organizations have a natural tendency to lock onto ideas and practices that have contributed to their success. Similarly, they want to reduce deviations from the organizational norm. They want to standardize around "best practices," spread them around the organization, and lock on. Leaders tend to become the champions and defenders of these successful operating practices. Indeed, it was probably the present leaders who pioneered them. Their understanding of the business is reflected in these practices, and their operating budgets keep them in play.

Here's a high-stakes example. According to a recent study, from the 1970s through most of the 1980s the CIA tended to overestimate the extent of the Soviet Union's power, but its sources were suspect. Pentagon intelligence on the Soviet Union "would never include anything that might threaten to reduce the Pentagon budget." And university "Sovietologists" had their research grants to protect. "Predictably, both the analysts and the organization [the CIA] as a whole found it difficult to relinquish views in which they were deeply invested. The economist Paul Samuelson . . . liked to say, 'We make progress in economic theory one academic funeral at a time.'"[1]

RIDING DEAD HORSES

"What is a conviction? It is a thought that has come to a stop."

—MILAN KUNDERA, *TESTAMENTS BETRAYED*

The tyranny of convention extends beyond operating practices ("*how* we do things around here") to our basic assumptions and strategies ("*why* we do the things we do"). No level of leadership is immune to supporting the status quo in the face of perfectly good reasons to reassess it. Sometimes the CEOs themselves are the leading defenders of standing pat ("We just need to stick to our knitting and we'll be okay" was a piece of advice one of us heard often from his company's chairman).

Why Is This So Hard?

It's hard, really hard, to be good at this business of criticism. First, there is the issue of challenging the very ideas and procedures that brought you to where you and the organization are today. It puts you in the position of challenging success. That makes anyone uncomfortable.

Second, playing out the role of critic makes others uncomfortable. When criticisms or questions come, people automatically assume they, and not the process or the procedures, are the objects of the criticism. You may think you're merely asking the question, "I wonder if we're doing this the best way possible?" But without a lot of advance leadership groundwork, your people hear a much different question, namely, "Why can't you do this the right way? It's your fault that it doesn't work better."

Third, by posing the critical questions, you are asking people to venture beyond the safety of the tried and true. And usually neither you nor your people know exactly where that adventure will take you. There is always an undercurrent, a tacit acknowledgment, that uncertainty and anxiety are part of this process. And there's at least one other reason why this is so hard: If you challenge and criticize too much, you risk losing your people in the sense they no longer see you as a leader to be followed, but merely an authority whose orders must be obeyed.

Holding on to Conventional Wisdom

There's a saying, cited in chapter 8, that "the quality of information declines as it moves upward through bureaucracies." Well, information can also deteriorate going in the opposite direction, as managers with vested interests deflect or distort new directives that might compromise their position. In fact, we become quite skillful and resourceful in deflecting the need for change, as the following piece of whimsy reminds us:

> Ancient wisdom holds that when you discover you're riding a dead horse, dismount. However, organizations often try other strategies, including:
>
> 1. Changing riders.
> 2. Using a stronger whip.
> 3. Falling back on "This is the way we've always ridden."
> 4. Appointing a committee to study the horse.

5. Arranging a visit to other sites to see how they ride dead horses.
6. Increasing the standards for riding dead horses.
7. Appointing a group to revive dead horses.
8. Creating a training workshop to improve riding skills.
9. Comparing dead horses in today's environment.
10. Changing requirements so the horse no longer meets the standard for death.
11. Hiring a consultant to show how to ride dead horses.
12. Harnessing several dead horses together to increase their speed.
13. Increasing funding to improve dead horse performance.
14. Declaring that no horse is too dead to beat.
15. Studying to see if outsourcing will reduce the cost of riding a dead horse.
16. Buying the latest computer program to enhance dead horse performance.
17. Forming a workgroup to find uses for dead horses.
18. Changing performance requirements for the horse.
19. Declaring a dead horse less costly than a live one.
20. Promoting the dead horse to a supervisory position.[2]

So it comes down to this: If you want to stimulate continuous improvement and seek continuous advantage for your organization, you must coldly and dispassionately scrutinize the ways things are done now and enlist others in this process. To sustain a culture that supports critique and introspection, you must work against the natural tendencies to preserve and resist critical review of a status quo you have helped establish. In this chapter, we focus on ways you can stimulate and encourage a healthy examination of conventional wisdom. We acknowledge some of the inherent barriers to challenging the status quo and talk about how to overcome them.

Countering Defensive Routines: Dealing with the Inevitable

Researchers have identified any number of mental and verbal defenses that come into play when work and work practices fall under scrutiny. Chris Argyris has argued persuasively that most professionals in organizations want to "avoid embarrassment or threat, feeling vulnerable or incompetent. In this respect, the master program that most people use is profoundly defensive."[3] And the defense takes the field instantly. We see strong implications in this profile of "defensive reasoning" for the ways you need to both *model and manage communications in your organizations.*

Argyris's defensive routines are essentially communication tactics—or, rather, noncommunication tactics designed to censor criticism and limit negative disclosure. To counter them and, more important, to head them off, you need to go on the offense. You need to coach your players to offer thoughtful critiques of present practice and reinforce them when they do. This different approach, going on the offense, as it were, might include five tactics to encourage scrutiny, feedback, and dialogue across the organization.

Communication Tactics to Counter Defensive Routines

1. *Acknowledge the difficulty of being a critic.* It would be foolish not to. We all have ambivalent feelings about poking holes in the things we've become accustomed to. Let people know that you understand their natural reticence, but also let them know there's just more to be gained by speaking out. You might also admit your own reluctance to rock the boat sometimes, along with the need to remind yourself that greater benefit is achieved through active commitment to a continuous improvement ethic.

2. *Drive out fear.* This important precept of the quality improvement initiatives of the 1980s takes on a special cast here. You must act to protect the messenger, to make it not only safe but advantageous to deliver bad, and possibly self-incriminating, news. For all the reasons why it might seem wiser to withhold comment (threatens authority, raises conflict, goes against traditional values, etc.), you should have explicit counters to offer ("Leaders are evaluated for continuous improvement," "Some

conflict can actually help an organization grow," "Our values need to change because the world is changing"). All such counters should be couched in the basic argument that the organization requires this kind of vigilance and feedback in order to survive and prosper.

You also need to publish clear procedures for bringing forward sensitive information, and clear guidelines for how such initiative will be protected and reinforced. The best "safety net" for employees is to see people, including their own leadership, rewarded and promoted, rather than punished, for speaking out. You need to make a point of recognizing and praising the behaviors of the alert monitor and the constructive critic.

After launching such a campaign to ensure safety for criticism and critics, including yourself, use a set of questions like these to check on the safety climate in your organization: Can people . . .

- ☐ Challenge an accepted procedure?
- ☐ Acknowledge a mistake they made?
- ☐ Ask for help to fix a mistake?
- ☐ Point out unsafe work practices?
- ☐ Criticize the actions of the team and its leadership?
- ☐ Report a loss to competition?
- ☐ Blow the whistle on unethical behavior . . . without incurring negative consequences, either immediate or delayed?

3. *Don't spare the warts.* Too many leaders don rose-colored glasses and ask their people to do the same. Thus, "good news" companies restrict their ability to learn from experience and mistakes. Instead, you must actively invite organizational critique and hard-nosed feedback from your people, circulate the news, and expect other leaders to follow up on it. You need to issue a hunting license to everyone. You also need to make it clear that avoiding difficulties and covering up problems hamper everyone's ability to act in the best interests of the organization.

4. *Bring the customer into the conversation.* Rather than consign research findings to the marketing department, circulate them throughout the organization. Call out what customers and other stakeholders see as deficiencies or weaknesses. Use them to justify change and target improvement goals. Challenge others to

share what they've heard from their own customer contacts, good or bad. Bring those findings to staff meetings or assign them to special task forces to recommend appropriate action. By making organizational examination and criticism a normal topic for meeting conversations, you can build a more effective learning organization.

5. *Put yourself on the line.* To set expectations of truth and candor from your direct reports, as well as peers and bosses, you need to start with yourself. You need to make yourself open to straight talk and occasional criticism, to step outside the protective cocoon of rank, to exercise some self-disclosure ("I have a tendency to lose sight of the big picture sometimes"), and even be ready to criticize yourself in the company of peers or subordinates ("I think I might have made a mistake here").

RAISING QUESTIONS

> *"The art of managing is the art of asking questions from a sound conceptual base."*
>
> —JERRY RHODES, *CONCEPTUAL TOOLMAKING*

The role of critic boils down to raising the right questions in the right ways and following up on the answers you get. Questions create critical focus. They open for examination subjects that would otherwise go unexamined. Donald Schon has observed that "many practitioners . . . find nothing in the world of practice to occasion reflection. They have become too skillful at techniques of selective inattention, junk categories, and situational control."[4] Questions put ideas and practices into play. When you raise the questions, you model a behavior you want to see others engage in. When you deputize others to be questioners, you make it okay to follow your lead.

You must help employees avoid being taken hostage by their own routines. When you ask about the preferences of customers (both internal and external), the best ways to get things done, the best places to find resources, the way the competition does it, etc.—

when questions like these are routinely raised, people are forced to think and reflect. When you question the reliability of conventional wisdom, you change its "off-limits" status. And when you express doubt about old data, you open doors for new truths.

Here are four strategic roles you can play to promote probing questions and solid reflection:

Questioning Strategies for Leaders as Critics

1. *Break the ice—jump in.* Sometimes people are aware of a problem, or at least a latent problem, but are reluctant to bring it forward. Sometimes people in an organization will acknowledge a concern but keep it at arms length because it's a sensitive subject or it resides in an "off-limits" territory. By taking the lead in raising the tough questions, you can break through the inertia and fear to reinforce critical review as an organizational priority. The CEO of a leading building products company once challenged his senior leadership team with the question, "What are the top five things we could do away with?" The question was a door opener and enabled a free-flowing discussion to take place that might not have occurred otherwise.

   When you are the de facto owner of a current policy or work procedure and volunteer it as a subject for scrutiny, you are acting in a related role, that of bell cow. The bell cow role invites others to follow, even to climb on, and allows discussion to proceed on a new level of candor and objectivity.

2. *Run tests—change the perspective.* Leaders need to continually put present practices under close review. You want your people to keep an eye out for flaws or loopholes. You want to ask questions that subject present performance to rigorous tests, such as this one used by art experts to reveal fakes: "One way to test a picture's integrity is to turn it upside down—a technique used not only by connoisseurs but also by artists trying to see their work with a fresh eye. When a fake is right side up, we anticipate the whole, and our brains automatically correct subtle gaps in logic. But upside down, the work becomes an abstract jumble of line and shape, and the mistakes pour off the page, from poorly proportioned heads to exaggerated shading."[5]

3. *Debrief—revisit what you've done.* Analyzing a project or an operation after it's been completed makes all kinds of sense, but few organizations find the time to do it. Even if there's a system in place to perform a postmortem, people are often reluctant to probe too deeply, particularly when the project was a failure or the proposal wasn't chosen. You need to decide how important this review process truly is and possibly make it a routine priority on the order of the following approach developed by the U.S. Army.

   The Army's After Action Review process employs a set procedure to guide teams of soldiers in evaluating the effectiveness of an action and to glean best practice ideas that might be passed on to successive teams. Discussion is organized by a series of questions designed to systematically examine data and to probe for lessons to be learned. A critical attribute of the process is the obligation participants have, regardless of rank, to a no-holds-barred analysis of the action. This includes the ability to criticize the performance of officers.[6]

   Some organizational leaders like to engage in "skip-level" conversations, typically with employees who are direct reports to their direct reports. Skip-level questioning can sometimes help you get closer to the action quickly. It can also send a signal to the managers in the middle that open communication channels are important and information filtering a hindrance to decision making.

4. *Investigate—probe a little.* Occasionally, you need to raise questions for which there might not be ready answers, questions that can be time-consuming and frustrating. Furthermore, it is often this kind of question that can undermine the prevailing wisdom of the organization. From a practical standpoint, such messy questions carry a "Don't go there!" warning. They present risks of complicating a world that is now simple and workable. But they also open up opportunities for cleaning out deadwood and identifying valuable alternatives. Leaders who want to step up to the plate here can frame questions that direct a special task force or simply an "outsider" without any baggage.

   UPS wanted to know how it might improve its impact as a strong corporate citizen in the local communities where its employees lived and worked. Corporate leadership put the question to representative teams of regional and district managers, who were then asked to come up with plans to tie together corporate philanthropy with active local volunteerism. No two plans were the same, and some were more workable than others. But the question instigated some creative problem solving, and actionable responses were the result.

Other lines of questioning that call for more systematic attention may involve the use of formal survey methods. Leaders who authorize regular customer and employee research are establishing questioning as a value-adding activity, which in turn can set a tone for the organization as a whole. One company we know wanted to strengthen its internal communications and asked employees to evaluate the present array of corporate and division communications vehicles. When focus groups responded with some unanimity that at least one vehicle was rarely read, let alone opened, leadership opted to kill the vehicle, thus saving corporate time and money.

Effective Questioning

To provoke a continuous review of the status quo, you need to skillfully orchestrate your questioning tactics. You need to develop questions that invite, rather than shut down, dialogue. Try applying these criteria to your questioning tactics:

❑ *Do questions invite thinking and opinion, or just information?* Closed-ended questions (requiring yes/no or other short, more definitive answers) can often lead to suspended conversations, where the responders see themselves as just filling a quick request for information rather than entering into a dialogue. Open-ended questions, the ones that ask for opinions or hypotheses or that begin with *how* or *why,* stand a better chance of engaging people in a more extended dialogue.

❑ *Do questions seem to build on each other?* When people sense that questions are going somewhere, that there's a logic being followed, they are better able to respond as they pick up the line of logic. Often a "question build" starts out with a simple request for observations, then graduates to more focused, opinion-based responses, possibly ending with an invitation to predict or to recommend. It leads the respondents into gradually more involved and sophisticated conversations.

❏ *Do questions invite questions?* If a question-driven dialogue simply follows a call-response pattern, it may not be as far ranging or useful as it could be if both parties were to pose questions or occasionally parried a question with a question. If your questions invite questions in return, a leveling of "status" occurs in the dialogue, along with a greater willingness to extend it and to speak candidly.

CHALLENGING ASSUMPTIONS

"[A] choice is posed between intellectual and administrative tidiness, on one hand, and flexibility for innovation, on the other."

—CHARLES LINDBLOM, *INQUIRY AND CHANGE*

Conventional wisdom is a familiar, trusted road, easy to navigate, and besides, everyone else travels on it too. Most of us have little occasion to seriously review our basic assumptions and beliefs about how (and what end) our organizations operate. Instead, we focus more on how to do the current work better, accepting as givens the thinking and reasoning that underpin present practice. It's only when we confront failures in the current system, hear criticism from customers or other outsiders, or entertain proposals for change that we consider looking beneath the surface and asking more fundamental questions about the right way to do things or even the right things to do.

The leader's role as perceptive questioner and critic of present practices carries with it the responsibility of periodically visiting basic "premises, inferences, and conclusions," both his or her own and those of others. Leaders require vantage points from which to see things differently. From a communications standpoint, this responsibility takes the form of modeling a process of self-review and helping others to engage in similar forms of examination. When leaders model a stance of readiness to question underlying assumptions, they might say things like the remarks in Figure 9-1.

Prompting Self-Review

In your role as critic of the status quo, you need to ask, and help others to ask, "why" questions such as, "Why do we do it the way we do it?" If such "why" questions are never asked, organizations might continue to travel down the same well-worn path while competition takes a shortcut. Two opportunities in particular exist for you and your colleagues to ask "why" questions that will prompt a challenge of the status quo: using performance data and debriefing after work or projects are completed.

Using Data Karl Weick has suggested that "organizations have a major hand in creating the realities which they then view as 'facts' to which they must accommodate."[7] For all of those organizations that want to think they "manage by fact," using reliable data to question the effectiveness of present practices is probably the first step in challenging the status quo. You need to get your hands on the right data, but more important, you need to use telling data in your discussions with colleagues and subordinates if you really want to stimulate hard-nosed scrutiny. Data can also serve to depersonal-

Figure 9-1. Scripts for questioning the status quo.

- ❏ "I tend to see things from this perspective; maybe I need to look from a different vantage point."
- ❏ "We get so used to doing things the same way, we forget why we decided to do it that way in the first place."
- ❏ "We tend to operate on autopilot a lot. Every once in a while, we need to take back the controls and see where we are."
- ❏ "Let's remind ourselves why we think this is the best way to get the job done."
- ❏ "Does it still make sense to be doing it this way?"
- ❏ "What if there's a better way to reach our goal but we're not even considering it?"

ize old loyalties and habits. As historian Alfred Crosby noted, when "you possess a quantitative representation of your subject . . . you can think about it rigorously. You can manipulate it and experiment with it. . . . It possesses a sort of independence from you."[8]

In recent years, the notion of a balanced scorecard has captured attention as a smart way to collect and use data to assess strategy.[9] We also see the balanced scorecard as a tool to widen the conversation about what gets measured and to involve more organization members in talking about what may be learned from such performance evaluation.

Anecdotal data can also serve as a powerful generator of critical review, and it's easier to grasp. In chapter 8 we noted how Cadillac supplied its dealers not only with quantitative findings from customer satisfaction research, but with videotaped interviews with groups of Cadillac customers as well. The review process that these tapes often precipitated for dealer leadership teams underscored the power of visual data to dislodge complacency and raise serious questions. Dealer leadership in many instances used the data to engage other members of their stores in productive and often highly creative, problem-solving conversations.

Debriefing After Completed Work The Army's After Action Review process, discussed earlier, is a questioning opportunity for everyone who was involved in the operation. The potential yield from serious, well-organized debriefings can go beyond stepped-out formulas for determining best practices. Debriefings can also challenge basic assumptions underlying conventional wisdom and lead to new thinking about how to accomplish specific objectives. You need to manage debriefing sessions in a way that the discussion is wide open. Instead of merely asking about what went right and wrong, you should raise more analytical questions and probe for alternative scenarios that might deliver different results.

Sources for Challenging Assumptions

Conventional wisdom and underlying assumptions go unchallenged in part because leaders often don't talk to the right people. You need to seek out people who might bring new perspectives to a review process. Four stakeholder groups in particular offer useful potential here.

Sources to Challenge the Status Quo

1. *Customers and Business Allies.* By inviting customers to voice their concerns and problems you can tap into this ultimate value perspective on the status quo. Key to getting substantive results from conversations with customers is to go beyond basic satisfaction surveys, where preset questions limit the range of customer response, and preset answers (yes/no or a scaled rating) limit their content. The in-depth, videotaped interviews with Cadillac customers, described in chapter 8, are a good example of the kind of yield leaders might expect from more extended dialogue. Another example, discussed in chapter 11, involved Wendy's Restaurants asking groups of customers to imagine themselves as new store owners with an opportunity to make changes.

    Other organizations go a step further and seek out trade allies and business partners to poke holes in the "way we do business now." Ameritech invited distributors of its voice and data products to a joint review and planning meeting in which the goal was to collaboratively identify the criteria for a successful distribution center. Ameritech sales and marketing people met in small group sessions with distributor representatives and together redefined best practice in several key dimensions of the distribution process.[10]

2. *New Employees.* New hires often arrive with fresh perspective, especially if they come from other organizations and have different work experiences. Most organizations want to quickly reorient new hires and fold them into their culture. But before newcomers lose their "otherness," you can interview them for the different perspectives they bring—other ways of seeing the world and getting work done.

    After a while, when they've had a chance to get to know the way things work in the new organization, leaders can ask again for their thoughts and insights. Since they'll no doubt maintain contact with people in other organizations (including the competition), you can use them as consultants in the future as well.

3. *Field People.* Employees who don't work in the headquarters office almost always have a different sense of how things work and what's important. Too often, headquarters keeps these people (and their special vantage points) at arm's length or disregards

their views completely. When leadership from Ford and American Airlines asked people at field locations to seek cost-saving possibilities, plant and airport personnel were able to tell them exactly where money was being lost and where alternative thinking could lead to savings to the tune of millions of dollars.[11]

The challenge for any organization's leadership is to create ways to tap into this cadre of "outside expertise." What kind of regular channels can you set up to manage a productive conversation with employees who will always know more about certain aspects of the business than central office leaders? Another dimension to this challenge is respecting and guarding the credibility of these "outside" voices who may not be so articulate or share the same professional or territorial perspectives as top leadership.

4. *Veterans and Retirees.* Sometimes leaders shy away from "old-timers," especially if they're looking for fresh new ideas. But some of the most valid challenges to current conventional wisdom can come from people who have been around long enough to have seen "wisdom" come and go and who can make studied comparisons between present and past versions. In an article titled "Elder Wizard," longtime basketball coach John Bach (with the NBA's Chicago Bulls and Washington Wizards) offered these thoughts: "Isn't it a smart man who knows what to let go of and what to retain? . . . That's what old guys like me bring to the game. We've seen all the strategies and situations and playing styles. . . . The more you know, the more you can adapt."[12]

Finally, there are the retirees who, while they went along with the status quo for years and didn't rock the boat, knew better. Now they can offer observations without any career risk and might feel truly gratified for being asked.

Prompting Status Quo Challenges

Leaders need to encourage others to monitor present effectiveness levels and to question current orthodoxies. In turn, employees need to feel that such behavior is not only safe, but highly desired as well. Pointing out the emperor has no clothes should earn definite positive reinforcement. A basic communication tactic, in addition to modeling the behaviors yourself, is to clearly establish for others the value to the organization and to them, of a readiness to challenge present practices. Four messages in particular are worth delivering on a regular basis to sponsor review and critique activity:

1. *The future success of the organization requires that everyone contribute to continuous improvement, even if improvement causes disruption or discomfort.* We have a common stake in targeting practices that are ineffective or outmoded. These messages can be delivered personally and reinforced by raising levels of business literacy.

2. *People who help pinpoint areas for improvement increase their chances for promotion and reward.* The substance of this message must be seen to be believed. You can recognize people who succeed here by placing recognition stories in corporate communication vehicles and by promoting people known as critics of the status quo. The message will come across.

3. *The two best places to look for improvement opportunities are your own work areas and the interfaces between your work and that of others, because nobody knows them better than you.* This message is especially apt for delivery in team and staff meetings: they're about work performance, talking shop, and making tacit knowledge more explicit.

4. *The two best sources of intelligence about improvement targets are your customers and your colleagues.* Nobody knows what someone else knows better than they do. So, you need to encourage the opening of channels and the free flow of information, especially that which may be critical or negative. "Praise the messenger" should be the watchword.

Testing Assumptions

"*We establish truth when we subject people's claims to rigorous tests. That allows us to see more clearly the causal processes embedded in those claims. That's transparency.*"

—CHRIS ARGYRIS, 1999 INTERVIEW

How can leaders best challenge the underlying assumptions behind current practices? How can they help colleagues and subordinates "surface their mental models" (a phrase made popular by advocates of the learning organization) and subject organizational "facts" to fresh scrutiny? Several communication tactics leaders can use follow.

Ways to Test Assumptions

❑ *Bring reasoning to the surface.* You can bring underlying assumptions into the open by routinely sharing your reasoning and then inviting others to do the same. This initiative is especially appropriate when the basis for an argument is not clear or obvious— either the other person's or your own. The two sets of script options in Figure 9-2 might provide some useful ways to take your conversation beneath the surface, and to test the thinking behind a position.

❑ *Play devil's advocate.* This tried-and-true technique is particularly appropriate for challenging assumptions that typically go unquestioned. When you announce your intention to play devil's advocate, you claim a license to question or criticize that is usually granted readily by others. But remember: You are assuming

Figure 9-2. More scripts for questioning the status quo.

Making *Your* Reasoning Visible

❑ "This is what I think my position means. Here's how I think it will affect us. Here's an example of what it might look like."
❑ "Here's how I've come to this conclusion. Here's the data I think supports my position. I'm assuming that. . . ."
❑ "Do you see any flaws in my reasoning? Is there anything I've overlooked, or need to consider more thoroughly?"

Making *Their* Reasoning Visible

❑ "What's the significance of that? I'm not sure I understand your position fully—can you walk me through it again?"
❑ "What led you to that conclusion? How did you come to that position? Can you help me understand your thinking here?"
❑ "How do your views differ from mine? Do you see any ways to bridge them? In what ways are they the same? Do you see any common assumptions?"

the devil's advocate stance both to suggest alternative approaches and to challenge accepted wisdom, not to shoot holes in everyone else's input. In Emerson's annual planning meetings, the corporate team regularly plays devil's advocate to draw out the reasoning and the justification for initiatives proposed by the business units.

❑ *Question the stories.* All organizations have stories that establish key beliefs and assumptions, define organizational values, and describe organizational heroes (and, by extension, what heroism looks like). The stories we tell about our organizations establish and confirm ways of thinking about the organization, bases for judging what's proper and what's important. Stories also influence behavior because they provide precedents and examples from the past.

To test underlying assumptions, leaders may have to question the stories that contain and express them. Do these stories still hold true? Are they still relevant? Are the values they embody still as important? Is this how we want present and future organizational heroes to act?

Raising questions about traditional stories or subverting their authority as guides for the future is in effect a version of playing devil's advocate. Since organizational stories are such powerful shapers of behavior, especially as they provide rationale for action, they are fair game for leadership attention that seeks to subject conventional wisdom to critical review.

❑ *Suggest a fresh start gambit.* One way to get out from under inherited ways of doing things or from other forms of conventional wisdom is to pose the question, "If we were just starting the organization, would we still do it this way?" By removing the floor of tradition, the way we've always done it, as a necessary platform to stand on, leaders can invite people to stand in different positions and apply new perspectives. The conversation that might ensue can both challenge traditional thinking and introduce new approaches to evaluate present performance.

"I Don't Get No Respect!"

Being a critic is not the easiest nor the most appreciated role you can play. But play it you must. Only when your people know you expect critical review and will not allow them to fall asleep behind the status quo will they be likely to come forward.

In fact, the leadership communication role of critic can take on an even more aggressive stance by sponsoring active debate and conflict to test present practices and to adopt new ones. In the next chapter, we examine the opportunities leaders have to manage argument and challenge as a kind of ongoing contact sport, to help the organization actively promote adaptation and renewal.

NOTES

1. Stephen Kotkin, "What They Knew (Not!): 44 Years of CIA Secrets," *New York Times* (March 17, 2001), A17.
2. "Business Humor: Organizational Wisdom (As Seen on the World Wide Web)," *Business Psychology News* [www.businesspsychologist.com] (2, 1998).
3. Chris Argyris, "Teaching Smart People How to Learn," *Harvard Business Review* (May–June 1991), 103.
4. Donald A. Schon, *The Reflective Practitioner: How Professionals Think in Action* (New York: Basic Books, 1983), 69.
5. Peter Landesman, "A Crisis of Fakes," *New York Times Magazine* (March 18, 2000), 38.
6. Richard T. Pascale et al., "Changing the Way We Change," *Harvard Business Review* (November–December 1997), 134.
7. Karl Weick, *The Social Psychology of Organizing,* 2nd ed. (New York: McGraw-Hill, 1979), 13.
8. Alfred Crosby, *The Measure of Reality* (New York: Cambridge University Press, 1997), 229.
9. See, for example, Robert S. Kaplan and David P. Norton, *The Strategy-Focused Organization: How Balanced Scorecard Companies Thrive in the New Business Environment* (Boston: Harvard Business School Press, 2001).
10. See Robert Mai, *Learning Partnerships: How Leading American Companies Implement Organizational Learning* (Chicago: Irwin/ASTD, 1996), 64–66.
11. Ibid., 115, 122.
12. Christopher McDougall, "The Elder Wizard," *New York Times Magazine* (January 13, 2002), 12.

10

Provocateur

> *"Held in debate, people can learn their way to collective solutions when they understand one another's assumptions. The work of the leader is to get conflict out into the open and use it as a source of creativity."*
>
> —JAN CARLZON, IN RONALD A. HEIFETZ AND
> DONALD L. LAURIE, "THE WORK OF LEADERSHIP"

Most organizations try to avoid conflicts. As individuals, we find conflict with other members of the organization unpleasant, and we attempt to protect both ourselves and others from experiencing negative feelings. Furthermore, internal conflict can signal lack of solidarity among members, a failing esprit de corps. Organizational infighting is seen as sapping the strength of the enterprise, wasting time that could be more productively spent on getting the job done. In short, verbal conflict in the everyday life of organizations is a sign that something has gone wrong.

Or is it?

ENTER CONFLICT, WEARING WHITE HAT

> "Contention is an ingredient of organizational life. Our mistake has been to ignore, suppress, or undermanage it."
>
> —RICHARD PASCALE, *MANAGING ON THE EDGE*

When leaders habitually shy away from conflict, they come to be seen as afraid to take a stand, or shoulder necessary responsibility. Conflict avoidance can erode workforce perceptions of leadership courage and resolution. Issues go unresolved at the risk of employee stagnation and dissension. Furthermore, avoiding conflict can deprive organizations of opportunities to actually solve problems, resolve issues, and make decisions necessary for moving ahead. When not addressed in timely fashion, they may indeed go away by themselves, but more often, they just become more difficult to deal with.

There's a famous management anecdote in which Alfred Sloan, the CEO who built General Motors into the most powerful automobile company in the world, expressed displeasure over his leadership team's reluctance to rock the boat. "I take it," said Sloan to his team, "we are all in complete agreement on the decision here. Therefore I propose we postpone further discussion of the matter until our next meeting to give ourselves time to develop disagreement and perhaps gain some understanding of what the decision is all about."[1]

Prompting disagreement so as to advance understanding— exposing more sides of an issue, more perspectives on a problem, etc.—has become, especially over the past twenty years, a smart thing to do in organizations. Disagreement and conflict are food for "the learning organization." They breed disequilibrium that can lead to positive change. They help root out buried failings and mistakes, increase accuracy in decision making, and prepare the ground for innovation and renewal.

Indeed, the business case for cultivating contention and conflict in an organization is readily made and has been launched under a variety of compelling metaphors: "Dynamic disequilibrium," "creative contention," "cognitive conflict," "constructive confrontation," "creative abrasion," "positive turbulence" (our favorite) are but some that come to mind.

But despite conflict's new standing, most leaders are still uneasy about stirring up the pot and fomenting arguments that expose others to blame and lead to hurt feelings. Therein lies the dilemma, and it's a bit of a paradox. Leaders are themselves conflicted over the need to sponsor and support confrontation within their organizations.

In this chapter we focus on using conflict and confrontation as a force for organizational benefit. Specifically, we believe leadership needs to effectively manage the rules of engagement: the communications that frame and contain contention, disagreement, and debate. We do not address "conflict management" per se, how to reduce the negative effects of interpersonal conflict. Instead, we look at how to bring conflict *into* discussions and utilize its power to challenge complacency and inertia.

We begin our discussion with an extended look at how the leadership team at Emerson, a company with a strong record of financial performance, uses deliberate, consistent confrontation to turn planning into a core organizational competency.

PLANNING AT EMERSON

With more than sixty operating divisions, each one with a branded product or service, coordinated planning at Emerson is critical. David Farr, Emerson's CEO, admitted in a 2001 speech that "some people think we do too much planning."[2] He said this with a twinkle in his eye, because clearly, planning is what lights Farr's fire and that of his predecessor, Chuck Knight. From the corporate level on down, planning at Emerson is in fact a process of focused conversations, with spirited dialogue that can become contentious, as we describe below.

The planning process, according to Farr, is an ongoing conversation about how Emerson can change the game to gain cost advantage, and to leverage its size, its combinations, and its operating efficiencies. The corporate planning process kicks off with a retreat in August attended by some some thirty senior leaders. This retreat is followed by a two-day corporate planning conference in October with all the division leaders. The October conferences are typically attended by some two hundred people from all of the divisions and combine information sharing with award presentations and occasional guest speakers on substantive topics.

But when Farr said senior leaders devote a lot of time to planning, he was referring to the ongoing planning discussions that take place afterward between a corporate team and each of the divisions at corporate headquarters in St. Louis. Paul McKnight, Emerson's vice president for organization planning, estimates that Farr and his senior managers spend upward of a third of their time meeting with division leaders. These meetings, described below, take place biannually, with a purpose to review and reshape each division's strategic plan.

In the year when there is not a formal division planning conference, David Farr (typically) and a smaller group of senior leaders make onsite visits to the divisions, when updated strategic plans are submitted for review. A parallel discussion goes on between another corporate team and the operations leadership of each division in the form of a profit-planning meeting. Additional conversations focus on promotable staff, and on what organizationally keeps division managers awake at night. Finally, each business leader has an annual planning meeting with each division president.

The division planning meetings are held at a retreat house outside the city. Since Emerson divisions range in size and annual revenue from $20 million to $2 billion, planning meetings typically last longer for the bigger divisions, sometimes carrying over into a second day. The meeting is staged around a U-shaped table, with the corporate team sitting at the head of the U. The meeting typically begins with some remarks by Farr on the state of the company and where it is headed. The division team then makes its presentation, focusing largely on its strategic marketing and sales plans. The team is headed by the division president, along with the Emerson business leader, a corporate executive who oversees the division. The team can include a mix of sales and marketing executives, as well as product and operations managers. Discussion in the daylong sessions focuses on last year's performance and the strategy for the coming year, and can also cover:

❏ Plans for expanding market share
❏ New product introductions
❏ New advertising programs
❏ Customer surveys (a required part of the meeting)

Planning as a Contact Sport

So far, the routine Emerson follows might not seem all that unusual. But here's where its planning process takes on its own special quality. The presentation by the division team is routinely interrupted by the corporate team, which demonstrates an unusually studied and pointed understanding of the division plan, along with the backup details presented in the division team's slides and charts. Hard challenges are thrown out: "I don't understand how you can make that point," or "I don't see how those two charts really corroborate each other." The challenges are not idle ones. For this process to work at the level it does, the executive team is required to be both well prepared and wide awake, attentive to a day's worth of numbers and nuances.

The sometimes contentious tone (Farr likes to refer to the "tension" inherent in the discussions) of the planning sessions is a legacy from former CEO Chuck Knight, who led Emerson for more than a quarter of a century, and who currently serves as chairman. The competitive tension is an ingredient that by all accounts "helps us to get to better decisions. When you bring forward a proposal that gets aggressively challenged by your CEO, you need to have your stuff together," according to McKnight.[3]

For instance, when division VPs argue that "our competition is moving out ahead of us and we need to add a new product," they can be quickly challenged and asked to defend their recommendations in the context of his competitive analysis or to tell whether they have fully considered alternative responses to the situation. Another tactic used by the senior leadership team, especially Farr, is to draw other division managers into the conversation with questions like, "Do you really believe the argument your boss just made?"

While such challenges are often aggressive and demanding, two rules help keep the meetings focused on making sound strategy and good decisions. Rule Number One is that nobody makes personal attacks. Rule Number Two is that discussion must always lead to an action recommendation, with both groups invested in getting there. This way, everyone has "skin in the game."

What the planning meetings have yielded for Emerson is an executive give-and-take that is more substantive, more data based, and more researched and rehearsed than the typical corporate planning meeting. Division teams go through a thorough kind of due diligence in preparing their plans, and it shows.

Avoiding the Potential "Dark Side" of Confrontation and Tension

Washington University's George Cesaretti, who works with Emerson on a leadership development project, notes there's a potential dark side to this tradition of aggressive, combative discourse. Despite the fact that Rule Number One is in force, confrontation and conflict aren't always easy to contain. Human beings don't normally keep emotions fully in check when arguing forcefully or staunchly defending a position. There's a natural potential for emotional spillover here.

Obviously, the planning exercise at Emerson requires some practice and some experience "under fire." Participants need to clothe their egos in a flak jacket and develop thick skins underneath in order to feel really ready for such a free-swinging engagement. But the most important way that division managers can prepare themselves for the planning conversations is to develop a communication strategy incorporating solid analysis, good supporting data, and clearly articulated reasoning.

This need for planning "discipline" presents a special challenge to the organization when it brings new people into a planning meeting. The problem is that younger managers or managers from newly acquired companies might see confrontation but miss the underlying commitment and goodwill necessary for reaching smart, well-argued decisions that people can live with.

So, with newly acquired companies, Emerson's practice is to observe a kind of "hands-off" policy for the first year or two. Acquired company officers report to an Emerson business leader rather than to a division president, and for the first year, new companies go through a less formal review.

Leadership style across all aspects of company management is at issue here, and Emerson doesn't want to send the wrong message to newcomers. Confrontation at Emerson is, as Cesaretti eloquently puts it, "an anvil on which you forge agreement."[4]

Leadership Development

One way Emerson works to strengthen collaborative planning discipline is through a well-orchestrated and fully supported leadership development program. Participants in the program include newly promoted managers as well as those newly hired (or acquired). The initial event is a retreat of several days' duration, attended by groups of about thirty-five to forty new managers along with members of the corporate leadership team.

An important objective of these retreats is to provide new managers with as much informal exposure to senior leadership as possible, in effect, to "humanize" senior leaders early so that later when these same leaders confront younger managers in planning sessions, there's a personal basis on which to engage in dialogue. At breaks, as well as in premeal social settings, senior leaders make a point of getting to know as many of the new people as they can. At one such meeting, Chuck Knight, the outgoing CEO, and his successor, David Farr, were both present. Afterward, a manager from a newly acquired company confessed he had worked at his former firm for fifteen years and had never met the CEO. "I've been at Emerson for less than a month, and I've met two."

Despite the breadth of the Emerson organization (which continues to expand), much is made of the importance of face-to-face communication and planning. The senior management team's regular meetings with the divisions are one illustration. Another is the Organization Room, a gallery of photos and profiles of every senior division manager, organized by both division and functional job category. By keeping track of faces as well as names, corporate leaders can reinforce the personal connection with division colleagues as they assess the talent pool or prepare for division visits. This personal connection, in turn, allows the planning meetings to play out on a more informal level and makes ongoing cooperation and support more personalized as well.

Another strategy for helping new managers become comfortable with, as well as adept at, participating in the planning process is to selectively invite them to planning conferences when they might not yet have a major role. By giving them a chance to present (and so be part of the conversation), as well as to observe their bosses interacting with their bosses, new managers can become better acculturated to the process that later they'll be asked to participate in more actively.

Getting the Right People in the Room

At the bottom of Emerson's commitment to managing its planning process through confrontational dialogue is a sense of trust and confidence in the people it appoints to lead its divisions. As Paul McKnight says, "If we get the right people in the room, we can solve any problem. And after we've worked through the planning process, people leave the room committed to making the plan work. I've been in other companies where people coming out of a high-level strategy meeting will start distancing themselves from the decisions and talk disparagingly about the process used to reach them—decisions that were often made before the meeting began and are now just in search of some ceremonial rubber stamp. That's not how it works at Emerson."

McKnight and Cesaretti both pointed out another important characteristic of the planning conversations: the requirement that all participants speak their mind, and not waste time trying to disguise their points or simply to withhold key opinions for fear of exposing themselves to unwanted criticism. "We don't have to look for the hidden message in somebody's comments," says McKnight. The planning process is less about the politics of decision making and more about getting well-supported positions out in the open so they can be worked into well-considered decisions.

In the long run, managers who show they can play in this arena are managers who demonstrate trustworthiness and reliability. Emerson has a strong track record for management retention within its industry. It promotes from within, and some 80 percent of the people on its annual "promotion recommendation lists" do in fact get promoted to higher levels of responsibility.

One of Emerson's most revered senior leaders offered a gloss on the issue of open communication at Emerson in some remarks made at a leadership development retreat. Asked why he had remained so long at Emerson despite opportunities to go elsewhere, he cited three reasons: the respect shown for people at Emerson, the opportunity to work for a winner, and an environment that was essentially absent of politics.

Emerson subscribes to the premise that managers who speak up and speak out are leaders who can make the planning conversation richer and broader. Surfacing new ideas, and pushing back on ideas requiring more scrutiny are valued leadership qualities at Emerson. When he was moving up through the ranks of the organization, David Farr apparently had a reputation of standing his ground with Chuck Knight. "But if you don't speak your mind," McKnight threw in, "you're letting people down."

Consider the significance of this last comment in describing the tenor of leadership communication and the culture of the organization. For Emerson to get the best thinking in play in its ongoing planning and strategy-making process, it demands that people don't hold back. Clearly the tactics for succeeding in a sometimes confrontational discussion are not to think defensively or avoid the risk of censure by keeping a low profile. Instead, a healthy conversation for both the company and its leaders is grounded in the importance of staying engaged, even if it means jousting with more powerful "opponents." What's most admired here are qualities of preparedness and a willingness to participate in the conversation, to engage in a contact sport with serious business consequences.

McKnight cited an example of how push-back can come from anywhere in the organization and be dealt with respectfully. Several years ago when Chuck Knight was still CEO, the company had decided, as a reaction to regulatory changes affecting personnel policy, to eliminate certain employee benefits. Among the benefits to be dropped was a component in the preretirement insurance program, and Knight directed his HR executives to move ahead with the changes. But an employee in a plant in Arkansas called Knight directly and complained, arguing that the reasons behind the decision were wrong. After some deliberation, Knight called his HR team to revisit the decision.

Commitment to Action, Control, and Follow-Up

Emerson firmly believes in the power of systematically challenging conventional wisdom and current practices through its planning. As Farr said in his business school speech, planning is a "dynamic process: we redo plans every year, and nothing is sacred." It's all part of a process that allows Emerson to stay ahead of the curve: "We keep stretching our industry—we push them."[5] This process, characterized as we have seen by a free-swinging dialogue, lies at the heart of a culture that trades on several other, complementary values. The first is a commitment to action and to assuming responsibility for taking action. The others are tied to carrying the plan forward in a conscientious, deliberate way.

The path that the leadership conversation takes on the way to building consensus starts then with a well-choreographed information-gathering phase, sparked by questioning and debate. When consensus is finally reached, decisions can be implemented with the full support of the organization. Commitment to action, as Farr noted, is the way out of the argument.

The objective of planning is action and the often fractious conversations that underpin the planning process are necessary to resolve concerns and allay doubts. One way to understand the questioning and the challenges voiced by the senior management team is that they are deliberate attempts to acquire sufficient information to be able to support a decision. It's all about Alfred Sloan's notion of the requirements for good decision making. The obligation of this kind of leadership communication at Emerson is therefore to build agreement out of disagreement.

When everyone is on board, *everyone owns the decision*. As Farr concluded, this process of involving all the key stakeholders in hammering out decisions helps make Emerson a "blameless organization," where implementation can't be hampered by residual doubts and people waiting to say, "I told you so." In other organizations without such commitment, there are two potential downsides to this kind of confrontational planning. Division teams could go away feeling defeated by and resentful of a senior management power play, or they could feel cheated and toyed with in what was merely a charade of shared decision making and "empowerment." "At Emerson, we gather the information, we make decisions, we get on with it," was Farr's summary of the process.[6]

Getting on with it involves close assessment, with an eye to altering the plan if necessary. As we noted before, the scheduled planning meeting is only the most dramatic part of an ongoing process that monitors results, integrates new developments, and involves a variety of players. Tight controls at the division level, subject to careful review by the corporate team, put teeth into the planning conversations, and make them uniquely about substance and performance, rather than people and politics.

PROVOKING CONFLICT AS A LEADERSHIP COMPETENCY

"It's about hand to hand mental combat about an issue—wrestling it to the ground intellectually, getting the answer and then owning it together, and taking the hill."

JACK WELCH, VARNEY INTERVIEW

The art of provoking conflict while seeking new harmonies is what leaders of dynamic organizations work to perfect. In most organizations, there is certainly potential to locate different views and opposing positions, if only because most organizations contain within themselves such diversity. Consider the ability to tease out discordant opinion from any or all of the following sources of difference:

- ❏ Headquarters and field
- ❏ Various (and sometimes competing) operating units
- ❏ Different professional backgrounds and problem-solving approaches
- ❏ Old guard/new guard (including new hires)
- ❏ Different "cognitive profiles" (e.g., the various Myers-Briggs types)

If the potential is there, the challenge is how to put confrontation and disagreement into play in the most productive, beneficial way. We examine this challenge on two levels: setting the stage and managing the process.

Setting the Stage

In an organization, a battle between points of view or opposing arguments is an intellectual contest whose resolution is intended to benefit the organization ("owning it together and taking the hill"). Leaders need to think of this as a kind of stage drama for which they are the directors. One early task is the identification of appropriate "cast members." Even though key cast members usually self-select, the leader needs to get others involved, especially when there are people who are not happy with prevailing views. "Err on the side of including people who disagree," suggests Daniel Yankelovich.[7] If they're excluded, the leader is sending a message that dissent or disagreement is not valued, or it is to be avoided.

Directing the action will invoke rules of engagement, and leaders must establish for cast members an etiquette, particularly for being confrontational about ideas rather than personalities. See Figure 10-1 for a beginning list of items for leaders to consider in preparing the ground for productive confrontation.

Figure 10-1. Preparing the ground for disagreement.

❏ *Establish (and continually keep in front of participants) a common purpose that serves organizational ends:* It's ultimately about building informed agreement and shared responsibility.

❏ *Remind participants of the strategy behind using confrontation and conflict:* It's not about changing people, but about testing positions and challenging ideas, which might then be changed.

❏ *Clearly identify participants and their standing with respect to issues being discussed:* Who are they and what's their stake in the contest?

❏ *Bring participants together, ideally in informal, social settings to build personal relationships.*

❏ *Set agendas for discussion:* What's worth focusing on, and what's not important?

❏ *Establish the importance of data to document and substantiate argument:* "In the absence of good data, executives waste time in pointless debate over opinions. . . . There is a direct link between reliance on facts and low levels of interpersonal conflict."[8]

Leaders can organize for confrontational dialogue on an ad hoc basis or, like Emerson and Intel, create structures that institutionalize it. For Emerson, that structure was its collaborative planning routine. For Intel, it involved a "two-in-a-box" principle: two executives with complementary skills heading up a business unit. The result of such a management structure is a built-in conversation that allows for multiple perspectives and the potential for self-checking at the top.[9]

Rules and Guidelines

Sponsoring ongoing dialogue that invites dissent and disagreement requires skillful process management. Otherwise, such discussions can lead to problems that are hard to undo and to lowered morale, dissension, reduced productivity, and even sabotage. To cultivate productive conflict, a leader needs to appear calm and under control, deploying a business-building strategy, not issuing a call to arms.

Because disagreement can so easily drift into personal attacks and animosities, leaders need to continuously monitor the level of discomfort that contention may be causing. In this regard, leaders serve as a pressure valve. When too much steam is being generated, the leader needs to help the sides cool down, refocusing on the issues, not the people. If need be, the leader should also consider acting like a soccer referee, handing out some equivalent of a "yellow card" to a player as a warning against continued untoward behavior. Helping antagonists regain their footing on a common ground, common cause basis helps, as does allowing them to regroup in a social setting.

Another process management task is to introduce new and different perspectives into the discussion, ideally by inviting new participants who represent these perspectives into the conversation. Having multiple positions or opinions in play can, on the one hand, slow down and confuse discussion. But on the other hand, considering several options instead of just two opposing alternatives can reduce interpersonal conflict and allow a freer, more open exchange. Multiple perspectives create a valuable diversity of ideas and enrich the ways teams attack and defend their position.

Finally, leaders might want to improve the effectiveness of confrontational discussions by resorting to specific discussion and debating formats and to some skills training, especially in the area of listening and negotiation. One of the potential benefits of taking part in an argument is the opportunity to learn from an opponent. Researcher Kathleen Reardon reminds us that "a persuader rarely changes another person's behavior or viewpoint without altering his or her own in the process. To persuade meaningfully, we must not only listen to others but also incorporate their perspectives into our own."[10]

In his "polarity management" format, Barry Johnson provides an approach in which opposing sides can both listen and learn in a confrontational discussion. At its essence is an attempt to begin by making sure you understand *their* position (before you start trying to convince them that yours is better). It is, as Daniel Yankelovich would say, an attempt to "initiate dialogue through a gesture of empathy."[11] *Polarity management* embodies a learned set of tactics that might prove useful as a method for handling confrontation in organizations. The sequence of "moves" Johnson suggests is a bit counterintuitive and occurs in this order:

1. Acknowledge the worth (and past contribution) of the present position—rather than trashing it (the more instinctive first move).
2. Admit to any weaknesses—real or potential—in your own thinking.
3. Describe your ideas or opinions as a better option.
4. (Only rarely) Point out the weaknesses of their thinking.[12]

Polarity management is only one possible communication method to work through conflict. A more traditional approach that starts with a logical questioning of stated positions (Emerson's procedure for conducting its planning dialogues, for instance) can also be effective if managed well. Some people, in fact, might find a reluctance to criticize as an insincere stance—better come out and say what you don't like first. Then, you can welcome in turn any criticism of your own position and work through to a discussion of the relative merits of each alternative.

MANAGING DEBATE

> *"The manager's task is no longer one of ensuring conformity and control; the over-riding challenge now becomes one of fostering a strong and constructive level of debate."*
>
> —MATTHEW KIERNAN, "THE NEW STRATEGIC ARCHITECTURE"

Debate is a managed discussion format for disagreement and confrontation. It provides a way for leaders to use conflict to champion organizational renewal. A well-managed debate is ultimately about substance and performance rather than people and politics, but it can fully engage both people and politics. At Emerson, the planning process frequently involves active debate, with senior management often playing the role of skeptic or devil's advocate, and division leadership arguing its case with thorough preparation and compelling data.

There is a tendency in many organizations to suppress real debate because leadership is uncomfortable with conflict. Leaders might in principle applaud open debate, yet not want their own positions to come under fire. But the benefits that can be gained through debating important issues, proposed plans, or key decisions are too strong to ignore:

- ❑ Broader, more thorough review and due diligence: more information and evidence offered; more alternatives considered
- ❑ Reality testing through trial and argument: more questions asked
- ❑ Improved practices or decisions: identification of added value possibilities, or problems that can be solved to add value
- ❑ Shaping of new ideas: opportunities for innovation and renewal
- ❑ Better informed, more knowledgeable key players
- ❑ Stronger consensus

Debates are discussion forums pitting two or more positions (and their advocates) against one another. There are a large number of tested debating tactics that we don't address here because our interest is how leaders can stage and facilitate debates, not win them. From the leader's perspective, debating has two primary objectives: improved intelligence and commitment to act. A well-managed debate should allow for a better, more complete examination of the subject debated. The result of the debate should be a stronger consensus around how to move forward, based on questions being answered, doubts removed, and benefits clarified. See Figure 10-2 for ten tasks that leaders can undertake to manage good debate.

Debates that are effectively resolved are often thought to be the product of compromise: incorporating different points of view,

Figure 10-2. Ways to manage good debate.

❏ *Level the playing field:* Don't pit higher ranking people against lower; keep the power balanced.

❏ *Remind everyone that the real winner of the debate must be the organization:* Redirect argument from people to task.

❏ *Create a positive, friendly, comfortable atmosphere:* It's a conversation among colleagues who want to develop solutions, not problems.

❏ *Assume an inquisitive, open stance:* Reinforce divergent, out-of-the-box thinking and risk taking.

❏ *Get agreement on procedural ground rules and expectations for participants, including items like these:*
  ○ Blaming and accusations are out of bounds.
  ○ All opinions are respected, as is the right to challenge them.
  ○ Participants must listen without interrupting.
  ○ Participants should paraphrase their opponents' input before responding to it.

❏ *Emphasize the importance of preparation:* Data, evidence, tested assumptions, etc. make for more convincing arguments.

❏ *Develop one or more debate* formats *that can work for you (e.g., polarity management):* Stick with them so that participants don't have to be concerned about remembering procedural rules and etiquette.

❏ *Use "collaborative media":* This can include flip charts, white boards, etc. that allow the group to keep subject and task continually in focus.

❏ *Translate one side's argument for the other:* Look for ways to combine, integrate points.

❏ *Make a point of socializing after a debate:* It's a critical ritual for reasserting bonds that may have been tested during the process.

blending ideas, etc. But as Richard Dawkins reminds us, "It's important to realize that when two opposite points of view are expressed with equal intensity, the truth does not necessarily lie exactly half way between them. It is possible for one side to be simply wrong."[13] That notwithstanding, debates in organizations are about the *organization,* and after the debate has ended, everyone needs to be on the "right" side. Organizational debates are rarely "winner-take-all" contests, because the losing side, if there is one, will need to join with the winners to carry forward with the action implications of the debate.

When a debate has reached closure or consensus, the leader should express gratitude to the group on behalf of the organization. He or she also needs to remind the group that tension and friction are normal byproducts of fully engaged debate, but that now is the time to close ranks again and move ahead with newly won decisions and resolutions.

This chapter on the leader as *provocateur* of disagreement, dissent, and conflict, along with the previous chapter on the leader as *critic,* sets the stage for the next communications role, that of *learning advocate,* which we address in chapter 11.

NOTES

1. Alfred Sloan, quoted in David Garvin and Michael Roberto, "What You Don't Know About Making Decisions," *Harvard Business Review* (September 2001), 115.
2. David N. Farr, speech delivered at the Dean's Breakfast, John Cook School of Business, St. Louis University (September 25, 2001).
3. Paul McKnight and George Cesaretti, interviewed by the author (October 12, 2001).
4. Ibid. All other quotes by McKnight and Cesaretti in this chapter are from this interview.
5. Farr speech (see note 2).
6. Ibid.
7. Daniel Yankelovich, *The Magic of Dialogue: Transforming Conflict Into Cooperation* (New York: Simon & Schuster, 1999), 107.
8. Kathleen M. Eisenhardt, Jean L. Kahwajy, and L. J. Bourgeois III, "How Management Teams Can Have a Good Fight," *Harvard Business Review* (July–August 1997), 79.
9. Sumantra Ghoshal and Christopher A. Bartlett, *The Individualized Corporation: A Fundamentally New Approach to Management* (New York: HarperBusiness, 1997), 122.
10. Reardon quoted in Jay A. Conger, "The Necessary Art of Persuasion," *Harvard Business Review* (May–June 1998), 87.
11. Yankelovich, *The Magic of Dialogue,* 82.
12. Barry Johnson, *Polarity Management: Identifying and Managing Unsolvable Problems* (New York: HRD Press, 1992), 66.
13. Richard Dawkins, quoted in Ian Parker, "Annals of Science: Richard Dawkins's Evolution," *New Yorker* (September 9, 1996), 41.

11

Learning Advocate

"To learn is to disorganize and increase variety. To organize is to forget and reduce variety."

—KARL E. WEICK AND FRANCES WESTLEY,
"ORGANIZATIONAL LEARNING:
AFFIRMING AN OXYMORON"

*A*ggressive, forward-looking organizations evolve to meet new situations and challenges. In recent years, we have come to call them "learning organizations," able to adapt to changing environments by rethinking or reinventing the rules for success. Much of the literature as well as the conventional wisdom about learning organizations emphasizes the role of the leader as champion of organizational change and renewal. What that role actually looks like—what behaviors you'd expect to see from such a leader—has not been so clearly delineated. Instead, it has been cloaked in metaphors or described as vaguely defined tasks like "systems thinking," "generative thinking," or "challenging mental models."

We intend to be more concrete about the tactics and behaviors used by leaders in the process of advocating organizational learning

and continuous improvement. We build directly on the two pre-
ceding chapters that describe the closely related communication
roles of *critic* and *provocateur*. And we examine how leaders in a variety of organizations manage the kind of dialogue that generates and
sustains continuous improvement thinking and action organization-
wide.

We start this discussion about leaders as *learning advocates* by focusing on an unusual leadership position. Called "process leader," it
functions within a successful continuous improvement project at
Cadillac. The role is described in a series of anecdotes as we follow
process leader Larry Bruozis in meetings and conversations with
dealership owners, department managers, and various others involved with customers at the stores. Over the course of several dealership visits, spanning two days, Bruozis demonstrates a wide range
of leadership communication strategies that stimulate and support
organizational learning in Cadillac dealerships.

LEARNING CONVERSATIONS AT CADILLAC

All through the 1990s, American vehicle manufacturers invested
heavily to raise levels of product and service quality. Cadillac insti-
tuted a sweeping continuous improvement initiative called Standards for Excellence (SFE). It involved an active collaboration
between Cadillac and its dealerships and led to a new dynamic
within the dealer organization that centered on Continuous Improvement Teams (CITs) of store employees. In concept, CITs
would convene ad hoc groups of employees around a specific problem to be solved. They would meet, discuss the problem, propose
solutions, and recommend their best ideas to dealer management.

Participating dealerships are supported by a cadre of specially
trained "process leaders," facilitator/coaches whose mission is to
work themselves out of a job. Each facilitator is assigned to work
with several dealerships, typically clustered in a major marketplace,
although in some cases spread over several states. As CITs become
more skilled at working together, team leadership transfers from the
facilitator to one or more local dealership people, called "site coordinators," who then run the meetings themselves.

Larry Bruozis was especially effective in helping CITs form and get started in a large Midwestern city. "At first," he had observed, "a CIT can seem like a bunch of high school kids sitting in detention. Everyone looks uncomfortable and wanting to be somewhere else. But later on, it's an awesome feeling to watch a CIT deliver recommendations to the leadership team, and the light bulb goes on for the dealer that those are his employees whom he's probably never seen in this way before."[1]

Our interest in Cadillac's initiative is how the facilitators and the local site coordinators, communicate with team members and how they create a climate of open, often argumentative, debate to support improvement at the dealership.

What follows are accounts of separate visits to three different dealerships and the communication tactics Bruozis and his local colleagues used to nurture conversation about improving business practices and rethinking the business.

Getting Comfortable with Sharing Responsibility

At the first CIT meeting in a new suburban store, participants had included the owner, most of the leadership team, and balanced representation from all dealership functions. Early on, some members of the leadership team had sounded skeptical. The service manager had shrugged off some early CIT recommendations ("We're already doing that") and even questioned the need for CIT teams ("That's *our* job"). The owner had also just brought on a young, rather brash general manager, and others in the group were unsure about how to deal with him. Most participants seemed afraid to contribute and said little.

The site coordinator, a woman, was the assistant leasing manager and had wanted to lead today's meeting herself. She believed women should assert more leadership in dealerships, particularly because most car buyers today are women. She was somewhat uncertain about how to handle the new general manager in the meeting. Before the session, Bruozis let her talk out her meeting strategy, which was to be direct, even confrontational, so as to clear the air and establish workable team ground rules.

The meeting rooms in Cadillac stores are usually found somewhere in the store's interior. They typically contain a long table with chairs, and most act as an impromptu storeroom as well. This leads to ritual table clearing and furniture moving before a meeting can be started. At this store, the site coordinator transformed the meeting room by covering the table with a bright, flowery table-cloth. Chairs were set in the round, up against the walls. Behind the site coordinator's seat was a whiteboard. Next to it, taped to the wall, was a flow chart of the service repair process. On an adjacent wall were four status charts, each tracking the trend lines for one of the customer satisfaction index reporting categories. Further props included trays of sandwiches and a strawberry shortcake (the owner helped himself to two pieces, so this move by the site coordinator was obviously good strategy).

The meeting was well attended and included the owner, the general manager, the service manager, the parts manager, the dealer prep manager, and a service consultant. The CIT's focus was the issue of "fixed right the first time." Early in the discussion, Bruozis acknowledged that in the first stages of the SFE initiative, most dealerships went for low-hanging fruit, with little risk and modest impact. Now, "fixed right the first time" called for "the ladder to get placed higher up the tree."

The group chose to zero in on how best to deal with customers whose expectations for timely repair work can't be met. Typically, the repairs on about three of every four cars are completed within the specified time. But with some cars, additional problems might show up during the repair work that could require ordering special parts or extended repair work. Owners who cannot be reached by phone to be alerted about repair delays are often unpleasantly sur-prised when they show up to retrieve their car, expecting it to be fixed and ready to go.

The challenge was how to effectively communicate these dis-coveries to owners so as to reduce the inconvenience and the disap-pointment (which sometimes led to angry complaints). Much of the group's discussion centered on the difficulty of reaching customers by phone to tell them a part had to be ordered or to explain other delays.

Recommendations ranged from preventive actions to concilia-tory tactics to a relationship-building gesture. The owner, a veteran in his late sixties, showed a flair for being up-to-date with a sugges-tion that the technicians fax their delay communication to the customers at their place of work. (Earlier, he had explained to the team, with some humor, that he was a *working* owner, not just a member of the "Lucky Sperm Club," an allusion to the tendency for dealerships to be handed down from one generation to the next.)

The service consultant suggested affixing a note to the repair order explaining the reasons for any delays, with an apology and a recommended course of action. A third suggestion involved a call to the customer sometime after the service work had all been done to see if the vehicle was operating satisfactorily.

After the meeting, the facilitator observed that although it was hardly ideal to have the CIT meeting so stacked with management, there was at least one strong positive consequence: When the owner and the general manger sit in on a session, they learn about process at a level of detail that might normally escape them. Furthermore, the owner's willingness to laugh at himself (although indirectly) helped pave the way for more active participation by other team members.

Problems Are About Process, Not People

Now to a second dealership. This Cadillac store was a longtime fixture on a busy commercial street in an old city neighborhood. The dealership was in its third year of SFE participation and had become adept at managing a productive dialogue about continuous improvement. Bruozis commented that "in looking at problems, the leadership team at first wanted to find people to blame. Now, they're more likely to see problems as being about process." Another good indicator of leadership's maturity was that after several leadership meetings attended by the facilitator, one manager had said to the facilitator, "You know, we need to talk about these meetings *outside* the meetings—they need to spill over into the way we do business, and everyone needs to hear about it."

Bruozis's agenda for the leadership team that day was to do a reckoning of "where we are in the SFE process." It was also an occasion to use a diagnostic tool that helps leadership teams assess their progress in building a climate for continuous improvement. "We're going to do a status check on the entire dealership," announced Bruozis, "to see how far SFE has penetrated the store."

The diagnostic tool, a matrix-like survey, asked users to pinpoint where they thought the dealership stood in five categories: process improvement, employee involvement, employee enthusiasm, improved capability, and customer focus. The team stayed with the exercise, with occasional disagreements over what stage the store was in on a specific item. These were often resolved by noting that differing perceptions reflected differences in how each department in the dealership had embraced the idea of continuous improvement. The entire store didn't necessarily advance uniformly across all the categories.

Another discussion focused on a new car launch and whether the leadership team would want to regard this event as a continuous improvement opportunity, and, by extension, should a new CIT be set up to examine how a different kind of product might warrant different ways of doing business. The service manager had strong feelings on this subject: "I'm against treating customers for this car any differently from the way I treat any of my other customers. Service is service, and just because this is a new product with a different pedigree, that doesn't mean I should treat these customers any better than I do the others."

The discussion brought out other concerns, most notably that Cadillac's requirements for becoming a dealer for the new vehicle were potentially disruptive and intrusive. One of these requirements was participation in SFE, including broad and active participation on CITs. A supervisor expressed skepticism about how much the service culture in the "back of the store" could accommodate new job expectations. "Techs are here for their paychecks, and that's all," he said. "When I've trained mechanics for years to stay on the line and turn wrenches and make money, and then I tell them to take time off to go to a meeting, they're going to have a problem with that."

The service manager admitted that he shared this concern. But subsequent discussion about the advantages of bringing out a dramatically different car to capture a new customer segment for Cadillac presented some grounds for seeking compromise. Eventually, the service manager agreed that they all would need to learn more about the expectations of a new and different Cadillac customer.

Solutions Are Where You Find Them

The third dealership was located in an older "borderline" neighborhood and was described as "landlocked," with no room to expand either its physical size or its market. It had a less affluent and older (by Cadillac standards) customer base. But despite these constraints, the store enjoyed an extremely impressive share of the luxury car market in its area.

When Bruozis arrived, he found that a scheduled leadership team meeting had been canceled. Bruozis chatted briefly with the site coordinator, a young woman who served as the store's comptroller. The problem the store wanted to address, related to the "fixed right the first time" theme, was peculiar to this dealership's clientele and its somewhat unusual setting.

Wednesdays and Fridays are days when service discounts are offered to senior citizens. This was a very successful promotion. Every Wednesday and Friday, the waiting room was crammed with seniors who brought their cars in for servicing and who chose to wait for them. Apparently, these customers, with time on their hands and not a whole lot of attractions in the neighborhood (there were no shopping malls, movie houses, or other diversions nearby), would rather hang out at the Cadillac store, with its opportunity to socialize in the comfortable waiting area.

The problem was that much of the waiting area conversation focused quite naturally on "things that went wrong with Cadillacs." Discussion can tend to accentuate the negative, serving to reinforce any existing dissatisfaction and even create some that didn't exist before. The CIT's thinking so far had concluded that the two most obvious recourses, reducing the wait time or offering to transport seniors to nearby destinations, were both impractical. The site coordinator felt that the CIT was in a rut.

Sometimes the SFE facilitator has to act as more than a facilitator, and this was such a time. Bruozis wondered aloud in the presence of the site coordinator and another team member whether they might create a different set of activities while customers waited, so they would be less likely to dwell on their car troubles. He suggested that possibly a local hospital might be interested in bringing in some routine, preventive diagnostic services (blood pressure tests, for example). Or maybe there might be some senior-oriented activities provided by a social service agency that could be made available at the dealership.

The site coordinator and her CIT colleague didn't jump at these ideas. But Bruozis suggested they might at least call some area hospitals to inquire about possibilities. He left the room with the expectation that this assignment might be carried forward.

Next stop was the owner's office. He was clearly pleased to see Bruozis, who had become a willing sounding board for the owner's issues and concerns. But today, the owner wanted to share his enthusiasm for his youngest and newest salesperson, and the only woman on the sales staff. This was her first job selling cars; she was formerly and unhappily a service writer at a Chevy dealership, where her husband still worked as a technician. She decided to try her hand at selling cars because she liked working with people and because she lived only eight minutes from the Cadillac store.

At thirty-one years old, the woman had already set all kinds of sales records for the dealership and was building a head of steam to start selling the soon-to-be-launched new car model. She had brought a different sales personality to the showroom, and her prospecting and follow-up tactics were energetic and innovative. Predictably, she targeted female buyers but also had a following with males who were impressed by her thoughtfulness as well as her automotive knowledge. Recently, the city had been laid low by a heat wave, and she had thought to inquire after the welfare of her older clients and prospects with a series of calls. This solicitude generated a lot of good feeling and several car sales.

Bruozis shifted the conversation to the new vehicle and suggested that it would be great if the owner formed a CIT to look into how to optimize the forthcoming launch. Maybe he could ask his star salesperson to head the team (the owner liked this idea). Bruozis also mentioned that the site coordinator was thinking about addressing the waiting room problem with a novel solution involving some onsite diagnostic health services, and that it sounded like it might be worth supporting. The owner liked that idea too, and Bruozis would use this later.

Next, Bruozis headed to the star salesperson's office, where they talked about how she liked her job now that she had become so successful, and the strategies she was using to build customer loyalty.

When Bruozis asked her about the new vehicle launch, she told him that she had a plan to hold a kind of "shower" when the car arrived at the dealership, to which she would invite as many women as she could. Bruozis asked if he could be invited to the shower. He also told her about his idea about forming a CIT to focus on the new car and suggested that she might be able to provide great leadership here.

On his way out of the store, Bruozis passed the site coordinator's office, stuck his head in the door, and mentioned the owner's "endorsement" of the waiting area idea: "He seemed excited about it. I'll call next week to see how it's coming along." And he did, too. By planting seeds, then inviting others to tend the garden (and reap the fruits), Bruozis combined thought leadership with cajolery and follow-through that made his role as a learning advocate especially effective.

LEARNING ADVOCATES PUSH AND PULL

> *"And so, in the last forty years, we have learned that work on improving any job or task begins with the people who actually do the work. They must be asked: 'What can we learn from you? What do you have to tell us about the job and how it should be done?'"*
>
> —PETER DRUCKER, *POST-CAPITALIST SOCIETY*

It's not so easy for leaders to get people to tell what they know and articulate their ideas for doing things better. Larry Bruozis spent much of his time teasing ideas out of people and then spreading them around so they'd be noticed. He amplified the voices of many people who wouldn't normally be heard and so extended the reach and scope of a conversation that helped people in Cadillac dealerships engineer change. He saw his role as both advocate and facilitator of learning and knowledge creation at Cadillac. He spoke with top leadership and with people who punched a clock and got them talking with, and listening to, one another. The communication tactics he used to spark and give shape to these conversations are described in Figure 11-1.

Bruozis's communications were both calculated and spontaneous. He laid plans for bringing certain individuals into larger conversations, and he seized opportunities as he found them to advance important messages and ideas. He connected people with different perspectives and helped them integrate what they knew for the common good. He worked to simplify issues so that they would be more accessible to discussion, especially by members of the cross-functional CITs.

But he also created more "complexity," as Rosabeth Moss Kanter describes it: "more relationships, more sources of information, more angles on the problem, more ways to pull in human and material resources, more freedom to walk around and across the organization."[2] By calling for "looser boundaries, crosscutting access, flexible assignments, open communications, and use of multidisciplinary project teams,"[3] Bruozis and Cadillac became successful advocates for organizational learning across the organization.

Getting People to Talk

Much of the expertise in organizations lives forever in the heads of individuals who don't feel comfortable or able to express that ex-

Figure 11-1. Communication tactics for continuous improvement conversations.

- ❐ *Telling stories*—about what different people in the organization are thinking about and doing
- ❐ *Seeding ideas* (and watering them too) that end up being owned and cultivated by others
- ❐ *Using questions and surveys* to pull out opinions, check status
- ❐ *Creating platforms* for those who might not be noticed or listened to
- ❐ *Encouraging underheard voices* to bring their ideas forward
- ❐ *Consulting on good meeting communication tactics* so that the discussion might become more productive and satisfying for participants
- ❐ *Acting as a gadfly* to stimulate thinking, advocate positions in different parts of the organization
- ❐ *Moving ideas around the organization*—brokering solutions and improvement suggestions
- ❐ *Recognizing and reinforcing initiative takers*—and those almost ready to take a step

pertise in words and therefore don't share it with anyone else. Many employees have ideas about how to improve products, services, work processes, and more, but they lack the confidence or the occasion to speak out. The flip side of this situation is that many equally reticent employees hold on stubbornly to outmoded ideas. Because they don't readily articulate their biases and beliefs, it's not so easy to sell them on better alternatives.

Growth and change require broad participation by as many organizational members as possible. Organizational learning is largely a social affair, with many conversations occurring among many people that give shape to new and different ways of doing things. Those close to the action, who deal directly with customers or who manufacture or service the product, are especially important participants in any dialogue about improvement and change. It is critical then for leaders to bring their people into such conversations and to manage them well.

Talking Shop

Perhaps the most challenging conversation to spark is the one with employees who aren't normally asked to speak their minds about improving work practices. Over the past twenty years, many organizations have held discussions around the subject of *best practices,* the most exemplary and effective ways of getting work done. As Donald Schon has argued (speaking about professional work practices), "We should start not by asking how to make better use of research-based knowledge but by asking what we can learn from a careful examination of artistry, that is, the competence by which practitioners actually handle indeterminate zones of practice," solving problems and creating shortcuts that fit their particular work situations.[4]

The purpose of most best practice discussions is first to bring descriptions of exemplary practices forward so they can be shared. Some organizations go further, collecting and codifying effective solutions to problems for wide use across the organization. Web sites and intranets have become the storage depot for many of these items.

The danger here is that the identification of better alternatives can lead to the creation of new orthodoxies and new rigidity. While spreading successful work practices, even standardizing them in some cases, has clear advantages, we must keep in mind that today's standards are tomorrow's constraints. Best practice discussions need to be continuous. Dynamic organizations never stop searching for better ways to work, and their leaders never cease their questioning, nor their advocacy for continuous improvement. And, as we'll see later in the section Communities of Practice, systematically gathering and storing best practice ideas in an accessible computer file ignores the vitality and richness of face-to-face, spontaneous conversations that contribute *ongoing* improvement ideas in real time.

How can you conduct or sponsor such exploratory conversations about work practice so as to create ongoing growth and improvement? At Saturn, this question came up in the context of the company's early successes in designing a new buying experience for car shoppers.[5] At a series of facilitated meetings, Saturn people from the most successful stores were asked to talk about what they were doing that was creating such high levels of customer satisfaction.

Meeting leaders found that at first participants tended to avoid specificity and behavioral description: "We just make the customer feel at home," or "We try to be friendly" were typical responses to questions about method and technique. For the meetings to be productive, leaders needed to know what was actually done to "make customers feel at home" and how sales team members actually communicated "friendliness." The meeting leaders eventually settled on a discussion routine that had participants describing their work tactics in a two-part statement, using an "I . . . by . . ." formula: "*I* make customers feel at home *by* offering them a cup of coffee or a soft drink." Once participants got into the rhythm of this routine, a lot of rich description flowed into the conversation, and participants were cued by one another to build on ideas or to offer alternatives.

Interestingly, participants said afterward that what they most profited from was the thinking they were prompted to do as they listened to others (and themselves!) describe their work. "How can I know what I think until I see what I say?"—Karl Weick's question about sense making in organizations[6]—applies to learning and continuous improvement, too.

MAKING THE TACIT EXPLICIT: SHARING
WHAT YOU KNOW WITH OTHERS

In 1966, philosopher Michael Polanyi introduced the now well-known concept of "tacit knowledge" and the notion that "we can know more than we can tell."[7] Some thirty years later, management theorists Ikujiro Nonaka and Hirotaka Takeuchi suggested that a useful strategy for creating organizational knowledge is to help make tacit knowledge become more explicit. "Organizational knowledge creation," they argued, "should be understood as a process that 'organizationally' amplifies the knowledge created by individuals and crystallizes it at the group level through dialogue, discussion, experience sharing, or observation."[8]

Seen in this light, organizational knowledge creation becomes largely a communications issue. Key to transforming tacit knowledge into organizational knowledge is how effectively leaders sponsor active dialogue, discussion, and experience sharing among their people. As fans of the St. Louis Cardinals baseball club, we're known to read the sports pages occasionally (but for no more than half an hour a day). Here are two examples of experience sharing between players that led to improved performance, both individually and organizationally.

The Cardinals' pitching staff had been decimated by several injuries and even a death to their cadre of starting pitchers. In desperation, since they were still in a pennant race, they acquired the thirty-nine-year-old veteran Chuck Finley, a pitcher whom sports journalists liked to say was laboring in the "twilight of his career." In a second move, the Cardinals reactivated Andy Benes, another veteran pitcher. Benes had earlier in the season announced his retirement from baseball (he changed his mind later) because of nagging injuries, including a lack of cartilage in his knee. Luck, however, was shining on the Cardinals. Finley turned out to have some gas left in his tank and pitched well over the rest of the season. But perhaps his most significant contribution was assisting Benes to develop a new pitch that helped the latter, gimpy knee and all, revive his career (at least briefly) and shore up a decidedly makeshift pitching staff.

Benes had seen his effectiveness decline over the past years, largely because he had lost velocity on his fastball and had no great variety in his other pitches. While on the bench, Benes noticed how Finley was able to get hitters out with an unusual pitch called a "split-fingered fastball," which actually came in slower to hitters, with a dramatic downward movement. "He showed me how he held it while we were playing around in the bullpen," Benes said. "I started throwing it, and pretty soon started developing confidence in it."[9] Over the next few weeks, the conversation continued on the bench and in the bullpen, with the result that Benes now had a pitch that was effective in itself, and helped his fastball seem faster as well.

In the second instance, about a month later, the Cardinals bolstered their hitting by trading for another player, Scott Rolen of the Philadelphia Phillies. And as with the earlier personnel change, the Cardinals reaped some extra benefit with this addition, too. Tino Martinez, their first baseman since the beginning of the year, had up to now endured one of his worst seasons in the major leagues. But watching and talking with Rolen as he moved into the Cardinals' lineup, Martinez was able to make some key adjustments to his hitting. Rolen, a big man, took a very compact, controlled swing at pitches rather than "swinging from the heels" to try for home runs. Duly inspired, Martinez shortened his own swing, described by a sportswriter as "an unwieldy hack." "'I was trying to drive the ball out of the park all the time instead of becoming a hitter,' Martinez said. 'It's really helped me since we got Rolen.'"[10]

Sitting around in dugouts is obviously a favorable situation for talking shop, but ballplayers, like any other workers, are also, to some extent, in competition with one another and not necessarily prone to giving away trade secrets. But on this team, management has apparently created an atmosphere in which workers are encouraged to learn from one another. In particular, the arrival of new employees had become an occasion to actively share craft knowledge and how-to tips such that other players were able to expand their skills and improve performance. It remains to be seen whether Finley will teach his split-fingered pitch to everyone on the staff, or if Rolen's technique will be adopted by other hitters. The point is, however, that individual exchanges can lead to more than some isolated individual learning events: They can change the performance of anyone who wants to get in the conversation and listen.

If you seek to be an advocate of learning and continuous improvement, you need to target all employees as potential knowledge creators, in particular those who know how the work gets done but don't often get to tell about it. You need to create opportunities for tacit knowledge to emerge in conversation so that it can be more broadly exposed and "amplified." To accomplish this, you must first make it clear to your organization how important this process is, how valuable employees' individual know-how and knowledge are to the rest of the organization. The following *message points* may help set this stage:

❐ People with customer knowledge and practical know-how can help the organization work smarter, and be more effective.

❐ An organization's success is based on its collective intelligence, and its ability to tap into the minds of all its people.

❐ Sharing your ideas and solutions to problems is a highly valued behavior and will be duly recognized and rewarded.

You can draw out employee thinking through a variety of leading questions and conversation prompts (see Figure 11-2). Midlevel and frontline leaders are especially well positioned to make this kind of conversation happen. They can help surface and circulate (or translate) practical know-how that might warrant broader application. They can also help employees better understand the potential for new ideas by clearly framing work practice within business goals and priorities. Frontline and middle managers can make sure that shoptalk and craft knowledge have a place in regular meeting agendas. By regularly prompting such discussion with questions about improvement opportunities ("What's not working well? How could we fix it?"), leaders reinforce the importance of sharing work experience as a key to organizational success.

FORUMS FOR ADVANCING KNOWLEDGE AND LEARNING

In chapter 8, we questioned the tendency of staff meetings to be dominated by leaders presenting information, instead of active participant dialogue. Staff meetings are among the best occasions to

Figure 11-2. Tactics to elicit employee thinking.

❏ *Challenge employees to scrutinize current routines and practices:* "Why are we doing it that way? How could we get better results?"

❏ *Incorporate performance data into meeting conversations:* "What does the data tell us about performance trends, opportunities for alternative approaches?"

❏ *Ask work teams (or even partners) to control part of a meeting agenda dealing with a specific aspect of work practice:* "How effective are we? What might we consider doing differently?"

❏ *Use process maps to draw out and cue dialogue:* "Given this (graphic) account of how the work gets done, is this the way it really happens?" (Is the map accurate, or is it a figment of management's imagination?)

❏ *Use narrative (storytelling) to describe how we do things now and ask people to build on or fill in:* "What happens next? How does this job get done?"

❏ *Regularly punctuate conversations about work practice with versions of the questions:* "Why do we do it that way? Are these the behaviors necessary to do the right things right?"

❏ *Ask employees to raise their own questions about process, without feeling responsible for having an answer:* "What areas do you think we might want to look at? What questions does our present approach raise in your minds?"

❏ *When employees speak up, recognize them publicly in some way, written or otherwise:* "We owe these people a round of applause for opening some new doors for us."

hold substantive conversations about work performance and performance improvement. Such conversations can be organized around leader-provided discussion questions like those listed in Figure 11-2. Or, they can be led by employees themselves, as in this account of an ambitious, planned series of school staff meetings in a school district.

The Staff Meeting as a Professional Development Session

Staff meetings hold great potential for learning conversations. In a suburban Denver district, every school schedules two hours per week for "professional learning," time that used to be budgeted for more traditional staff meetings. One school has set up a rotating schedule of four differently focused professional development sessions. The principal has asked that she be allowed thirty minutes at the staff meetings every other week, but only if something comes up. Her allotted time still follows the planned agenda for the day.

The first day in the rotation typically involves outside experts addressing specific learning topics. At the second session, teachers meet in grade-level teams to discuss applications of ideas explored in the previous week's meeting. During the third week, teachers meet in self-selected study teams of three to four to address specific teaching topics of interest to them. At the fourth week's session, teachers meet with colleagues in other grades to discuss examples of student work and how to improve curriculum and instruction at the school.[11]

Besides staff meetings, leaders can create or support other forums to explore improvement opportunities. On the more formal side, Cadillac's CIT meetings or GE's Crotonville Workout sessions focus participants on specific discussion topics or questions that can have far-reaching consequences for organizational learning. Cadillac dealers initially saw the SFE initiative as a way to identify operations problems and develop fixes. But over time, the leadership teams realized their entire operation could be seen as an integrated process and needed to be addressed as such. One service manager noted that *process* was initially the cause of a 41 percent comeback rate (vehicles returned for additional service), which after the initiative improved to 17 percent.[12]

Cross-functional teams like Cadillac's CITs make for richer, more insightful discussion. Development project teams are another way to foster more integrative conversations about the organization and its work. Nonaka and Takeuchi suggest that organizations need to "build a high-density field of interaction at the front line," where "tacit knowledge is converted into explicit knowledge" through lively conversations involving various work perspectives.[13]

Taking the Learning Conversation Outside

Participants in these conversations are typically all employed by the same organization, but learning can be equally well advanced through discussions with outsiders as well. In chapter 8, where the leader was examined as *linking agent,* we described several potential contributors to organizational learning, including an organization's customers. Wendy's Restaurants went so far as to use customers as continuous improvement consultants.

Wendy's, like its competition, regularly surveys its customers for their opinions about products and services. But Wendy's leadership decided customers could provide something more: advice on how the restaurant experience could change so as to provide even greater satisfaction and value. Accordingly, Wendy's convened group discussions with customers around this question: "Imagine you're part of a family who had just inherited a fast food chain. How might you make the business better able to serve customers?" To add perspective, Wendy's also asked separate groups of store employees and headquarters staff to address the same question.

The facilitated discussions first produced a lot of ideas. The groups then reviewed the ideas and established priorities. End products included a variety of valuable insights regarding customer preferences and practical suggestions for improvement in areas ranging from food preparation, customer handling, and ergonomics, to how to keep customers entertained while they waited for their order. Wendy's had staged an unprecedented conversation with customers and other stakeholders that brought new value to store operations.[14]

Communities of Practice

Communities of practice are groups of people with similar or related work responsibilities who come together on their own, and whose conversation supports a special kind of peer learning and knowledge creation. The teaching staff discussed above is a good example. Another is the group of Xerox customer service reps who met for breakfast, mentioned at the end of chapter 8.

Communities of practice are largely self-directed and identify their own "leadership" from within. They can meet and converse in scheduled, more formal sessions or, as is more frequent, informally and spontaneously. Our interest in communities of practice lies in the ways organizational leaders can make it easy for these communities to pursue and be productive with continuous improvement and learning and development agendas.

In one sense, we're back to the water cooler phenomenon and the need to create places and environments where colleagues can bump into one another and talk. A study of Corning engineers, conducted by researchers at MIT, found that "80 percent of their ideas arose from face-to-face contacts, but the engineers typically were unwilling to walk more than 100 feet from their desks. Corning responded by equipping a new building with a dozen discussion areas, with coffee machines and blackboards, as well as open stairs, escalators and ramps."[15]

Sigma-Aldrich, a supplier to research labs, recently opened a new R&D center designed "to bring scientists together, inside and outside their laboratories." ("It's amazing how much in science happens by random interactions," says the company's R&D director.)[16] The center features different kinds of gathering places, including coffee bars on each floor and a reading room on the main floor. Architectural designs aside, organizational leaders can support water cooler conversation in several ways (see Figure 11-3).

In preparing this chapter and the next, we've made a somewhat artificial distinction between communication that supports learning and continuous improvement and communication that fosters more

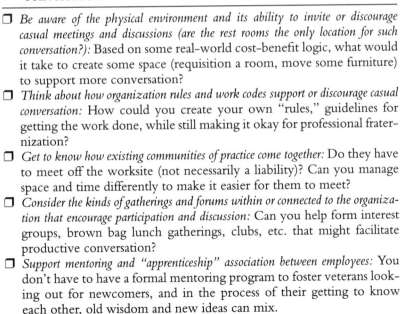

Figure 11-3. Tactics for inviting more water cooler conversation.

❏ *Be aware of the physical environment and its ability to invite or discourage casual meetings and discussions (are the rest rooms the only location for such conversation?):* Based on some real-world cost-benefit logic, what would it take to create some space (requisition a room, move some furniture) to support more conversation?

❏ *Think about how organization rules and work codes support or discourage casual conversation:* How could you create your own "rules," guidelines for getting the work done, while still making it okay for professional fraternization?

❏ *Get to know how existing communities of practice come together:* Do they have to meet off the worksite (not necessarily a liability)? Can you manage space and time differently to make it easier for them to meet?

❏ *Consider the kinds of gatherings and forums within or connected to the organization that encourage participation and discussion:* Can you help form interest groups, brown bag lunch gatherings, clubs, etc. that might facilitate productive conversation?

❏ *Support mentoring and "apprenticeship" association between employees:* You don't have to have a formal mentoring program to foster veterans looking out for newcomers, and in the process of their getting to know each other, old wisdom and new ideas can mix.

fundamental change and innovation. In one sense, the difference is only a matter of degree. But different communication strategies drive each of these endeavors at organizational renewal, so in chapter 12 we describe still another role for leadership communication: the leader as innovation coach.

NOTES

1. Larry Bruozis, interviewed by Robert Mai (July 31–August 1, 1996). All quotes by Bruozis are from this two-day observation and interview.
2. Rosabeth Moss Kanter, *The Change Masters: Innovation for Productivity in the American Corporation* (New York: Simon & Schuster, 1983), 148.
3. Ibid.
4. Donald A. Schon, *Educating the Reflective Practitioner: Toward a New Design for Teaching and Learning in the Professions* (San Francisco: Jossey-Bass, 1987), 13.
5. See Robert Mai, "How Communication Can Foster the Learning Organization," *Strategic Communication Management* (June–July 1998), 24.
6. Karl E. Weick, *The Social Psychology of Organizing,* 2nd ed. (New York: McGraw-Hill, 1979), 165.
7. Michael Polanyi, *The Tacit Dimension* (Garden City, N.Y.: Doubleday, 1966), 4.
8. Ikujiro Nonaka and Hirotaka Takeuchi, *The Knowledge-Creating Company* (New York: Oxford University Press, 1995), 239.
9. Joe Straus, "Credit Should Be Split for Benes' Revival," *St. Louis Post-Dispatch* (August 18, 2002), C9.
10. Straus, "6-Run 9th Extends Cards' Streak," *St. Louis Post-Dispatch* (August 16, 2002), B1.
11. Joan Richardson, "Meeting Expectations: Turn Staff Gatherings Into Learning Opportunities," *Tools for Schools* [National Staff Development Council newsletter] (December 2001–January 2002), 2.
12. Larry Bruozis interview.
13. Nonaka and Takeuchi, *The Knowledge-Creating Company,* 230–31.
14. Robert Mai, *Learning Partnerships: How Leading American Companies Implement Organizational Learning* (Chicago: Irwin/ASTD, 1996), 82–83.
15. Fred Andrews, "Learning to Celebrate Water Cooler Gossip," *New York Times,* Sunday Business Section (February 25, 2001), 6.
16. Virginia B. Gilbert, "Sigma-Aldrich Laces Technology Center With Better-Way Features," *St. Louis Post-Dispatch* (December 9, 2001), F1, 8.

12

Innovation Coach

> *"It is this ensemble of problem framing, on-the-spot experiment, detection of consequences and implications, back talk and response to back talk, that constitutes a reflective conversation. . . ."*
>
> DONALD SCHON, *EDUCATING THE REFLECTIVE PRACTITIONER*

O rganizational renewal is about evolution, adapting to new situations, taking advantage of new opportunities, and becoming a new and different organization in the process. Over the past decade or so, management literature has championed organizational renewal ("reinventing ourselves") as a critical survival strategy for sustained success. But despite all of the compelling stories of new product development, "skunk works," and "incubators" that appear on business bookshelves, it remains difficult for most leaders to put wheels on the concept of renewal and innovation. We see the challenge for leaders to be one of communicating the importance of innovation and renewal and creating conditions that allow their organization to learn and to change.

HOW BIRDS DO IT

Former Shell executive Arie de Geus suggests that the question "How does an organization—as distinct from an individual—learn?" might be addressed by looking at birds. Citing the work of biochemist Allan Wilson, de Geus offers the hypothesis that organizations can improve their ability to exploit opportunities in the environment if they are able, like certain species of birds, to demonstrate these three performance "characteristics:

> 1. *Innovation.* Either as individuals or as a community, the species has the capacity (or at least the potential) to invent new behavior. They can develop skills that allow them to exploit their environment in new ways.
> 2. *Social Propagation.* There is an established process for transmission of a skill from the individual to the community as a whole, not genetically, but somehow through direct communication.
> 3. *Mobility.* The individuals of the species have the ability to move around, and (more importantly) they actually use it! They flock or move in herds, rather than sitting in isolated territories."[1]

As metaphors go, this one about bird behavior provides valuable and usable insights. As we examine how leadership communication nurtures adaptation and innovation, we organize our approach around the three conditions for species learning:

1. *Innovation:* Challenging creative people to be inventive, both inside and outside "the box"
2. *Sharing:* Establishing and managing the communication channels for good ideas to be adopted by others and institutionalized by the organization

3. *Socializing:* Creating *flocking* opportunities and a climate that sponsors active dialogue about ideas

"INNOVATION": PAVING THE WAY FOR IDEAS

> *"How then to invent a form which provokes discovery?"*
> —RICHARD SENNETT, *THE CONSCIENCE OF THE EYE*

New possibilities emerge in organizations when individuals reshuffle old ideas or combine them with new ones. We like to tell stories about how acts of invention, like the famous account of how Post-it® Notes were conceived, are really the result of very bright (and sometimes strange) people tinkering or experimenting until they experience a dramatic breakthrough. More often, breakthrough ideas are the result of cumulative work by individuals and teams over time. In either case, an organization's leadership can be instrumental in sponsoring successful innovation at four levels:

1. Communicating the importance of, and the contexts for, problem solving and innovation
2. Creating conditions within the organization for creativity to flourish
3. Inviting people with potential to develop new possibilities to tinker, experiment, and explore
4. Actively facilitating knowledge creation and idea generation processes

We examine these activities as four important leadership communication agendas. First, however, we want to discuss several barriers to these agendas. They're actually communication habits leaders fall into that can block new ideas and knowledge that bubble up from talented people in the organization.

Bad Habits

Leaders may themselves go through a protracted thought process, involving considerable research and discussion, before arriving at a solution to a problem or a new course of action. But what they share with their people may be a highly compressed version of their thinking. They assume that others don't need to know about the logic they used, or that people can shortcut the learning process they went through and fully understand (and accept) the end product of that process.

This habit is typically a consequence of time factors: Leaders have already "done the thinking," and now they're in a rush to move ahead with implementation. But withholding critical information can undermine the ability of colleagues to offer feedback, critique, elaboration, or expansion. If they're not privy to the steps in the logic chain, or they simply don't understand the ideas well enough, they can't add value.

Related to the first bad habit is a more general one of leaders seeing themselves as the primary solvers of problems and generators of ideas. Many leaders got where they are today because they were adept at solving problems. It's not just a habit; it's who they are. In some situations, this identity becomes an unspoken compact with their people: "Leave the thinking to us and you'll have one less thing to worry about." While such a compact might be a comfort for both sides, it's clearly not in the interests of any organization that values knowledge creation to reduce the number of people who *think* on its behalf. On the contrary, it reinforces rigid dependency relationships, limits perspective, and compromises organizational creativity.

The leader as lone problem solver, or as new-idea hero, is a recipe for intellectual stagnation and lowered organizational morale. Unfortunately, many leaders are sucked into this identity because of another temptation: to be regarded as *the* person responsible for planning (like the CEO in our chapter 1 fable). When planning is the exclusive province of a few organizational leaders, it risks becoming an exercise based on the *illusion of control* over events and forces.

Effective planning requires a range of input and collaboration. It's more likely to occur opportunistically, apropos new market data or competitive intelligence, or an intimation of how a new technology might be harnessed to the organization's advantage. It's linked to leader conversations that continually monitor and share thoughts with others about what's happening and how to define or redefine future opportunity.

Coaching for Knowledge Creation

Because you aren't the only idea person in the organization, you need to see yourself as a *coach* of a broadly shared responsibility for problem solving and idea generation. Your challenge is to *communicate as a coach* and help others communicate effectively as co-owners of the knowledge creation process.

Donald Schon describes the challenge this way: "The coach works at creating and sustaining a process of collaborative inquiry. Paradoxically, the more he knows about the problem, the harder it is for him to do this. He must resist the temptation to tell . . . [an employee] how to solve the problem or solve it for her, but he must not pretend to know less than he does, for by deceiving her, he risks undermining her commitment to their collaborative venture."[2]

This challenge takes shape around several communication agendas, each of which places the leader in a coaching role that supports employees as creators of new knowledge the organization can use.

Agenda 1: Establishing Context and Direction

"Leaders need to spend more time framing the environment that allows more strategic initiative and debate to emerge from below."

ANDY GROVE, IN GHOSHAL AND BARTLETT, *THE INDIVIDUALIZED CORPORATION*

By making your team more aware of context, you can also communicate why the problem needs to be tackled in the first place, along with any sense of urgency that may apply. Peter Drucker has suggested that one of the first communication requirements for leaders "to raise the yield of existing knowledge (whether for an individual, for a team, or for the entire organization) is *problem definition*—even more urgently perhaps than . . . the currently fashionable methodology for 'problem solving.' "[3] Richard Pascale adds that defining a problem is about setting a context, so a critical leadership competency is "perceiving, articulating, and exploiting the changes in context . . ."—keeping people up-to-date on the state of the environment and current priorities.[4]

Communicating context for the goals and actions of an organization and its people was a topic of the discussion on meaning-making in chapter 3. One of the key tasks for leaders as meaning-makers is "framing": building a context that gives special meaning to the work. By extension, framing communications can also focus on problems to be solved or areas in which newly developed knowledge could lead to organizational advantage.

When a leader like Emerson's David Farr discusses global market projections and priorities for investing corporate resources, he also signals opportunity targets for business unit leadership to pick up on and incorporate into its planning. His expectation is that business unit leaders will carry this thinking forward and work up their own creative strategies to capture business advantage.

Establishing context is an ongoing communication function, because context must be continually redefined. Sometimes the context that gets redefined is a larger one, the reigning business paradigm or "theory of business." More often it's a redefinition of a work process, a customer requirement, or a technology application. The contexts within which new organizational thinking is focused and creative energies are deployed are the product of continual framing conversations that leaders have with various colleagues. These conversations are driven by questions as well as explanations, but they always seek to create a kind of scaffolding on which employees can stand somewhat apart from actual work and gain useful perspective.

Agenda 2: Creating a Push for Creativity

"The most gifted members of the human species are at their creative best when they cannot have their way."

—ERIC HOFFER, IN PASCALE, *MANAGING ON THE EDGE*

Composer Igor Stravinsky once offered this insight on his creative process: "My freedom will be so much the greater and more meaningful, the more narrow my field of action and the more I surround myself with obstacles. Whatever diminishes constraints, diminishes strength. The more constraints one imposes, the more one frees one's self of the chains that shackle the spirit."[5] The paradox here is that while leaders want to free up their people to be "thought leaders" in their own right (and not to monopolize this role themselves), they can do so in part by imposing various constraints and difficulties.

The good news is that for most organizations, this comes naturally. We work within limited budgets; we're accountable to customers, stockholders, boards, regulators, et al.; and time is rarely on our side. Leaders can also employ other forms of tension and constraint that more directly impact efforts at problem solving or idea generation and do so in ways that force out greater thought and ingenuity.

See Figure 12-1 for communication tactics leaders can use to create some healthy discomfort for problem solvers and potential innovators.

Agenda 3: Getting the Right People

Researchers on creativity and idea generation have long known that different perspectives can spark different lines of thinking, that het-

Figure 12-1. Communicating discomfort to problem solvers and idea generators.

❏ *Continually challenge basic premises and rationales:* "What are you basing your idea on? Is that premise still viable?"

❏ *Question validity and sufficiency of evidence and data:* "Have you looked at it from every angle? Is that data reliable?"

❏ *Invoke a sense of crisis (but only if justified!), for which new ideas and solutions are urgently required:* "If we don't come up with some new ideas here, competition will eat our lunch."

❏ *Suggest alternatives, and demand a response:* "What would happen if we went in the opposite direction?"

❏ *Bring likely opponents or people with other interests into the conversation:* "Have you checked this out with _____?"

❏ *Tighten the screws:* "Okay, you've met the objective, but now I'd like you to get the job done in half the time."

> *"I like Bartok and Stravinsky. It's a discordant sound—and there are discordant sounds within a company. As president, you must orchestrate the discordant sounds into a kind of harmony. But you never want too much harmony."*
>
> TAKEO FUJISAWA, IN PASCALE, *MANAGING ON THE EDGE*

erogeneous teams develop richer, more complex ideas than teams whose members all work in the same job function. Given this knowledge, what might leaders do to take full advantage of it?

The conventional wisdom in forming teams to create new insight and direction is to make them cross functional. So far so good. But the problem with cross-functional teams is that they can't always speak one another's language. As we suggested in chapter 8, on the leader as linking agent, leaders can make diversity work more successfully by serving as translator, interpreter, and summarizer, and, sometimes, as referee. Leaders of teams with diverse membership shouldn't take for granted that the team will willingly unpack all of its multiple perspectives on a given problem or issue. Instead, leaders of such initiatives should be prepared to draw people out, to create platforms from which more reluctant speakers can hold forth.

One group of participants who warrant inclusion in knowledge creation conversations are those whom psychologists call "low self-monitors"—"people who are especially insensitive to subtle, and even not so subtle, hints from others about how to act." ("High self-monitors are likely to be yes-men and -women; they can't stop themselves from telling others what they think they want to hear.") Low self-monitors are bound to add range and variety to the conversation because "they don't notice—or don't care about—pressures to follow the herd."[6] Since low self-monitors can also be social misfits, leaders should take extra steps to welcome them into the conversation and accord them the same respect as other group members receive.

By inviting people with different ways of seeing the world to speak their mind, leaders can program diversity into everyday conversations. Baseball manager Tony La Russa once called a player into his office to congratulate him on signing a big new contract.

" 'I asked him to sit in the dugout and tell me what he would do if he was managing. . . . So, he comes in, and he has about five ideas. Unfortunately, most of them were good. . . . So, that makes me have some real doubt about what I'm doing.' "[7]

Figure 12-2 contains a set of communication tactics leaders can use to optimize diversity in knowledge creation activity.

Agenda 4: Asking and Telling

> *"Our problem, rather, is achieving consciousness of what we so easily do automatically."*
>
> JEROME BRUNER, *THE CULTURE OF EDUCATION*

Many techniques are available today to facilitate creative, divergent thinking in organizations, but our particular slant is not so much about thinking techniques as it is about what leaders can say and do to make inquiry happen. We're interested in how leaders can coach for higher levels of collaborative inquiry in their organizations. We've chosen to look at a couple of communication coaching

Figure 12-2. Tactics for putting diversity to work.

❐ Remind people that multiple perspectives bring multiple benefits: Aside from getting beyond the conventional and the obvious (and the "low-hanging fruit"), they can clarify, expand, extend, and combine with each other or trigger new, fresh insights and ideas.

❐ Make it clear that although there is a natural tendency for organizations to want to reduce the number of options considered in the interests of time and "getting on with it," you will oppose that tendency.

❐ Feed the potential for diverse, alternative thinking with information: routinely monitor different sources; use electronic clipping services; make team participants serve as "delegates" to specific constituencies, carrying the conversation to them, and then back to the team.

❐ Use open-ended questions to surface alternative points of view:
  ○ "I tend to see the problem this way. What about you?"
  ○ "I've heard people in other departments saying . . . What do you think about their idea?"
  ○ "If your group were in charge of the whole organization, what things would you change?"

methods that are both fundamental and versatile: posing questions and telling stories.

Posing Questions We've discussed leader's questioning tactics in chapters 9 and 10 in the context of two related roles: the leader as *critic,* and as *provocateur.* As innovation coaches, leaders must also pose questions that challenge existing beliefs and orthodoxies and that open doors to new rooms for thinking (or simply get out of the proverbial box). Figure 12-3 suggests several question leads that might open doors, create new perspectives, and stimulate fresh thinking.

In general, innovation coaches get a lot of knowledge creation mileage from regularly asking two basic kinds of questions:

Why

- ❒ Do we do it that way?
- ❒ Did we do it that way in the past?

Figure 12-3. Questions to stimulate fresh thinking.

- ❒ What are the basic assumptions and beliefs we hold about our business? Are they still valid today? Which ones might we sidestep or simply try to ignore?
- ❒ What things did we do right that are no longer so right for the organization now and in the future? Do we still do them from force of habit? What things should we consider discontinuing?
- ❒ What's happening with our traditional customers? Are they the same groups as before? Do they have the same needs and requirements?
- ❒ What's happening with our allies and partners? Are they moving in new and different directions? What are the implications of these movements for us?
- ❒ What are we good at doing? What do we need to be better at? What happens if we don't get better?
- ❒ What things that we don't do now might help us be successful in the future? Who's good at doing them? How do we mobilize, expand, learn?
- ❒ What people in our own organization might have new and different perspectives? How might we hear what they have to say and engage them better in planning conversations?
- ❒ How might we benefit from new technologies? In what ways have we misused technology or missed opportunities to use it well?
- ❒ Where are the biggest gaps between what we see in our service population/market, and how we're geared to serve it?

❐ Do you think that's the right way to do it?
❐ Do you hold that opinion?
❐ Etc.

What if . . .

❐ We challenged that belief?
❐ We discontinued that practice?
❐ We went after a new kind of customer?
❐ We did it another way?
❐ Etc.

Telling Stories If we view knowledge creation and innovation as a learning process, then we need to remind ourselves that learning occurs more readily when people can encounter information in the form of a story (see chapter 4). For leaders concerned with sponsoring new and creative thinking, setting a challenge or a request in a story format, and asking others to add to, resolve, or create an ending for the story, might be a better way to engage them in the solution or knowledge creation process. A story format would have these basic components:

❐ *Setting:* Our organization or division, a specific market or service territory, time frame
❐ *Characters:* Customers and providers, allies and competitors; product and service prototypes
❐ *Plot:* Events and forces driving the action, with a variety of possible endings

Typically, leaders are primarily responsible for establishing setting and characters, the frame for the story or scenario. They can also get the plot off the ground by "bringing us up to the present" through a retelling of past events. The conversation and story design work thereafter shifts to the groups or teams invited to shape new possibilities for the organization.

Simulations and Prototypes

Creating future products, services, work processes, or any dimension of organizational life that will reshape the present way of doing things often involves the design of simulations or prototypes. As Michael Schrage suggests, designing a prototype is the basis and the stimulus for an ongoing conversation that involves playing with ideas, reacting to them, proposing alternatives, and the like. ("Prototypes are a way of letting you think out loud.")[8] The conversation grows like a story line, taking the design forward, with occasional setbacks and the need for redesign.

Thus simulations and prototypes are attempts at creating and evaluating story lines. The dialogues triggered by these designs in progress constitute a continuous testing and refinement process. Schrage states that they are not so much "about finding optimal solutions; they're about discovering what stories make sense."[9]

Organizational leaders, with a stake in the success of design development and knowledge creation, can assist in this conversation by extending a story line or by resolving difficulties. They can also interject "what if" questions to prompt different endings or alternative paths the plot may follow. Finally, leaders can open the conversation and the design exercise to outsiders like customers or vendors to get still another reading on the story line.

"SHARING": GETTING NEW IDEAS ADOPTED

> *"The only relevant learning in a company is the learning done by those people who have the power to act."*
>
> —ARIE DE GEUS, IN WALLY WOOD,
> "SO WHERE DO WE GO FROM HERE?"

The second attribute of species learning in birds is the ability to communicate new skills and behaviors throughout the flock. With organizations, or learning organizations, we talk about idea implementation or institutionalization. The definitive work on this subject is probably Everett Rogers's *Diffusion of Innovations*.[10] We don't aim to be definitive here (but we do recommend Rogers). Instead, we want first to introduce a leadership communications hero, and a real coach (in more ways than one), to illustrate how knowledge creation and innovation might be effectively nurtured and adopted.

Reinventing the Game at Grinnell

A few years ago *The Wall Street Journal* ran a story on a college basketball program with an unusual formula for success.[11] The school led the nation in both team and individual scoring and also gave up the most points to the opposition! The story featured Grinnell College, a prestigious liberal arts school located in a small Iowa town of the same name.

The college fields intercollegiate sports teams for men and women, but the school's emphasis is decidedly on academics. Grinnell offers no athletic scholarships and therefore attracts a more modestly talented group of student athletes. When a new coach was hired for men's basketball (and women's tennis), he inherited a particularly undistinguished basketball tradition and a twenty-seven-year streak of losing seasons! The good news was that not a lot of people, especially the students, seemed to care.

The new coach, Dave Arseneault, assessed the basketball situation realistically. A fair number of young men turned out for the team, and they seemed reasonably enthusiastic. They weren't especially tall but were clearly above average in intelligence. The team probably looked a lot like the ones who had achieved failure in the past twenty-seven years. Arseneault's conclusion was blunt and to the point: "All the clues were there that a complete overhaul of playing style would be the only course of action."[12]

Reframing the Dialogue, and Keeping People in the Conversation

In the conventional approach to fielding a basketball team, there are typically seven to eight players who get in the game. The rest are mainly practice players, honing their skills for the future or just supplying scrimmage competition for the first string. But at Grinnell, a school where intercollegiate athletics is not a high priority, there is little honor in being a benchwarmer on a losing team, and other college demands exert a strong pull on a player's time. Not surprisingly, many players would quit the team as the season wore on, while those who stayed displayed varying levels of commitment and solidarity with the program.

Arseneault's initial goal was to keep the program viable. In an interview, he disclosed that maybe by rethinking (something his team was good at) their basic approach to the game, he might have a shot at accomplishing objectives like these:

- ❏ Reducing the attrition rate and fielding enough players to have adequate numbers during practice sessions ("so we could improve throughout the season.")
- ❏ Increasing team morale through increased player participation (in planning as well as execution)
- ❏ Giving players the opportunity to attain some significant individual goals
- ❏ Turning around a losing record
- ❏ Finding a niche to "make a name for ourselves" that would allow for more successful recruiting of scholar athletes[13]

Arseneault decided to first identify and build on "strengths." These turned out to be two: team intelligence (including analytic intelligence) and at least one player who could shoot 3-pointers (long-distance shots) fairly well. Not exactly a winning combination yet, but at least a place to start.

Coach Arseneault also had an idea he wanted to try. He was familiar with at least one instance in which a team platooned so as to create a faster, more active style of play. The platooning approach had not secured for the teams he knew a significant competitive advantage, but Arseneault wanted to ratchet up the approach. And given the caliber of talent at Grinnell, the answer "couldn't be a conventional running game. We needed to go to extremes."[14]

Design as a Learning Conversation

Coach Arseneault presented his basic concept to a group of ten players, not exactly a full roster by most college standards. His plan was to create two platoons and move them in and out of the game, much like a hockey team deploys shifts in successive waves to ensure continuously fresh legs. The team considered other options as well, including a slow-down approach with elaborate play patterns.

When Arseneault had them vote on which one they thought would be best, his main counsel was "Extreme is better."

The team decided to go with a "run and gun" platoon strategy, with two key components: constant pressure on the opposition (with the intention of running the other team ragged) and launching as many 3-point shots as possible (since Grinnell players aren't very tall, their long-range shots are less likely to be blocked by taller opponents clustered close to the basket). Victories didn't come at once, but the team scored a lot more, and everyone played.

Data-Based Learning Conversations

During Year One of the new program, players and coaches tracked as many statistics as they could identify, looking for different indicators that might provide useful feedback for further strategy design. As the season progressed, the team would systematically analyze performance data and revise strategy as necessary. Several students created class projects around this tracking and analysis exercise. The end result was the identification of forty relevant measures, from which five reliable success indicators were derived:

1. Force the opponent to run up and down the court at least 150 times per game.
2. Take at least 94 shots per game (instead of the traditional 60 to 80) . . .
3. . . . half of which would be 3-pointers.
4. Retrieve at least 33 percent of missed offensive shots (not that difficult, since long shots lead to long rebounds).
5. Force at least 32 turnovers.

Basically, the Grinnell design for success evolved over much experimentation, significant analysis, and a lot of conversation about implications for strategy. Arseneault acknowledged that, from the outset, the team had treated both their practice sessions and their games as a forum in which to experiment. During the game, each shift receives immediate feedback on the quality of its play with respect to key indicators. After each game, the team goes through a fairly structured analysis, again using the key statistical indicators as an organizer. "Over the years, the system has continued to change. Shooting strategies, for example, have been radically changed, and we continue to look to the data, and to the changing make-up of successive teams, to improve our performance. We also have to react to new defenses opposing coaches come up with."[15]

Conversations About Buy-In and Support

In Arseneault's third year at Grinnell, the team achieved its first winning season in twenty-eight years. Since then, the team has continued to win and earned several conference championships while setting NCAA scoring records (in the 2002 season, the team averaged 125 points per game, more than any NBA team!). Once the team became a winner, the squad expanded to seventeen positions that are actively competed for each year. That's at least three platoons, or shifts, of players Grinnell can throw at the opposition, and on this team, everyone plays.

Working together well is especially important on a team that assigns particular roles to each player (the good long-range shooters become *the* shooters, with others assigned different responsibilities). At the beginning of each season Arseneault asked each player to rank order "the ways in which he felt he could best help our team, and had them forward me a list of the players they most enjoyed playing with. Whenever possible I tried to match together people who were comfortable with one another and complemented each other."[16]

Not surprisingly, players enjoy having input in the design strategy. "By showing confidence in our players' abilities through the assessment process, involving their thoughts as the playing roles and units were assigned, we created a positive, trusting environment in which the athletes were much more likely to succeed."[17] With ten years' experience in reinventing a style of play they could win with, Grinnell teams have bought into a system that still seems counterintuitive to many other coaches and players.

Arseneault's formula has indeed become institutionalized, embraced even by fans who at first shook their heads over play that produced:

❐ Giving a lot of easy shots to the other team—opposition shooting percentage averages an unheard of 67 percent (one opponent actually shot at an 85 percent rate, and Grinnell won)

❐ Double-digit deficits, typical at the end of the first half (before the hectic pace wears the opposition down and Grinnell catches up in the second half)

Arseneault philosophized about what it took for players and fans to stay committed: "You can't think of where you are at present—you have to think about where you're going."[18] With game attendance up, more players trying out for the team, and better high school players showing more interest in Grinnell, the coach has come a long way.

Spreading Innovation

Coach Arseneault's experience at Grinnell presents, albeit on a modest scale, a picture of a leader playing all the roles of a champion for organizational renewal. Arseneault is both an innovative coach and an effective coach of innovative thinking. In larger organizations, where the work is more extensive and the stakes are higher (not to minimize the importance players attach to winning games), a leader who coaches for knowledge creation and new ideas would still do well to follow many of Coach Arseneault's communication strategies, including the ones listed in Figure 12-4, in particular.

In organizations more complex than a basketball team, new ideas, however brilliant, don't always get adopted or institutionalized because they fail to get communicated to the right people in the right ways. Rosabeth Moss Kanter has observed, "Experience after experience with innovations that fizzle after a bright start, be they new participative work systems or new products, shows that external relations are a critical factor; the connections, or lack of them, between the area initially producing the innovation and its neighborhood and beyond."[19] Sometimes, ideas fall into the "not-invented-here" trap. Other times, they simply encounter resistance from people whose budgets are threatened or whose ownership in the status quo is under attack.

Figure 12-4. Ways to foster new thinking.

☐ Expand participation. The more people in the "conversation," the richer will be the yield.

☐ Invite input regarding personal interests, motives and preferences. Support "win-win" opportunities for individuals and the team.

☐ Challenge people to think and talk "outside the box" ("Extremes are best").

☐ Use data to question and to reflect on current performance (as well as experiments and prototypes); then build and sustain a conversation around data.

☐ Keep new ideas in play and open to further refinement and improvement.

☐ Invite people to draw inferences from the data and to act on them.

☐ Encourage people to take responsibility for shaping new ideas and making appropriate decisions.

☐ Be religious about sharing feedback.

☐ Defend (and rationalize) new and different behaviors.

☐ Recognize and celebrate accomplishment.

Clearly, the responsibility of the *innovation coach* extends beyond your own team or area of responsibility. From a communication standpoint, you want to be able to get the word out to a wide, yet select, network and effectively build support for an idea. Taking a cue from Coach Arseneault, you can "socialize" an idea in its early stages of development, seeking reactions and inviting comments, including data that might add shape and substance to it. Ideas that are passed around within larger networks can grow in scope (and value) like a snowball rolled along the ground.

Ideas that get shared are ideas that can improve, especially when they are batted back and forth. In the idea generation model used by Ford and American Airlines,[20] suggestions developed by teams were reviewed by designated coaches, typically middle managers with a broader purview and a stake in the action. They offered "friendly" criticism as required and helped ideas get better. Evaluators, senior leaders who could make budget decisions, were also encouraged to coach originating teams if they felt an idea had promise but lacked enough detail.

Finally, we would be remiss if we didn't remind you once again to use your storytelling techniques to socialize and promote new ideas. Storytelling is not just a way to enhance understanding and memory. Hearing a well-told story allows us to fit new perceptions and ideas into old plotlines, as a way to make sense of new story material. Often, you can persuade others to buy in to an innovation by challenging them to rewrite their own stories, especially by helping them see an innovation as an acceptable and plausible "ending" to an older storyline: "You know, for years we've had success in using this method. Now we have an opportunity to get even better results, and I'll bet you can figure out how we can pull it off."

"Socializing": Flocking as a Team Sport

> "The challenge is to create collaborative tools and environments—techniques and places that enable people to be themselves while they are being more than themselves."
>
> MICHAEL SCHRAGE, *Shared Minds*

Management author Henry Mintzberg tells the story of Zubin Mehta being asked what it was like to conduct the Israel Philharmonic, where all the musicians think of themselves as soloists. His reported reply was "I'm the only Indian; they're all the chiefs."[21] Not every organization is made up of chiefs, but knowledge workers and others increasingly say that being heard and having their voices count is critical to job satisfaction. There's a little "chief" in most of us, apparently.

The key leadership task here is the one that Mehta faced: helping a group of talented individuals come together as a team. Unfortunately, organizational structures and the habits they enforce often deter diverse players from getting together. Kanter notes in her classic management book *The Change Masters,* "The structural barriers to communication, to exchange of ideas, to joint effort to solve problems, are matched by attitudes that confine people to the category in which they have been placed, that assume they are defined by that category, and that fail to allow them to show what they can contribute beyond it."[22] Too often there's a caste system problem that inhibits information sharing and collaboration, and that communicates status and power differences among people working toward common goals.

The antidote to this dilemma is a version of the birds' flocking strategy. Leaders need to give people license to think and act beyond the place they occupy on the organizational chart. By creating cross-functional teams and task forces that bring different people together, you help ideas spread while connecting people with one another across the organization. Leaders, in other words, need to foster continuous dialogue among many different groups and individuals. They need to initiate and support discussions in which people move around to solve problems and think out loud about better ways of doing things in the organization.

Communication for Collaboration

Bringing people in organizations together to drive learning and innovation involves the creation of a sense of shared purpose and common stake. It involves relationship building that in turn can support active, intelligent dialogue among "equals." And it involves staging conversations where participants feel both comfortable and energized. In a book called *Learning Partnerships,* Robert Mai describes the ways over a hundred companies, including American Airlines, Ford, and Georgia-Pacific, created programmatic efforts to stage successful idea generation initiatives.[23] These initiatives called for voluntary, often mixed, employee teams to submit improvement ideas and be significantly rewarded for those that were accepted for implementation.

The most prevalent *communication themes* for these team-based initiatives included:

☐ Good ideas could come from anywhere, and anybody.
☐ Teams, particularly heterogeneous ones, could be counted on to generate bigger, richer ideas than individuals.
☐ No ideas that made people or their jobs vulnerable would be considered (the flock would be protected).
☐ Good ideas would create value for the organization and pay off for teams as well.
☐ Innovation would make the organization stronger, more competitive, and a better employment option for the future.

Most of these initiatives involved special programs that were not ongoing. But they succeeded not only in producing measurable, value-adding innovations but a stronger, sustained sense of community, of employees pulling together to achieve unusual accomplishments. Kanter described collaborative efforts like these as requiring "parallel organizations" outside the normal organizational hierarchy, where flocking and collaboration are constrained by rank and function. "Indeed, involvement in the parallel organization—membership in a task force or action team—may be the closest to an experience of 'community' or total commitment for many workers. . . ."[24]

Today companies continue to form parallel organizations to address problem solving or new idea agendas. Self-directed teams proliferate in knowledge industry companies. Information technology allows more employees to have greater access to information they require to think creatively about process improvement and productivity advances. Interest in strengthening "internal communications" has grown considerably among corporations seeking to leverage the collective thinking power of the workforce. All these factors are *potential* contributors to successful collaborations that solve organizational problems and cultivate new ideas.

So how do leaders turn this potential into actions and outcomes? How do they prompt and support the kind of dialogue that allows groups to generate usable ideas and solutions together? Schrage suggests, "What's necessary isn't more communication but rather a different quality of interaction—which is precisely what collaboration is. . . . Collaboration means that people are less interested in displaying data than in creating a shared space to play collectively with ideas and information."[25] Figure 12-5 lists nine leadership communication ideas for managing "a different quality of interaction," and for making collaboration happen.

The "Gift Community"

A final note on fostering a collaborative climate: Lewis Hyde has explored the notion that idea *exchange* within certain "coherent communities," like a community of practice or a group of scientists engaged in similar research, is like gift giving. That is, ideas are allowed to be passed around freely within the community but are

Figure 12-5. Communication guidelines to support effective collaboration.

❏ *Clearly and forcefully set a common purpose for group collaboration:* What organizational goal can people rally around together?

❏ *Invoke a commonly held motive:* Remind people how participation can lead to reward and gratification.

❏ *Establish rules of equality:* Suspend the normal pecking order—all voices are equally important.

❏ *Guard and protect the "space" where people talk and share ideas:* Keep time and territory safe from incursion and the atmosphere free from fear.

❏ *Convey (and model) empathy:* Employ Yankelovich's "gestures of empathy," including paraphrasing and summarizing, to confirm understanding and establish common ground and interests.

❏ *Convey (and model) respect:* Be ready to commend people's thinking and its legitimacy (even though you may disagree with their ideas).

❏ *Help collaborators stay in touch with one another and with one another's ideas:* Use collaborative tools and media to record, store, disseminate, and provide feedback to thought contributions so they can be built on and extended.

❏ *Acknowledge participation:* Positively reinforce "tries" so as to invite more input.

❏ *Celebrate winning:* Focus praise and gratitude on the products of collaborative thinking and on the relationships that support productivity.

---

not so freely passed outside. "A gift community," suggests Hyde, "puts certain constraints on its members, yes, but these constraints assure the freedom of the gift." Hyde adds that such "gift exchange is an economy of small groups. When emotional ties are the glue that holds a community together, its size has an upper limit."[26] With respect to collaboration for the purpose of learning and inventing together, the free exchange of ideas as a kind of collaborative communication might work best when the size of the flock is kept within reasonable parameters.

NOTES

1. Arie de Geus, *The Living Company* (Boston: Harvard Business School Press, 1997), 133.
2. Donald A. Schon, *Educating the Reflective Practitioner: Toward a New Design for Teaching and Learning in the Professions* (San Francisco: Jossey-Bass, 1987), 296.
3. Peter F. Drucker, *Post-Capitalist Society* (New York: HarperBusiness, 1993), 193.
4. Richard T. Pascale, *Managing on the Edge: How the Smartest Companies Use Conflict to Stay Ahead* (New York: Touchstone, 1990), 54–55.

5. Igor Stravinsky, *The Poetics of Music* (Cambridge, Mass.: Harvard University Press, 1970), 87.
6. Robert Sutton, "The Weird Rules of Creativity," *Harvard Business Review* (September 2001), 98.
7. Rick Hummel, "Tatis, Cards Agree on 4-Year Contract," *St. Louis Post-Dispatch* (March 12, 2000), D14.
8. Michael Schrage, *Serious Play: How the World's Best Companies Simulate to Innovate* (Boston: Harvard Business School Press, 2000), 166.
9. Ibid., 174.
10. Everett M. Rogers, *Diffusion of Innovations,* 4th ed. (New York: The Free Press, 1995).
11. Frederick C. Klein, "On Sports: Grinnell's Scoring Machine," *The Wall Street Journal* (January 22, 1999), W5.
12. Richard Ridgway, "Arseneault Reveals Formula for Courting Success," *The Grinnell Magazine* (spring 1998), 7.
13. David M. Arseneault, interviewed by Robert Mai (March 9, 1999).
14. Ibid.
15. Ibid.
16. David M. Arseneault, *The Running Game: A Formula for Success* (Spring City, Pa.: Reedswain, 1999), 10.
17. Ibid.
18. Arseneault, 1999 interview.
19. Rosabeth Moss Kanter, *The Change Masters: Innovation for Productivity in the American Corporation* (New York: Simon & Schuster, 1983), 125.
20. See Robert Mai, *Learning Partnerships: How Leading American Companies Implement Organizational Learning* (Chicago: Irwin/ASTD, 1996), chapters 10 and 11.
21. Mehta, quoted in Henry Mintzberg, "Covert Leadership: Notes on Managing Professionals," *Harvard Business Review* (November 12, 1998), 144.
22. Kanter, *The Change Masters,* 31–32.
23. Mai, *Learning Partnerships,* chapters 6, 11, and 12.
24. Kanter, *The Change Masters,* 203.
25. Michael Schrage, *Shared Minds: The New Technologies of Collaboration* (New York: Random House, 1990), 31.
26. Lewis Hyde, *The Gift: Imagination and the Erotic Life of Property* (New York: Vintage Books, 198), 82.

13

Assessment

"*Payment by results,*" *Osnard said.* '*Only way. Agreed?*' . . . '*Andy, that has been a principle of mine ever since we opened shop,*' *Pendel replied fervently, trying to think when he had last paid anyone by results.*"

—JOHN LE CARRÉ, *THE TAILOR OF PANAMA*

*W*e don't mean to suggest that the "results" of effective leadership communication are readily definable, and that you should reconstruct your leadership compensation plans accordingly. But we do think that communication needs to be considered deliberately in terms of organizational strategy and assessed in terms of key organizational outcomes.

In this last chapter, we want therefore to offer several approaches you might take toward assessing leadership communication in your organization. Since leadership communication is a combination of tactics and skills, we think that leaders themselves would be well served by some self-assessment activity: Which of the roles we've described have you already taken on, and how are you exercising them? We suggest a question-driven framework you can use to more pointedly assess your role-specific behavior.

Following these suggestions for self-assessment, we present a parallel framework for organizing an outcome assessment and help you inquire about the impact your communication practices are having and with what results to the organization.

A Leadership Communication Profile

One way to tie together the ten leadership communication roles and align them with your own communication practices is hold them up as a mirror and have a look. We don't intend to create a ready-to-use behavioral instrument to measure communication performance because it would not be in keeping with the spirit of this book. In chapters 3 through 12, we wanted to lay out guidelines and illustrate with anecdotes and vignettes—not to be overly prescriptive or formulaic. However, we offer you a list of questions, four per communication role, that you might use to focus your own assessment of where you are and where you want to be with your communication practices.

Developing a Communication Profile: Questions You Can Ask

Meaning-Maker (Chapter 3)

- ❏ Do I talk about the organization as a community that we all "belong" to and have a stake in? (Do I talk "team," and walk the talk?)
- ❏ Do I communicate supportiveness to people on my team? (Do they know I and the organization are in their corner?)
- ❏ Do I talk about work in terms of a larger mission and values?
- ❏ Do I discuss current work and tasks in the context of a bigger picture?

Storyteller (Chapter 4)

- ❏ Do I use anecdotes and vignettes to make a point?
- ❏ Do I encourage others to share their anecdotes and stories (in conversation and in meetings)?
- ❏ Do I talk about where I see the organization going (and where it's been)?

☐ Is my planning conversation more about numerical targets or a story of where you want to go (and what you want to be)?

Trust Builder (Chapter 5)

☐ Do I regularly make myself visible and accessible?
☐ Do people know what I stand for (and what I know and can do)?
☐ Do I make an effort to explain myself and my thinking?
☐ Do I listen well and willingly share "airtime"?

Direction Setter (Chapter 6)

☐ Do I use data to set direction (or just to report where we've been)?
☐ Do I actively and consistently share information about the organization?
☐ Do I regularly invite questions and concerns from my people?
☐ Do I tie organizational goal achievement to individual reward and recognition in my conversations?

Transition Pilot (Chapter 7)

☐ Do I let my people know about change ahead of time (and ahead of outsiders)?
☐ Do I communicate concern for individuals during times of organizational transition?
☐ Do I communicate a steadfast attention to organizational objectives and required tasks during disruptions and restructurings?
☐ Do I stay in touch with people at different levels of the organization (especially with frontline supervisors)?

Linking Agent (Chapter 8)

☐ Do I create forums for all my people to speak their mind and input their concerns and ideas?
☐ Do I make it easy for outsiders (remote locations, business allies, customers, etc.) to connect with me and my team?

❐ Are my staff meetings mostly a monologue or a dialogue?

❐ Do I solicit the perspectives and ideas of "outsiders"?

Critic (Chapter 9)

❐ Do I question the status quo in conversations and meetings?

❐ Do I actively invite others to do the same?

❐ Do I create conditions of safety for people to speak candidly and openly?

❐ Do I challenge the underlying assumptions of conventional wisdom?

Provocateur (Chapter 10)

❐ Do I invite disagreement and argument about work policy and practice?

❐ Can planning be confrontational (but with common resolve as the outcome)?

❐ Do I sometimes provoke conflict as a way to explore more than one perspective?

❐ Do I have acknowledged and accepted rules for debate within my team?

Learning Advocate (Chapter 11)

❐ Do I encourage people to talk shop among themselves and with me?

❐ Do I draw out improvement ideas from my people (and do I seed ideas for development)?

❐ Do my staff meetings invite discussion about process improvement and new ideas?

❐ Do we talk with customers and other outsiders about how we could be better?

Innovation Coach (Chapter 12)

❐ Do I make it easy for team members to collaborate on problem solving and idea generation?

❐ Do I let people know that idea generation is everyone's responsibility, not simply my prerogative as leader?

❐ Do I make new ideas and innovation a priority and challenge my people accordingly?

❐ Do I acknowledge and reinforce people for their suggestions
and ideas?

Again, we recommend that you consider these questions not so
much as a forty-item battery, to be administered in a kind of formal
self-assessment, but as a way to begin to profile yourself as a leader
who communicates effectively. You might choose to target one role
only, or a cluster of roles (perhaps as they reflect a combined approach to one of our three critical leadership agendas).

In any case, the four questions listed beneath each communication role are meant to be suggestive, a way of framing more specific
communication behaviors that describe your approach to real leadership challenges in your own organization. We feel strongly that
assessing your own communication habits and behaviors provides a
valuable starting point for any kind of strategy development involving your people, their performance, and their commitment.

MEASURING OUTCOMES

At the same time that you think about yourself in terms of the
communication strategies and tactics you currently practice, you
have the opportunity to employ other means to complete your
communication assessment. The most valuable source of information would of course be the people with whom you communicate:
their insights about your effectiveness, as well as their own communication behavior.

Here again we present clusters of four questions for each communication role, only this time the focus is on impact and effect.
Given our three organizational goals of developing community,
keeping everyone aligned and on task, and fostering renewal and
innovation, these questions help assess how well leadership communication serves those goals.

Assessing Impact: Questions You Can Ask

Meaning-Maker (Chapter 3)

❐ To what extent do people see their own jobs and work serving larger organizational goals?

☐ Do employees think and talk about their work in terms of larger meanings and values?

☐ To what degree do people feel their leaders support them and their careers?

☐ Do employees feel proud to be a part of the organization?

Storyteller (Chapter 4)

☐ What stories do employees tell about the organization and its future?

☐ How do the stories of veteran employees resemble or differ from those of new people? How do they both resemble or differ from those told by leaders?

☐ Are there one or more consistent story lines that people use to describe the organization and its purposes?

☐ To what extent do employees feel they have a role in shaping the future of the organization?

Trust Builder (Chapter 5)

☐ Do employees feel they are listened to?

☐ Do employees have trust in their leaders, including the senior leadership team?

☐ Do your people feel they understand your positions on key issues and concerns?

☐ Do your people feel they can talk with you when they need to and get straight answers?

Direction Setter (Chapter 6)

☐ How well informed do your people feel about leadership's decisions?

☐ Do your people feel they have input to decisions that affect them?

☐ Do your people feel they know where the organization is going, and why?

☐ Do employees feel that praise and recognition are contingent on, and closely related to, achievement of stated organizational goals and objectives?

Transition Pilot (Chapter 7)

☐ Do people feel they know about new directions and moves in good time (and ahead of the general public)?

❐ Do employees feel their welfare is being considered and looked after during transitions?

❐ Does productivity suffer because people are confused and demoralized?

❐ Do your people feel your decisions about change are well informed, logical, and fair?

Linking Agent (Chapter 8)

❐ Are there pockets of people who feel they are not really connected to the organization?

❐ Do "outsiders" feel they have a voice and that it's valued?

❐ Do people feel they have opportunities to sound off, register concerns, or suggest improvement ideas?

❐ Do your people regard staff meetings as opportunities to participate, or simply to listen?

Critic (Chapter 9)

❐ Do people see leadership locked into the status quo or ready to question and challenge it?

❐ Do employees raise questions about work practices and the way we do business in staff meetings and other conversations?

❐ Do employees regard data and its use to be a tool to explore performance options or a stick to punish performers?

❐ Do employees feel they'll be protected from backlash and retribution if they offer criticisms (will they be heroes or whistle-blowers)?

Provocateur (Chapter 10)

❐ Do people feel it's relatively safe to argue about organizational issues?

❐ Are there regular opportunities for debating decisions?

❐ Is the organization's planning process an occasion for give-and-take or more of a slam dunk?

❐ Do people stand behind group decisions, even if they didn't win the battle?

Learning Advocate (Chapter 11)

❐ Do employees feel that continuous improvement is a priority, where they will be recognized for their contributions?

❏ Do people feel they have ample opportunities to offer suggestions for improvements and be listened to seriously?

❏ Is it easy for frontline employees to communicate concerns and ideas registered by customers?

❏ Do employees regard each other, as well as their leaders, as sources of knowledge and process improvement?

Innovation Coach (Chapter 12)

❏ Are team and staff meetings a time during which problems are examined and worked on by the group?

❏ To what extent do employees submit suggestions and ideas for improvement, new approaches, etc. (how many submissions per employee)?

❏ Do employees feel their ideas are treated seriously and implemented, if the ideas are worthwhile?

❏ Does the organization champion people who come up with new ideas and acknowledge (if not reward) their accomplishments?

Most organizations use employee attitude surveys from time to time to take the pulse of their workforce. We recommend that you incorporate questions like these in such surveys as a way to evaluate the impact of leadership communication, among other things. Convening focus or discussion groups of employees to probe more deeply into issues of communication effectiveness, or to explore how well the organization is handling either or all of the three agendas we've discussed, is another useful assessment strategy.

In any case, our assumption is that measuring the impact of leadership communication in your organization can simply be a matter of targeted observations (e.g., listening to the stories people tell about the organization), and co-opting already deployed assessment practices (e.g., the annual employee survey). It shouldn't require either major expenditure or significant additional time requirements.

TAKING ACTION

Your assessment activity should provide you with a clearer picture of your own strengths as a communicator and a manager of communication, and with a better sense of which specific communication practices might best address your present organizational needs and priorities. Implications for action, for changing existing practices, developing certain skills, employing different tactics, will spring from your conclusions about potential for added value and itches that need to be scratched. Figure 13-1 is a kind of scorecard that might help you sort out communication strengths and weaknesses and decide where action might best be taken.

MOVING AHEAD

The other return on your investment in such assessment activity (and action follow-through) is of course that you'll grow more *conscious* of communication as a strategy for achieving organizational aims. We recognize how easy it is to *not* think about communication because we're always doing it. By choosing to call out and examine different communication *roles* and how they contribute to the health and success of your organization, you're bringing leadership communication into sharper focus. And if any leadership subject warrants sharper focus, this is it.

You'll have to excuse our bias (again), but to our mind, paying this kind of attention to what's being said, who's in the conversation, and how well the organization supports questioning, criticism, and debate is of the utmost importance. At the outset of this book, we also stated that communication was *the* key competency for leaders. For this competency to grow and develop, one of the first orders of business is for leaders to create for themselves a clearer picture of communication as a force to enact strategy. You need to know what effective communication might look like before you can attempt to improve how it's exercised. Having a plan to examine present communication practice within a well-defined framework of roles and tactics should help here.

After that, it's a matter of continuing to communicate about communication. Make it a subject to talk and reflect about, not just the means (and an unexamined means!) for passing around information and staying in touch. Leadership communication begs more sustained, systematic attention, as with any important element of strategy.

Figure 13-1. Leadership communication assessment matrix.

	Self-assessment: strengths, weaknesses, gaps	Impact assessment: strengths, weaknesses, gaps	Action priority: Which gaps are most troublesome? Which have best potential for gain?	Action steps and timeline: Who needs to do what, when?
Meaning-maker				
Storyteller				
Trust builder				
Direction setter				
Transition pilot				
Linking agent				
Critic				
Provocateur				
Learning advocate				
Innovation coach				

Bibliography

Adams, Scott. *The Dilbert Principle*. New York: HarperBusiness, 1996.

Ainspan, Nathan D., and David Dell. *Employee Communication During Mergers,* Report No. 1270-00-RR. New York: The Conference Board, 2000.

Andrews, Fred. "Learning to Celebrate Water-Cooler Gossip." *New York Times,* Sunday Business Section (February 25, 2001).

Argyris, Chris. "Teaching Smart People How to Learn." *Harvard Business Review* (May–June 1991).

———. "Good Communication That Blocks Learning." *Harvard Business Review* (July–August 1994).

———. "A Chat With Chris Argyris." Interviewed by Donna Abernathy. *Training and Development* (May 1999).

Armour, Terrence E. "Bulls Fans Get Their Phil." *Chicago Tribune,* Sports Section (May 6, 1999).

Arseneault, David M. *The Running Game: A Formula for Success.* Spring City, Pa.: Reedswain, 2000.

Autry, James. *The Servant Leader*. New York: Prima, 2001.

Bennis, Warren. "The Leader as Storyteller." *Harvard Business Review* (January–February 1996).

Block, Peter. *Stewardship: Choosing Service Over Self-Interest*. San Francisco: Berrett-Koehler, 1993.

Bridges, William. *Managing Transitions: Making the Most of Change*. Reading, Pa.: Addison-Wesley, 1991.

Brown, John Seely, and Paul Duguid. "Balancing Act: How to Capture Knowledge Without Killing It." *Harvard Business Review* (May–June 2000).

Bruner, Jerome. *Acts of Meaning*. Cambridge, Mass.: Harvard University Press, 1990.

————. *The Culture of Education.* Cambridge, Mass.: Harvard University Press, 1996.

Buckingham, Marcus, and Curt Coffman. *First, Break All the Rules.* New York: Simon & Schuster, 1999.

Burke, Kenneth. *Permanence and Change: An Anatomy of Purpose.* 2nd ed. Indianapolis, Ind.: Bobbs-Merrill, 1965.

"Business Humor: Organizational Wisdom (As Seen on the World Wide Web)." *Business Psychology News* [www.BusinessPsychology.com] (2, 1998).

Byrne, John. "Jack Welch: A Close-Up Look at How America's Number 1 Manager Runs GE." *Business Week* (June 3, 1998).

Cappelli, Peter. *The New Deal at Work: Managing the Market-Driven Workforce.* Boston: Harvard Business School Press, 1999.

————. "Managing Without Commitment." *Organizational Dynamics* (spring 2000).

Carr, David. "Narrative and the Real World: An Argument for Continuity." In *Memory, Identity, Community,* edited by Lewis P. Hinchman and Sandra K. Hinchman. Albany: State University of New York Press, 1997.

Chase, Richard, and Sriram Dasu. "Want to Perfect Your Company's Service? Use Behavioral Science." *Harvard Business Review* (June 2001).

Cialdini, Robert. "Harnessing the Science of Persuasion." *Harvard Business Review* (October 2001).

Clymer, Adam. "Defining a Leader First by His Words." *New York Times* (September 16, 2001).

Conger, Jay A. "The Necessary Art of Persuasion." *Harvard Business Review* (May–June 1998).

Crosby, Alfred. *The Measure of Reality: Quantification and Western Society, 1250–1600.* New York: Cambridge University Press, 1997.

Davenport, Thomas H., and John C. Beck. "Getting the Attention You Need." *Harvard Business Review* (September–October 2000).

De Geus, Arie. "The Living Company." *Harvard Business Review* (March–April 1997).

————. *The Living Company.* Boston: Harvard Business School Press, 1997.

Denby, David. "Does Homer Have Legs?" In *Best American Essays*

1994, edited by Tracy Kidder. Boston: Houghton Mifflin, 1994, pp. 57–84.

Diamond, Jared. *Guns, Germs and Steel: The Fates of Human Societies.* New York: W. W. Norton, 1999.

Drath, Wilfred H., and Charles J. Palus. *Making Common Sense: Leadership as Meaning-Making in a Community of Practice.* Greensboro, N.C.: Center for Creative Leadership, 1994.

Drucker, Peter F. "The New Society of Organizations." *Harvard Business Review* (September–October 1992).

———. *Post-Capitalist Society.* New York: HarperBusiness, 1993.

Dunbar, Robin. *Grooming, Gossip and the Evolution of Language.* Cambridge, Mass.: Harvard University Press, 1996.

Eisenhardt, Kathleen M., Jean L. Kahwajy, and L. J. Bourgeois III. "How Management Teams Can Have a Good Fight." *Harvard Business Review* (July–August 1997).

Farr, David N. Speech delivered at the Dean's Breakfast Series, John Cook School of Business, St. Louis University (September 25, 2001).

Ferrazzi, Keith E. "Plugging in Change." *Across the Board* (October 1995).

"The First 100 Days: New Leadership Outlines Its Priorities." www.sbc.com (May 1998).

Fisher, Anne B. "Making Change Stick." *Fortune* (April 17, 1995).

Fitz-enz, Jac. *The 8 Practices of Exceptional Companies.* New York: AMACOM, 1997.

———. *The ROI of Human Capital: Measuring the Economic Value of Employee Performance.* New York: AMACOM, 2000.

Fredrickson, George M. "Wise Man" (review of *Hanging Together: Unity and Diversity in American Culture,* by John Highham). *New York Review of Books* (February 28, 2002).

Freiberg, Kevin, and Jackie Freiberg. *Nuts! Southwest Airlines Crazy Recipe for Business and Personal Success.* New York: Broadway Books, 1998.

Fukuyama, Francis. *The Great Disruption: Human Nature and the Reconstitution of Social Order.* New York: Free Press, 1999.

Fullan, Michael G. "Turning Systemic Thinking on Its Head." *Phi Delta Kappan* 77 (February 1996), pp. 420–23.

Garvin, David, and Michael Roberto. "What You Don't Know

About Making Decisions." *Harvard Business Review* (September 2001).

Geertz, Clifford. *The Interpretation of Cultures.* New York: Basic Books, 1973.

Ghoshal Sumantra, and Christopher Bartlett. *The Individualized Corporation: A Fundamentally New Approach to Management.* New York: HarperCollins, 1997.

Gilbert, Virginia Baldwin. "Sigma-Aldrich Laces Technical Center With Better-Way Features." *St. Louis Post-Dispatch* (December 9, 2001).

Gleick, James. *Chaos: Making a New Science.* New York: Viking, 1987.

Goffee, Robert, and Gareth Jones. "Why Should Anyone Be Led by You?" *Harvard Business Review* (September–October 2000).

Goldberg, Robert. "Talking About Change." *Issues & Observations,* Center for Creative Leadership newsletter (nos. 1–2, 1997).

Goode, Erica. "Anthrax Offers Lesson in How to Handle Bad News." *New York Times, Science Times* (October 23, 2001).

Gould, Stephan Jay. "Cordelia's Dilemma." In *Best American Essays 1994,* edited by Tracy Kidder. Boston: Houghton-Mifflin, 1994, pp. 173–82.

Hackett, Brian. "What's New About the New Deal?" In *The New Deal in Employment Relationships,* Report No. 1162-96CR. New York: The Conference Board, 1996.

Hamel, Gary. "Strategy as Revolution." *Harvard Business Review* (July–August 1996).

Hefling, Kimberley. "A Farewell to 4 Fallen Americans." *St. Louis Post-Dispatch* (December 11, 2001).

Heifetz, Ronald A. *Leadership Without Easy Answers.* Cambridge, Mass.: Belknap Press/Harvard University Press, 1994.

Heifetz, Ronald A., and Donald L. Laurie. "The Work of Leadership." *Harvard Business Review* (January–February 1997).

Hellenga, Robert. *The Fall of a Sparrow.* New York: Scribner, 1998.

Hinchman, Lewis P., and Sandra K. Hinchman, eds. Introduction to *Memory, Identity, Community: The Idea of Narrative in the Human Sciences.* Albany, N.Y.: State University of New York Press, 1997.

Hummel, Rick. "Tatis, Cards Agree on 4-Year Contract." *St. Louis Post-Dispatch* (March 12, 2000).

Hyde, Lewis. *The Gift: Imagination and the Erotic Life of Property.* New York: Vintage Books, 1983.

———. *Trickster Makes This World: Mischief, Myth, and Art.* New York: Farrar, Straus & Giroux, 1998.

Johnson, Barry. *Polarity Management: Identifying and Managing Unsolvable Problems.* New York: HRD Press, 1997.

Kanter, Rosabeth Moss. *The Change Masters: Innovation for Productivity in the American Corporation.* New York: Simon & Schuster, 1983.

Kaplan, Robert S., and David P. Norton. *The Strategy-Focused Organization: How Balanced Scorecard Companies Thrive in the New Business Environment.* Boston: Harvard Business School Press, 2001.

Kerby, Anthony Paul. "The Language of the Self." In *Memory, Identity, Community,* edited by Lewis P. Hinchman and Sandra K. Hinchman. Albany: State University of New York Press, 1997.

Kiernan, Matthew. "The New Strategic Architecture: Learning to Compete in the Twenty-First Century." *Academy of Management Executive* (February 1993).

Kim, W. Chan, and Renee Mauborgne. "Fair Process: Managing in the Knowledge Economy." *Harvard Business Review* (July–August 1997).

Klein, Frederick C. "On Sports: Grinnell's Scoring Machine." *The Wall Street Journal* (January 22, 1999).

Kotkin, Stephen. "What They Knew (Not!): 44 Years of C.I.A. Secrets." *New York Times* (March 17, 2001).

Kotter, John. "What Leaders Really Do." *Harvard Business Review* (May–June 1990).

Kouzes, James M., and Barry Z. Posner. *The Leadership Challenge: How to Get Extraordinary Things Done in Organizations.* San Francisco: Jossey-Bass, 1991.

Kristof, Nicholas. "Fortune Cookie: Your Ignorance Clouds Asian Joy." *New York Times* (August 13, 1995).

Kundera, Milan. *Testaments Betrayed: An Essay in Nine Parts.* Translated by Linda Asher. New York: HarperCollins, 1995.

Landesman, Peter. "A Crisis of Fakes." *New York Times Magazine* (March 18, 2001).

Larkin, T. J., and Sandar Larkin. *Communicating Change: Winning*

Employee Support for New Business Goals. New York: McGraw-Hill, 1994.

————. "Reaching and Changing Frontline Employees." *Harvard Business Review* (May–June, 1996).

Le Carré, John. *The Tailor of Panama.* New York: Alfred A. Knopf, 1996.

Lilienthal, Peter. "Tune in If You Want to Turn on Employees." *Reputation Management* (May–June 1998).

Lindblom, Charles E. *Inquiry and Change: The Troubled Attempt to Understand and Shape Society.* New Haven, Conn.: Yale University Press, 1990.

Lohr, Steve. "He Loves to Win. At IBM, He Did." *New York Times* (March 10, 2002).

Mai, Robert. *Learning Partnerships: How Leading American Companies Implement Organizational Learning.* Chicago: Irwin/ASTD, 1996.

————. "How Communication Can Foster the Learning Organization." *Strategic Communication Management* (June–July 1998), pp. 22–26.

————. "Branding Begins in the Home." *Journal of Employee Communication Management* (September–October 1999), pp. 19–35.

McCarthy, Joseph L., ed. *A Blueprint for Managing Change,* Report No. 1149-96-CH. New York: The Conference Board, 1996.

McDougall, Christopher. "Questions for John Bach: The Elder Wizard." *New York Times Magazine* (January 13, 2002).

Milligan, Patricia. "Regaining Commitment." In Brian Hackett, *The New Deal in Employment Relationships.* New York: The Conference Board, 2001.

Mintzberg, Henry. "Musings on Management." *Harvard Business Review* (July–August 1996).

————. "Covert Leadership: Notes on Managing Professionals." *Harvard Business Review* (November–December 1998).

Mirvis, Philip. "Can You Teach Your People to Think Smarter?" *Across the Board* (March 1996).

Nonaka, Ikujiro, and Hirotaka Takeuchi. *The Knowledge-Creating Company: How Japanese Companies Create the Dynamics of Innovation.* New York: Oxford University Press, 1995.

Parker, Glenn, Jerry McAdams, and David Zielinski. *Rewarding Teams: Lessons from the Trenches.* San Francisco: Jossey-Bass, 2000.

Parker, Ian. "Annals of Science: Richard Dawkins' Evolution." *New Yorker* (September 9, 1996), pp. 41–45.

Pascale, Richard Tanner. *Managing on the Edge: How the Smartest Companies Use Conflict to Stay Ahead.* New York: Simon & Schuster Touchstone, 1990.

Pascale, Richard, et al. "Changing the Way We Change." *Harvard Business Review* (November–December 1997).

Pfeffer, Jeffrey, and Robert Sutton. *The Knowledge-Doing Gap: How Smart Companies Turn Knowledge Into Action.* Boston: Harvard Business School Press, 2000.

Polanyi, Michael. *The Tacit Dimension.* Garden City, N.Y.: Doubleday, 1966.

Prahalad, C. K. "An Interview with C. K. Prahalad." Interviewed by Joel Kurtzman. *Strategy and Business* (3rd quarter 1996).

Rhodes, Jerry. *Conceptual Toolmaking: Expert Systems of the Mind.* London: Basil Blackwell, 1991.

Richardson, Joan. "Meeting Expectations: Turn Staff Gatherings Into Learning Opportunities." *Tools for Schools* [National Staff Development Council newsletter] (December 2001–January 2002).

Ridgway, Richard. "Arseneault Reveals Formula for Courting Success." *The Grinnell Magazine* (spring 1998), p. 70.

Rogers, Everett M. *Diffusion of Innovations.* 4th ed. New York: The Free Press, 1995.

Rucci, Anthony J., Steven P. Kim, and Richard T. Quinn. "The Employee-Customer-Profit Chain at Sears." *Harvard Business Review* (January–February 1998).

Sayles, Leonard. *The Working Leader.* New York: The Free Press, 1993.

Schama, Simon. "Rescuing Churchill." *New York Review of Books* (February 28, 2002).

Schank, Roger C. *Tell Me a Story: A New Look at Real and Artificial Memory.* New York: Charles Scribner's Sons, 1990.

Schein, Edgar H. "Three Cultures of Management: The Key to Organizational Learning." *Sloan Management Review* (fall 1996).

Schon, Donald A. *The Reflective Practitioner: How Professionals Think in Action.* New York: Basic Books, 1983.

———. *Educating the Reflective Practitioner: Toward a New Design for*

Teaching and Learning in the Professions. San Francisco: Jossey-Bass, 1987.

Schrage, Michael. *Shared Minds: The New Technologies of Collaboration.* New York: Random House, 1990.

——. *Serious Play: How the World's Best Companies Simulate to Innovate.* Boston: Harvard Business School Press, 2000.

Senge, Peter M. *The Fifth Discipline: The Art and Practice of the Learning Organization.* New York: Doubleday Currency, 1990.

Sennett, Richard. *The Conscience of the Eye: The Design and Social Life of Cities.* New York: Alfred A. Knopf, 1990.

Smircich, Linda, and Gareth Morgan. "Leadership: The Management of Meaning." *Journal of Applied Behavioral Science* 18 (1982).

Stewart, Thomas. "The Information Wars: What You Don't Know Will Hurt You." *Fortune* (June 12, 1995).

——. "Company Values That Add Value." *Fortune* (July 8, 1996).

Straus, Joe. "6-Run 9th Extends Cards' Streak." *St. Louis Post-Dispatch* (August 16, 2002).

——. "Credit Should Be Split for Benes's Revival." *St. Louis Post-Dispatch* (August 18, 2002).

Stravinsky, Igor. *The Poetics of Music.* Cambridge, Mass.: Harvard University Press, 1970.

Sutton, Robert. "The Weird Rules of Creativity." *Harvard Business Review* (September 2001).

Terkel, Studs. *Working.* New York: Pantheon Books, 1974.

Troy, Kathryn. *Change Management: Communication's Pivotal Role,* Report No. 1122-95-CR. New York: The Conference Board, 1995.

United States Securities and Exchange Commission. *A Plain English Handbook: How to Create Clear SEC Disclosure Documents.* Washington, D.C.: SEC (Office of Investor Education and Assistance), 1997.

Weber, Eugen. *France, Fin de Ciècle.* Cambridge, Mass.: Harvard University Press, 1986.

Weick, Karl E. *The Social Psychology of Organizing.* 2nd ed. New York: McGraw-Hill, 1979.

Weick, Karl E., and Frances Westley. "Organizational Learning: Affirming an Oxymoron." In *Handbook of Organization Studies,* edited by Stewart R. Clegg, Cynthia Hardy, and Walter R. Nord. Thousand Oaks, Calif.: Sage, 1996, pp. 440–58.

Welch, Jack. "An Interview with Jack Welch." Interviewed by Geoffrey Colvin at the University of Michigan Business School. C-Span 2 (April 9, 2001).

——. "Jack Welch: Icon of Leadership." Interviewed by Stuart Varney at Fairfield University. *CEO Exchange,* WTTW Chicago (December 30, 2001).

Wong, Edward. "A Stinging Office Memo Boomerangs." *New York Times* (April 5, 2001).

Wood, Wally. "So Where Do We Go From Here?" *Across the Board* (March 1997).

Yankelovich, Daniel. *The Magic of Dialogue: Transforming Conflict Into Cooperation.* New York: Simon & Schuster, 1999.

Index

LIBRARY. UNIVERSITY OF CHESTER